The state of Russia, under the present Czar. In relation to the several great and remarkable things he has done, as to his naval preparations, the regulating his army, ... By Captain John Perry.

John Perry

The state of Russia, under the present Czar. In relation to the several great and remarkable things he has done, as to his naval preparations, the regulating his army, ... By Captain John Perry.
Perry, John
ESTCID: T105640
Reproduction from British Library
Errata slip pasted to the verso of the final leaf of 'The preface'.
London : printed for Benjamin Tooke, 1716.
[8],280p.,plate : map ; 8°

Eighteenth Century
Collections Online
Print Editions

Gale ECCO Print Editions

Relive history with *Eighteenth Century Collections Online*, now available in print for the independent historian and collector. This series includes the most significant English-language and foreign-language works printed in Great Britain during the eighteenth century, and is organized in seven different subject areas including literature and language; medicine, science, and technology; and religion and philosophy. The collection also includes thousands of important works from the Americas.

The eighteenth century has been called "The Age of Enlightenment." It was a period of rapid advance in print culture and publishing, in world exploration, and in the rapid growth of science and technology – all of which had a profound impact on the political and cultural landscape. At the end of the century the American Revolution, French Revolution and Industrial Revolution, perhaps three of the most significant events in modern history, set in motion developments that eventually dominated world political, economic, and social life.

In a groundbreaking effort, Gale initiated a revolution of its own: digitization of epic proportions to preserve these invaluable works in the largest online archive of its kind. Contributions from major world libraries constitute over 175,000 original printed works. Scanned images of the actual pages, rather than transcriptions, recreate the works *as they first appeared.*

Now for the first time, these high-quality digital scans of original works are available via print-on-demand, making them readily accessible to libraries, students, independent scholars, and readers of all ages.

For our initial release we have created seven robust collections to form one the world's most comprehensive catalogs of 18th century works.

Initial Gale ECCO Print Editions collections include:

History and Geography
Rich in titles on English life and social history, this collection spans the world as it was known to eighteenth-century historians and explorers. Titles include a wealth of travel accounts and diaries, histories of nations from throughout the world, and maps and charts of a world that was still being discovered. Students of the War of American Independence will find fascinating accounts from the British side of conflict.

Social Science
Delve into what it was like to live during the eighteenth century by reading the first-hand accounts of everyday people, including city dwellers and farmers, businessmen and bankers, artisans and merchants, artists and their patrons, politicians and their constituents. Original texts make the American, French, and Industrial revolutions vividly contemporary.

Medicine, Science and Technology
Medical theory and practice of the 1700s developed rapidly, as is evidenced by the extensive collection, which includes descriptions of diseases, their conditions, and treatments. Books on science and technology, agriculture, military technology, natural philosophy, even cookbooks, are all contained here.

Literature and Language
Western literary study flows out of eighteenth-century works by Alexander Pope, Daniel Defoe, Henry Fielding, Frances Burney, Denis Diderot, Johann Gottfried Herder, Johann Wolfgang von Goethe, and others. Experience the birth of the modern novel, or compare the development of language using dictionaries and grammar discourses.

Religion and Philosophy
The Age of Enlightenment profoundly enriched religious and philosophical understanding and continues to influence present-day thinking. Works collected here include masterpieces by David Hume, Immanuel Kant, and Jean-Jacques Rousseau, as well as religious sermons and moral debates on the issues of the day, such as the slave trade. The Age of Reason saw conflict between Protestantism and Catholicism transformed into one between faith and logic -- a debate that continues in the twenty-first century.

Law and Reference
This collection reveals the history of English common law and Empire law in a vastly changing world of British expansion. Dominating the legal field is the *Commentaries of the Law of England* by Sir William Blackstone, which first appeared in 1765. Reference works such as almanacs and catalogues continue to educate us by revealing the day-to-day workings of society.

Fine Arts
The eighteenth-century fascination with Greek and Roman antiquity followed the systematic excavation of the ruins at Pompeii and Herculaneum in southern Italy; and after 1750 a neoclassical style dominated all artistic fields. The titles here trace developments in mostly English-language works on painting, sculpture, architecture, music, theater, and other disciplines. Instructional works on musical instruments, catalogs of art objects, comic operas, and more are also included.

The BiblioLife Network

This project was made possible in part by the BiblioLife Network (BLN), a project aimed at addressing some of the huge challenges facing book preservationists around the world. The BLN includes libraries, library networks, archives, subject matter experts, online communities and library service providers. We believe every book ever published should be available as a high-quality print reproduction; printed on-demand anywhere in the world. This insures the ongoing accessibility of the content and helps generate sustainable revenue for the libraries and organizations that work to preserve these important materials.

The following book is in the "public domain" and represents an authentic reproduction of the text as printed by the original publisher. While we have attempted to accurately maintain the integrity of the original work, there are sometimes problems with the original work or the micro-film from which the books were digitized. This can result in minor errors in reproduction. Possible imperfections include missing and blurred pages, poor pictures, markings and other reproduction issues beyond our control. Because this work is culturally important, we have made it available as part of our commitment to protecting, preserving, and promoting the world's literature.

GUIDE TO FOLD-OUTS MAPS and OVERSIZED IMAGES

The book you are reading was digitized from microfilm captured over the past thirty to forty years. Years after the creation of the original microfilm, the book was converted to digital files and made available in an online database.

In an online database, page images do not need to conform to the size restrictions found in a printed book. When converting these images back into a printed bound book, the page sizes are standardized in ways that maintain the detail of the original. For large images, such as fold-out maps, the original page image is split into two or more pages

Guidelines used to determine how to split the page image follows:

• Some images are split vertically; large images require vertical and horizontal splits.
• For horizontal splits, the content is split left to right.
• For vertical splits, the content is split from top to bottom.
• For both vertical and horizontal splits, the image is processed from top left to bottom right.

THE
STATE
OF
RUSSIA,

Under the Present CZAR.

In Relation to the several great and remarkable Things he has done, as to his Naval Preparations, the Regulating his Army; the Reforming his People, and Improvement of his Countrey.

Particularly those Works on which the AUTHOR was employ'd, with the Reasons of his quitting the CZAR's Service, after having been Fourteen Years in that Countrey.

Also an ACCOUNT

Of those TARTARS, and other People who border on the Eastern and extreme Northern Parts of the Czar's Dominions, their Religion, and Manner of Life: With many other Observations.

To which is annex'd,

A more accurate MAP of the Czar's Dominions, than has hitherto been extant.

By Captain JOHN PERRY.

LONDON,

Printed for BENJAMIN TOOKE, at the *Middle Temple-Gate* in *Fleetstreet*. 1716.

THE PREFACE.

HERE being no Account of Russia *publish'd since the Czar's being in* England, *and the many Years I lived there,* and the Works I was employ'd upon, having given me an Opportunity of observing the State and Condition of that Countrey, with the several Improvements which the Czar has made among his People since his Return from his Travels, whereby he is become formidable to his Neighbours, and has gain'd universal Applause, I thought the following Relation might not be unacceptable to the Publick.

The PREFACE.

I have first given an Account of my being taken into the Czar's Service, and of the Work I was employ'd in for making a Communication between the Caspian and Black Sea, and of my being commanded from thence to another Work at Veronize, *for repairing his Fleet design'd against the* Turks, *which I did, by artificially raising the Water for laying the Ships dry on the Land, without the help of the Tide, to answer the same Use as our Docks in* England, *with this Advantage, that the Water is only raised when required, and that as our Docks in* England *are usually made to receive but one or two Ships at a time, by the Method of artificially raising the Water, by the placing a single Sluice, without the Charge of making Docks, the first time I raised the Water I laid fifteen Ships at once on the Land to be repair'd, which I chose to be particular in, because the same has not been practised in any other Place that I have heard of. I have mention'd another Work I was employ'd on, for*

ma-

The PREFACE.

making the River Veronize *navigable for the Passage of Ships of* 80 Guns, *which the* Czar *has built there for forming a Navy against the* Turks.

I have also spoken of the Czar's *Designs for laying his Ships on that side in a dry Haven in Time of Peace, to preserve them from Decay, and of my being employ'd to survey the Rivers in the Province of* Petersburgh, *for making a Communication from thence to the great River* Wolga, *and the Methods and Resolutions which the* Czar *has taken to bring the Trade of his Countrey thither, to make* Petersburgh *the Capital of his Empire.*

This is what I first writ, without any Intention of going any farther, as the Reader will easily discern; but I was prevailed upon by the Persuasions of some Friends, to proceed in giving a more particular Account of the Czar's *Dominions, and of his Intentions to discover a Passage from the North East Part of his Dominions to* China *by the Tartarian Sea; of the Inhabitants of those*

Nor-

The PREFACE.

Northern Parts, their manner of Life in the Extremity of Cold, of the Conquest of Siberia, *and the Trade and Correspondence which is at present maintain'd through that Countrey to* China *by Land-Carriage, with a Description of the several Hordes of* Tartars *who inhabit on the Eastern Parts of the* Czar's *Dominions, having had the Opportunity of observing many Particulars in their Way of Life, whilst I was employ'd on that side the Countrey.*

I have laid down some Observations of the Quantity of Waters which fall into the Caspian Sea *by the* Wolga, *and the many other great Rivers; and have given my Thoughts touching the Opinion advanced by some Men of a subterraneous Passage for their Discharge, and which, according to the approved Experiments made by the learned Mr. Professor* Halley, *of the Evaporations of Waters, I have made an Attempt to prove that there is no such subterraneous Passage. I have farther offer'd some Reasons to prove the Nature and Necessity*

The PREFACE.

cessity of the Circulation of Dews from the Surface of the Earth, and falling down again in Rain, drawn from some Observations of my own that I made in Russia, which I submit to the Opinion of the more judicious and learned.

I have farther shewn the Occasion of the Czar's first Thoughts of building Ships, the Reason of his Travels into Europe, of the several Rebellions in his Countrey, his regulating his Government at his Return, reforming his People in their Customs and Habits; of the Method he has taken for the establishing Knowledge and Learning among them; of the Temper of the People; of the Manufacture and Trade of Russia; and of many other remarkable Things relating to the Improvement of his People in the Art of War. All which, though I may have been irregular in my Method, and incorrect in my Language; yet I hope the Sincerity and Truth of the Relation, which I have with great Care perus'd, will sufficiently recompense for it.

AN

ERRATA.

PAG. 9. l. 4. r. *Stems*. p. 30. l. 17. r. *Molds*. p. 32. l. 14. r. *Ability*. p. 62. l. 4. after *that is* dele , p. 65. l. 19. for *thick* r. *thin*. l. *ult*. r. *on their*. p. 76. l. 25. r. *to Death*. p. 77. l. *ult*. r. *the manner*. p. 79. l. 17. r. *Czaravich*. l. 30. r. *and Tabollsky*. p. 89. l. 8. r. *with*. l. 9. dele *have*. p. 93. l. 24. r. *the Persians*. p. 94. l. 5. r. *of time*. p. 99. l. 11. r. *Turtle*. p. 106. l. 19. r. *the several*. p. 121. l. 28. for *Colours* r. *Clouds*. p. 125. l. *ult*. dele *be at*, and after *rest* dele , p. 128. l. 21. for *break* r. *brush*. p. 130. l. 1. r. *Fogs*. l. 9. r. *made its*. p. 137. l. 8. r. $46\frac{1}{2}$ *Degrees*. p. 145. l. 6. r. *Allexavich*. p. 168. l. 23. dele *all*. l. 28. r. *Souda Sea*. p. 169. l. 13. r. *Cozens*. l. 27. r. *War*. p. 202. l. 19. r. *the Boyars*. p. 210. l. 23. r. *burn or*. p. 217. l 35. after *but* add *their own arbitrary*. p. 222. l. 1. r. *Paint*. p. 245. l. 14 r. *Rivers become*. l. 27 r. *of Oak and Fir*. l. 32. r. *both Oak and Fir Timber*. p. 254. l. 12. after *at least* r. *that tho'*.

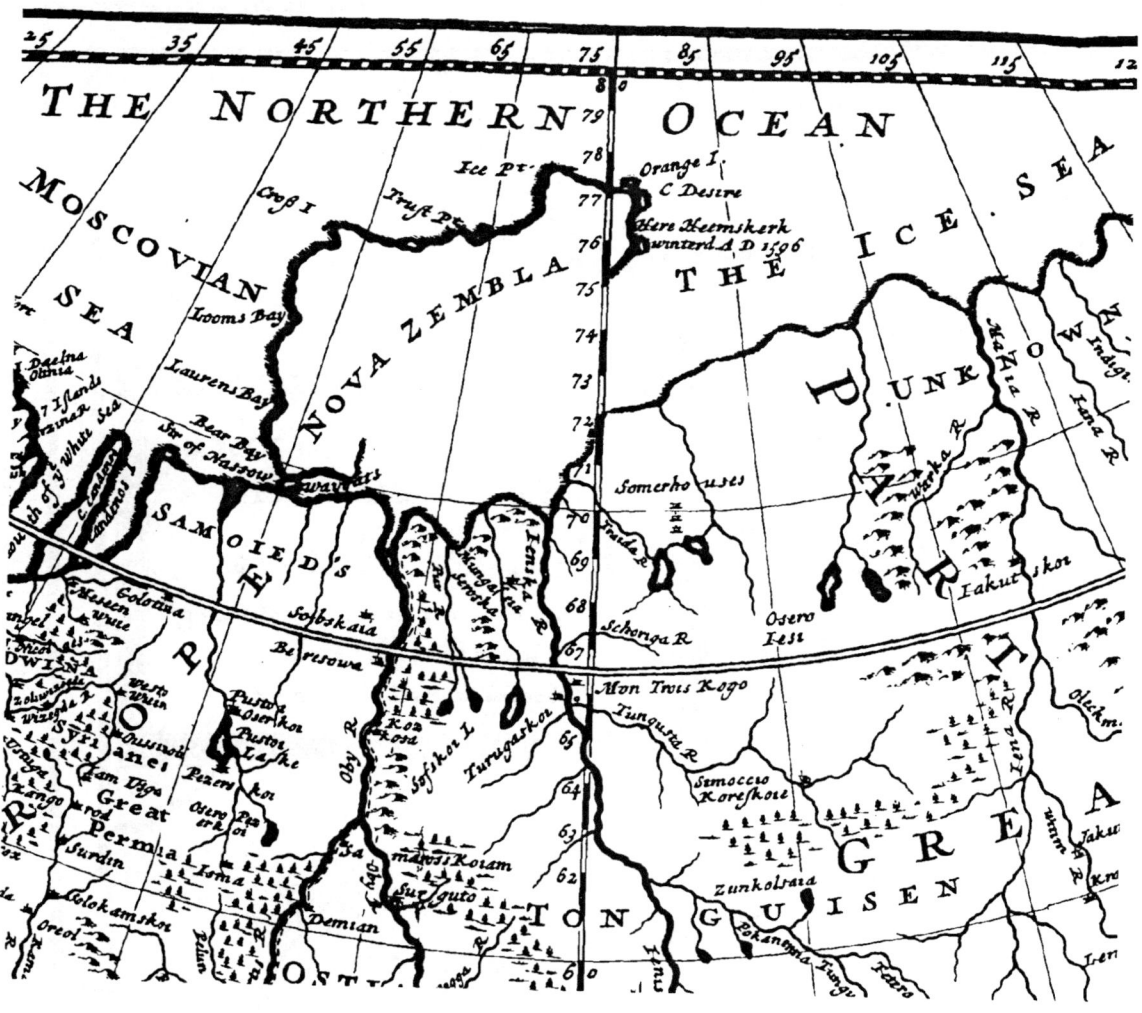

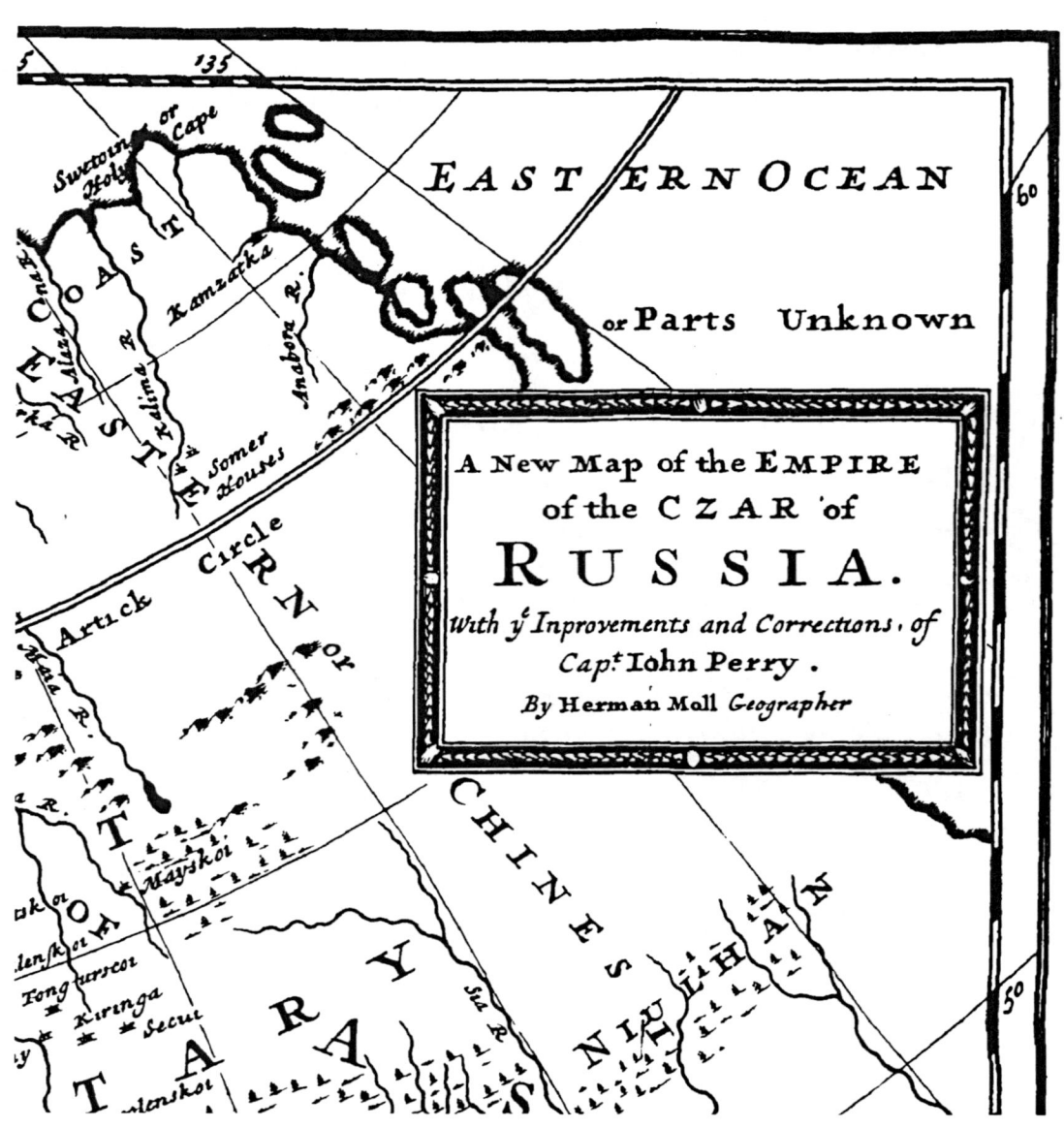

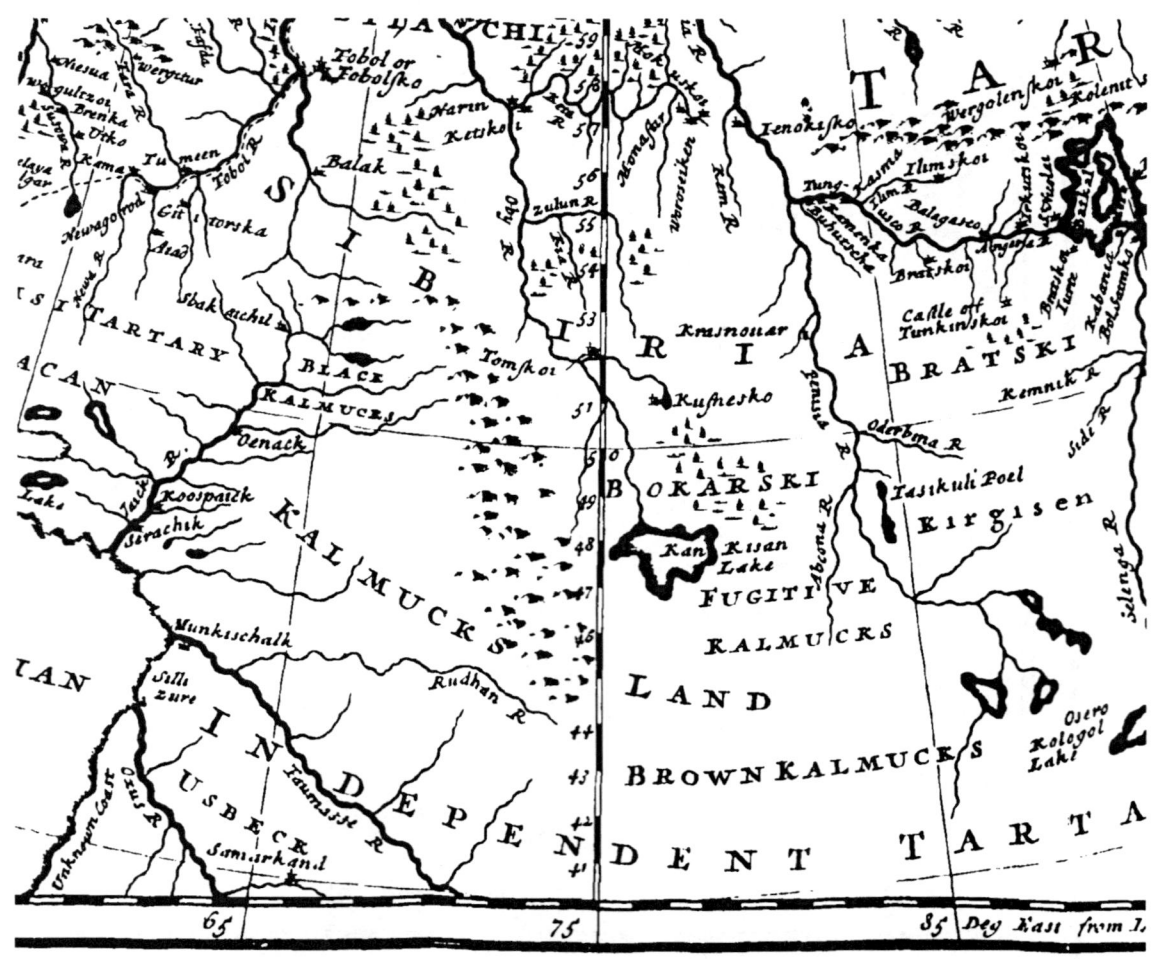

AN ACCOUNT OF RUSSIA,

Particularly of those remarkable Things done by the present CZAR.

IN the Year 1698, his Czarish Majesty being then in *England*, making his Observations of our Arts in building and equipping out our Fleets, among several Artificers, &c. whom he was then pleased to entertain, I was recommended to him by the
then

then Lord Marquifs of *Carmarthen*, Mr. *Dummer*, (then Surveyor of the Navy) and some others, as a Person capable of serving him on several Occasions, relating to his new Designs of establishing a Fleet, making his Rivers navigable, &c. After his Majesty had himself discoursed with me, particularly touching the making of a Communication between the River *Wolga* and the *Don*, I was taken into his Service by his Embassador Count *Gollovin*, who agreed with me for the Salary of 300 *l.* Sterling *per Ann.* to be paid me, with my travelling Charges and Subsistence Money upon whatsoever Service I should be employ'd; besides a farther Reward to be given me to my Satisfaction at the Conclusion of any Work I should finish.

Soon after my Contract was made, the Czar going from hence to *Holland*, took me along with him thither, and after I had made such Observations as I had there an opportunity to do, I was sent directly to *Mosco*, with Orders for my being immediately dispatch'd from thence into the Province of *Astracan*, about a thousand *Wurst* (or *Russ* Miles) beyond *Mosco*, to survey a Work, which his Czarish Majesty had before design'd, and another Person been employ'd upon for the making of the abovesaid Communication for Ships of War, as well as trading Vessels of Burden, to pass between the *Caspian* and the *Black Sea*, by way of the said two great Rivers, the *Wolga* and the *Don*. The first of which

which Rivers, after running between 3 and 4000 *Ruſs* Miles * through the Czar's Countrey, falls into the *Caspian* Sea; and the other, after running near half as far, falls thro' the *Palus Meotis* into the *Black Sea*.

The Distance of which Communication between the said two great Rivers is about 140 *Ruſs* Miles by the way of two other small Rivers, the one called the *Lavla*, which falls into the *Don*; the other the *Camiſhinka*, which falls into the *Wolga*; upon these small Rivers Sluices were to be placed to make them navigable, and a Canal of near 4 *Ruſs* Miles to be cut through the dry Land where the said two small Rivers come nearest together; which Work, if finished, would be of very great Advantage to the Czar's Countrey, especially in case of any War with the *Turks* or *Crim-Tartars*, or with *Perſia*, or any of the Countreys bordering upon the *Caspian* Sea. A Draught of which intended Communication is laid down with the general Map of the Countrey, which is hereto annex'd.

The said Work was first begun by one Colonel *Breckell* a *German*, who was a Colonel in the Czar's Army, and who had the Reputation of a very good Engineer as to Fortifications, and the like: But he very little understanding this Business which he had taken upon him, and having unaccountably design-

---

* Note, *A* Wuſt *or* Ruſs *Mile contains* 3504 Engliſh *Feet, which is about two Thirds of an* Engliſh *Mile.*

ed the Canal, and the first Sluice which he placed being blown up, that is, having given way at the Foundation, and the Water taking its course underneath, at the first shutting of the Gates, he therefore, upon his coming to *Mosco* the Winter following, obtained a Pass to be given as for one of his Servants, whom he pretended to send for Necessaries for the Work, and himself went off with the said Pass, and made his Escape out of the Countrey.

The Czar had Advice of this whilst he was in *England*, and therefore he was pleased to send me immediately forward to examine whether the Work was practicable or not. Accordingly I went and survey'd it the same Year that I was retained; and upon the Draught and Report which I deliver'd to the Czar upon his Return from his Travels to *Mosco*, in which I shew'd the Reasons why the said Work that was begun by *Breckell* was not properly design'd, and of which the Czar had a true Notion. His Majesty was pleased to order me to take it upon me, and to begin the Canal in a new place, that I proposed as more practicable for it, where there would be both a great deal less Labour of digging Work, and be also much more convenient in the placing of the Sluices.

Upon which Work I was employ'd three Summers successively, having demanded 30000 Men for it, but never had half that Number, and the last Year not 10000 Men given me, nor the necessary Artificers and Materials that were wanting, sufficiently provided; of which I every Winter, at my Return to *Mosco*, gave a List into the Czar's own Hand, setting forth the Necessity of being better supplied with what was wanting, particularly for making the Sluices. But the Czar having about this time lost the Battel of *Narva*, and the War with *Sweden* being like to continue, which required more immediate Supplies of Men and Money; in the latter end of the Year 1701, I received Orders to let that Work stand still for a while, and to leave one of my Assistants there to take care of what was done, (there being several Sluices near finish'd, and the Canal above half dug) and to come my self, with the rest of my Assistants, to *Mosco*; from whence I was sent to do another Work at *Veronize*; and *Kneaz*, (or Prince) *Allexyeavich Gollitzen*, who had the Government of the Kingdom of *Astracan*, where the Work for the said Communication was situated, was displaced by the Czar from his Command, for his having actually discouraged the Work, and not having supplied me with the necessary Men and Materials that were wanting for it; for which the said Prince, upon his being displaced by the Czar, ever after became my irreconcileable Enemy, and by his Interest (being allied to the greatest Families) influenced the next Lord, under whose Command I afterwards served, (on another Work) very much to my Prejudice.

Besides the general Dislike which most of the old Boyars had to all new Undertakings which the Czar, by the Advice of Strangers, engaged in, beyond what his Predecessors ever had attempted to do; one Occasion which made the Lord *Gollitzen* particularly dissatisfied with the said Work, was this: After the aforesaid *Breckell* had unskilfully fix'd his first Sluice, which upon the first Tryal of the Waters gave way and blew up, finding his Inability to carry on a Work of this kind, and fearing the dangerous Consequence that might fall upon him in an Arbitrary Government, deserted as aforesaid, and afterwards writ a Letter of Complaint to the Czar against the said Lord *Gollitzen*, alledging, that he had not been supply'd with Necessaries for the Work, and particularly complained of the ill Usage that he had received from the said Lord, who was then an Enemy to the Work, and who had struck him with his Cane, and threaten'd to hang him. This happen'd whilst the Czar was abroad upon his Travels; and the Czar having accused the said Lord, on his coming home, as not having discharged the Trust that was reposed in him, he thereupon became irreconcileable to the Work, and made Reflections upon it, as a thing impossible to be done by the Hands of Men. He represented it as burthensome to the Countrey by the Numbers of Men that were employ'd in it, and used all his Endeavours to have had it given over as impracticable, declaring it as

his

his Opinion, that God had made the Rivers to go one way, and that it was Presumption in Man to think to turn them another.

As soon as I arrived in *Mosco*, by Order as aforemention'd, I petition'd for my Salary that was then due to me, and which I was in hopes to have received, having as yet not been paid a Penny of it, but only my Subsistence Money, at 25 Rubles *per Month, settled and confirm'd by the Czar at my first coming into the Countrey to be paid me apart, besides my Salary beforemention'd of 300*l. per Annum*, for which I then petition'd.

At this time my Lord *Apraxin* (whom the Czar had a little before sent to supervise the said Work for a Communication, and who had then the chief Inspection of building the Czar's Navy, and is since made Lord High Admiral, &c.) was pleased to discourse me concerning his Majesty's Ships at *Veronize* †. which being built of green Timber, were in a very short time so decay'd, that they would not bear lying upon the Careen to be refitted, and were ready to sink in the River. I told his Lordship that there was a Method which I believed might be put in practice upon that River, or somewhere near it, without careening, or the least straining of the Ships, to

---

* *A Ruble is* 100 *Rub Copeeks, which was then each Copeek full an English Penny Value, but since the Czar has recoined his Money, it is little more than half the former Value*

† *Veronize is a City situated upon a River of that Name, which falls into the* Don.

place

place them upon the dry Land to be refitted, by damming up the Course of the River, and to fix a large Sluice with a Set of draw Doors sufficient to let off the Floods, and another Sluice apart to be made with a pair of great Gates for the Passage of Ships, which being at pleasure shut to, would swell and raise the Water in the River high enough to lift his Majesty's biggest Ships on and off the Land at any time; which his Lordship told me would be a very acceptable Service to his Majesty on the present Occasion, could it be performed; assuring me that I should be better assisted with Men and Materials than I had been with Prince *Gollitzen*; and that he would not only justly pay me my Wages whilst I was under his Command, but that he would be my Patron, and help me to all my Arrears which I then petition'd for, as soon as I had done this Work, which would be of great Use to the Czar in the establishing his Navy design'd against the *Turks*.

Accordingly in the Year 1702, I was sent down to *Veronize*, and pitched upon a Place at the Mouth of the River, which I found most proper for raising the Water to the height that was required, for placing of the said Ships to lie dry upon Blocks above the ordinary Surface of the River; which in little more than 16 Months, I perform'd to Satisfaction, and the first time that the Sluces were shut, I plac'd 15 Ships (some of them of 50 Guns) upon the Land, to be re-fitted,

fitting

sitting upright upon Blocks like as in our dry Docks in *England*, and which Ships as they were found defective, were stripp'd down and repaired; some of them their Timbers, and others their Stems and Stern-posts being shifted, and then taken off the Land again, and others set in their Places.

But although this Work was perform'd to their full Satisfaction, yet when I demanded my Salary and Arrears that was due to me, and which I hoped to have received according to Promise, I was again farther put off by the said Lord *Apraxin*, until I had done another Work which I was ordered to do on the same River, and that then I should not fail of having all my Money together given me.

The Czar at the Time when the foresaid Work was finished, came himself to *Veronize*, and gave Directions for repairing his said Ships that sate upon the Land; and was then farther pleased to command me to survey the River, whether by the fixing of another large Sluice higher up upon the *Veronize*, the same could be made navigable the whole Way from the City, for Ships of 80 Guns, (such as he intended to build) to be launched and come down into the River *Don* at any time of the Year.

Accordingly when I had survey'd and made my Report to his Majesty, that the same was practicable, he was pleas'd to command me to take it in hand, which I began *Anno* 1704:

And

And the Year following I finish'd the same to Satisfaction, as I was commanded; the Sluices being 43 Foot broad, and of Depth proportionable to swell the Water for the Passage of the said 80 Gun Ships; fix'd also with Draw-Sluices in manner aforesaid, sufficient for the Discharge of the Floods, which in that Countrey upon the sudden melting of the Snows in the Spring of the Year, overflow all the Works, and come down with a Drift of Ice and Torrent that is not easie to be described; and yet the Dams that I have fix'd on those Rivers, are so secure, that they suffer no Damage by the said Floods, so as to be in any Danger of giving way so long as the World endures. Which Works have been seen by several Persons who are now in *London*.

When this last Work at *Veronize* was also finish'd to Satisfaction, I again moved my Lord *Apraxin* for my Wages, but I found the Honour of his Word and Promises made to me, was but little regarded; for I was again put off as before, and was as far from receiving my Money as ever; his Lordship then telling me, that my Money would not go away from me, that I was not in any immediate Want of it, and pretending at the same time, that he could not adjust my Accounts without Count *Gollovin*, who first took me into his Majesty's Service. However, after performing each of the said Works, his Lordship, to keep me in some Temper,

(11)

Temper, gave me a small Present to the Value of about 250 *l*. Sterl.

The fixing of Sluices that are to bear but little Weight of Water, for the making Rivers and Streams navigable for small Vessels for inland Carriage, where the Floods are not great, is easie and practised every where; but I do not know of any River that has before been made navigable for Ships of near so great Dimensions: And the Ground where I was oblig'd to place the last Sluice being extreamly bad, when I came to dig below the Surface of the River, I met with such extraordinary Force of Springs, that all the Pumps that could be placed, could not discharge the Water for to carry down the Foundation of the Sluice to the Depth that was required for it, which obliged me to let the Works stand still six Weeks, till I had made an Engine on purpose for throwing out the Water, which wrought Night and Day for several Months together, and would easily discharge ten or twelve Ton of Water in a Minute. The Czar happening to come again to *Veronize*, when I was oblig'd to use this Engine, he came several times to see it work with several of his Lords with him, and was extreamly pleas'd with it, it being an Improvement of an Engine which I first made at *Portsmouth* Dock above 23 Years since, when I was Lieutenant of the *Mountague* that came there to be refitted.

Whilst

Whilst I was doing this last Work at *Veronize*, a Person that was a *Pole* by Birth, and had taken upon him the *Russ* Religion, and who had been employ'd on the making of a Dock in the Czar's artificial Haven at *Taganroke*, on the side of the *Palus Meotis**: This Person was ordered to make a new kind of Docks on the River *Veronize*, for building his Majesty's said 80 Gun Ships, with Chests fix'd to the Bottom of them, to float them down the *Don* and over the Bar at *Azoph*, being from the Mouth of the River *Veronize* (as the Stream runs) above 1000 *Russ* Miles, which Docks the Czar ordered when he was at *Veronize*, as before mention'd, some little time before my last Work was finish'd.

It being then in the Winter, and his Majesty, upon the Arrival of a Courier from *Poland*, going suddenly from thence, he was pleas'd the Night before he went, to leave Orders with my Lord *Apraxin* in Writing, for my making some particular Observations at the coming down of the Floods, and that my Opinion, together with his three Master Ship-Builders, (which were two *English*,

---

* *Which Haven was design'd for entertaining of the Czar's Navy, but being built off a Point into the Sea, in a Place where there was but very little Depth of Water, to a great Distance without the Point, the Sands gathered round the Work as fast as it was carried out, and the Haven intended became in a manner choaked up before it was half finished. And upon the late Peace concluded with the* Turks, *has been since demolished, as will be hereafter shewn.*

Mr.

Mr. *Cozens* and Mr. *Ney*, and one *Russ* should be taken, touching the Place to be pitched upon for building the said Docks: But quite different from my Opinion, a Place was chosen for it, and the Work was resolv'd to be carried on in a sandy Foundation, and by a Method that was no way proper for it; I therefore first verbally urg'd to my Lord *Apraxin*, the ill Consequences that were to be feared in the making these Docks, more especially in the Place and Manner that was designed for it; that upon the coming down of the Floods, the Foundation of the Work would blow up, and perhaps destroy the Ships when they were half built (as it afterwards happen'd). But his Lordship perhaps thinking me only desirous to advance my own Opinion, and not suspecting the Judgment of the Person that was to make these Docks, who was positive of the Success; and adhering also to the Persuasion of the Czar's aforesaid *Russ* Builder, and another Person of the same Nation who had their private Interest in it, having a small Village in the Place that was marked out for the said Work, for which they were to have a much better given them in the room of it: I found his Lordship did not mind my Words, therefore for my own Justification, I drew up my Reasons in Writing, and deliver'd them to the said Lord *Apraxin*, wherein I represented the Danger that would inevitably ensue in case of carrying on the said Docks in the Place and

Manner

Manner which was designed for it, and presented a Draught to his Lordship at the same time, in what Place and in what Manner I proposed them to be built; to which I annexed a mathematical Figure, shewing thereby the Weight of Water that would press against such Docks, according to the Height of the Floods in the Spring of the Year, which was very necessary on this Occasion to be considered, and which I did to demonstrate and explain to them the Reasons which I had laid down, that the Work would be unsuccessful.

But notwithstanding all my Representations, his Lordship was pleased to let the Work go on in their own Way; and the building Place for the Czar's Navy, that was before at the City of *Veronize*, was on this Occasion order'd 7 *Russ* Miles lower down upon the River, and the Houses of the Czar, and several of the Lord's (being framed of Wood to take down at Pleasure, as is the Way of *Russia*) with all the Houses of the Master-Builders, Artificers, and Labourers, were carried thither, and a large Fortification with regular Bastions was with all Expedition made round this new Place; which, after the Expence of many hundred thousand Rubles, and above three Years wearied Experiments and Endeavours to maintain the same, they were at last obliged to quit and lay it wholly aside; by reason that the Floods still undermined the Foundation, and came in upon them. Which made

(15)

made the said Lord *Apraxin* after become very uneasie with me, fearing lest one time or other it should come to the Czar's Knowledge, that he had commanded the said Work to go on; in direct opposition to the Arguments and Reasons that I had given him against it: Which, together with another thing, that about the same time I had proposed to his Lordship, for the preserving of his Majesty's Ships that were built at *Veronize*, from Decay, in time of Peace, for which the Czar was very much displeased with him for his not having faithfully represented it to him, the Circumstances of which would be too tedious here to relate, made his Behaviour ever after prejudiced and injurious towards me.

All which Proceedings in the Affair aforesaid, relating to the said Docks, with the Copy of the Draught and Arguments I had laid down, setting forth what would be the Consequence of that Undertaking, and that it would at last oblige them to quit it, I shew'd to her late Majesty's Envoy Extraordinary, the honourable Mr. *Whitworth*, to the *English* Consul Mr. *Goodfellow*, and some other *English* Gentlemen, at my coming to *Mosco*, *Anno* 1706, which was above two Years before they found themselves mistaken and were obliged to give over the said Work as impracticable, and to seek out another new Place to build lesser Ships without Docks, as formerly.

After

After I had finished my last Work at *Veronize*, I continued some Months in *Mosca* without any Orders; and then it being his Majesty's Pleasure to think of putting in practice the Work abovemention'd for preserving his Ships at *Veronize* from Decay in time of Peace, *viz.* by laying them up under Sheds in a dry Haven, with a Sluice to be placed, by which to swell and raise the Water for the Entrance into such dry Haven, to take Ships in and out at any time required for it; which said Work I proposed to be made for the laying his Majesty's Ships according to the several Rates in Divisions apart, to lie 10 or 20, more or less, in a Division, as should be best approved of by his Majesty, to sit upon Blocks like as in our Docks in *England*; and that when after some time lying dry the Plank should begin to shrink, and the Oakham thereby grow slack in the Seams, then to have it raved out for the better Passage of the Air to the Timbers, with their Ports and Hatches, to be kept constantly open, &c.

Which Proposal I grounded on this Principle, namely, that all sorts of Timber, or whatsoever is built or made of Wood, being exposed to the Injuries of Wind and Weather, does soon moulder and decay, more particularly in the case of Shipping, the falling of Mists and Rains from above in the Winter, the scorching Heats in Summer, the Leakage and Damps from the Water in the Hold rising up in the Rooms among the Timbers

Timbers, between the outward and inward Planks of the Ships, where there is no Passage for the circulation of the Air, is the evident Cause of a Ships soon rotting. Whereas on the other hand I represented, that whatsoever is not exposed to the Injuries of Wind and Weather, but either kept constantly wet or constantly dry, will last and hold good Time out of Mind; and that there was great Reason to presume from thence, that by putting Ships in a Posture to lie wholly dry in time of Peace, they would last at least twice, if not three or four times as long, as usual, without Occasion for Repair.

I represented also, that such a dry Haven, if made in a proper Place for it, would not only be convenient for examining and keeping his Majesty's Ships in a Condition always ready for Service in Time of Peace, but be of extraordinary Use also in Time of War, for putting Ships in and out to be refitted with Expedition and Pleasure; in like manner as I had before placed 15 Ships together on the Land to be refitted at the Mouth of the *Veronize*, to be done by swelling and raising the Water in the River whenever required; only with this Difference, that such dry Haven should be made not to float all the Ships together, but with an Entrance apart to be made to each Division of Ships, to take in and out at any Time, only such Number as there should be Occasion, and such Haven to be moated and walled round, the better to be

secured

secured against any Accidents of Treachery and Fire: That a continual Trouble and vast Treasure would thereby be eased for ever, in the building and repairing of his Majesty's Ships, and the Charge of making and maintaining such dry Haven would be very inconsiderable, in proportion to such annual Expence which must otherwise always be continued.

My Lord *Apraxin*, when I first spoke of this Proposal to him, and told him that I was ready to make it appear if commanded, whereby his Majesty's Ships should in a very great Measure be undoubtedly preserved from Decay, desiring him to acquaint the *Czar* of it: He misrepresented it to his Majesty, as if I had gone about to impose upon him a thing that was impracticable; but a more true Representation being afterwards made of it by my late very worthy Friend Mr. *Henry Stiles*, and being stated in Writing, and afterwards laid before the *Czar*, he readily apprehended and approved of it; and I was thereupon appointed to attend his coming to *Mosco*, where, when I had waited some Months without doing any Business, as has been mentioned, his Majesty was pleased to send his Orders from *Poland*, that I should go down upon the River *Don*, and survey a proper Place for the doing of the said Work.

Accordingly I proceeded, and surveyed the Situation of the Mouths of five small Rivers that fall into the *Don*, which were mentioned in my Orders for that purpose, and return'd to my Lord *Apraxin*, who was in *Mosco*, with the Report of the most proper Place for the Work, and a List of the Men and Materials that were necessary for it: Which Report and Account his Lordship took with him to *Petersburg*, whither he was then going to attend the coming of the *Czar*, and his Majesty was thereupon pleased to direct that the Timber should be cut in Readiness for the Work, but that the taking the Work in hand, should not be begun until he had Leisure to come himself and to view the Place which I had marked out for it, and to give his particular Orders in it.

In the mean time, his Lordship upon his returning again to *Mosco*, informed me, that he had Orders from the *Czar*, to pay me my Arrears, and he gave Directions to his Deputy, to bring in the Account of what was due to me; so that I thought my self now sure of my Money: But the next Time I waited upon his Lordship, in Discourse he told me, that his Majesty was so taken up with the Affairs of the Army in *Poland*, that it would perhaps be a long Time before he would come again to *Mosco*, and have Leisure to go and view the Place, and to give his Orders for the Work aforesaid; and pleasantly asked me, what I would do with my self in the mean time? Upon which I proposed to his Lordship, that since his Majesty had deferr'd the said Work till his coming from the Army, and that there was no immediate Business for me, that he would therefore give me Leave to take a short Turn to *England*, to see my Friends, and that I should serve his Majesty with the greater Satisfaction in what I was commanded, when I came back again; which I proposed to do in eight or ten Months at farthest, and which his Lordship, when I first proposed it to him, seemed readily to approve of, and told me, that I should give him a Petition for that purpose, and that he would write to the *Czar* for Leave for me.

But this innocent Request of mine, afterwards proved a Snare to me; for instead thereof, he represented to the *Czar*, that I had a Design to leave his Service, and that I had applied my self to the *English* Envoy for that Purpose, who had writ to *England* on my Behalf, and recommended the same Proposal for preserving the *English* Navy from Decay in Time of Peace, which I had given for the Preservation of his Majesty's Shipping that were then rotting at *Veronize*; and that therefore he had put a Stop to the Payment of my Money: Which his Lordship afterwards frankly acknowledged to me, telling me, that he was well informed, that I had applied my self to the *English* Envoy to recommend the like Proposal which I had given to his *Czarish* Majesty, who had accordingly sent the same forward to *England*; and that I having desir'd Leave of him to go out of the Countrey, he must take Care of his own Head: That therefore he had put a Stop to the Payment of my Money, which he could not now give me without his Majesty's farther particular Orders in it, to whom he had writ concerning me.

After which, the *Czar* being long in *Poland*, I continued still in *Mosco*, without either having my Arrears, or any Employment. At length his Lordship told me, that he had received an Answer from the *Czar*, and that he had Orders to send me upon Service; but would not tell me whither, or upon what particular Business, but that I must sign a new Covenant to serve his Majesty where and upon whatsoever Occasions I should be commanded for the future; without which, I was not to receive my Arrears, or any Part of them; and with this farther Hardship, that my Account which was then offered me to sign, was made at above 38 *per Cent*. Loss, according to the Course of Exchange at that Time, occasion'd by the *Czar*'s having recoined his Money; of which ill advised Project I shall hereafter give a more full Account in its proper Place.

These new Demands being not only very unreasonable, but dishonourable; and farther to be confin'd in a Countrey where I had been too long ill treated already, went very much against my Mind, for which Reason I could not accept nor comply with them: Whereupon his Lordship, who was then going again to *Petersburg*, to meet the Czar, be-

fore

fore he went, left Orders with his Deputy, to take away my Subsistence Money from me, and the *Denshicks*, or Soldiers, that had hitherto been given to attend me; thinking thereby to force me to a Compliance, and charging me with the Crime of obstinately disobeying the *Czar's* Orders. Whereupon I represented in a Memorial, the Hardships offered to me, and solicited for my Discharge to be given me, resolving to go out of the Countrey, and to leave my Money behind me; but my Discharge being refused, I was obliged to continue at *Mosco* till the *Czar* return'd from his Army.

About this Time the King of *Sweden* having dethroned King *Augustus*, and forced him to such a Peace as he was pleased to impose upon him, the *Czar* was left by himself in the War; and it being then rumour'd, that his *Swedish* Majesty intended to march out of *Saxony* directly to *Mosco*, and force the *Czar* to a Peace also, Orders were immediately given to fortifie the City of *Mosco*, by laying on Bastions all round the second Stone-Wall. And for this Work two Engineers were principally appointed, Mr. *Carchmin* his Majesty's chief *Russ*. Engineer, (whom I shall hereafter mention on another Occasion) and one *Sparitor*, who was Lieutenant Colonel of the *Czar's* Artillery. Of which Bastions there was a Necessity to place several upon the Side of the *Neglena* (a small Rivulet that falls into the *Mosco* River) in a

swampy

swampy Ground. Upon which, after I had observed them to begin to lay out the Foundation of the said Bastions, that were to be raised to a considerable Height before they could command the high Ground at a small Distance opposite to them, I accidentally met with the said Lieutenant Colonel one Day at Mr. *Whitworth*'s the *English* Envoy's House in *Mosco*; and in Discourse told him, that the Method which they took to build the Foundation of these Bastions, would never be sufficient to secure and bear the great Weight of Earth that was to come upon them, but would settle out at the Foot and tumble down before they were half finished: Which Discourse happened to be in the Presence both of her late Majesty's Envoy aforesaid, and the *English* Consul Mr. *Charles Goodfellow*; and I do not doubt but they still remember it. After I had made this Observation, being willing to shew my Readiness for his *Czarish* Majesty's Service, and believing that I might perhaps oblige my Lord *Apraxin* on this Occasion, (whose Command I was then under) I drew up a small Proposal, setting forth the Insufficiency of the said Work; and sent it to the said Lord, to whom the *Czar* had then given both the Command of the Fleet and the Army at *Petersburg*, offering my Assistance to make good the said Work; but his Lordship was not pleased to take any Notice at all of it. The Work went on as it was begun, and within six

Weeks

Weeks after my said Writing, several of the Bastions began to give way at the Foot; settled one Part from the other, and tumbled down before they were half built, and three of them which happened to be in the worst Ground, tumbled down a second Time the same Year; and though again built up the third Time, yet to this Day are not secured at the Foundation, nor raised to the proper Height required for it. But as things afterwards fell out, there was no Occasion for the making any Use of them.

For the King of *Sweden* who had deposed King *Augustus*, as has been mentioned, and who marched out of *Saxony* with an Army of 36000 chosen Men, might (as 'twas believed by Persons of the greatest Judgment in Affairs of that Time) have then easily obliged the *Czar* to honourable Conditions of Peace also, had he not been too rash and unadvised in his Proceedings; but there were two Things to which all his Misfortunes have been since principally imputed, and therefore I believe it may not be unacceptable to the Reader here to mention them.

The first of which is, that upon the *Russes* retiring before him through *Poland*; and he having got the Victory in the first Action, before he cross'd the *Nieper*, (near a Place called *Haloftzin*) he therefore did not wait for the coming up of his other Army that were on their March from *Riga* to join him, commanded by Lieutenant-General *Levenhaupt*,
which

which were 16000 Men more; who were afterwards entirely ruin'd at the Battel of *Lefno* by the good Management and perſonal Behaviour of the *Czar* in that Action; the greateſt part of the ſaid 16000 Men being either killed or taken upon the ſpot, with all the Artillery and Waggons that were carrying Ammunition of all ſorts to the King's Army. The ſecond is, that King after he had croſſed the *Nieper*, the *Czar* having burnt all the Houſes and Forage to a great diſtance on both Sides of the Road toward *Moſco*, he paſſed within 40 *Ruſs* Miles of *Smolensko*, without ſecuring any Place or Magazine behind him, but filed off to the Right, and march'd ſtill farther directly into the *Ukraine*.

He being invited by General *Mazeppa* (or the Hetman) of the *Coſſacks*, who inhabit that Countrey, and are under the Protection of the *Czar*, as they formerly were under that of the *Poles*; and who being now made uneaſy by the Breach of their Privileges and Exactions from them during the War, this General *Mazeppa*, as it afterwards appeared, correſponded near two Years with the King of *Sweden*, and promiſed to revolt to him upon his Arrival on that ſide of the Countrey, on Conditions to be re-inſtated under the Protection of the *Poles*. But by the Interception of ſome Letters and Circumſtances concurring, the Deſign was diſcovered, and the ſaid *Mazeppa*, with ſeveral of the great Officers, eſcaped to the King of *Sweden*. Upon the
Diſcovery

Discovery of this Conspiracy, Prince *Mentzicoff* immediately surprized the Garrison of *Butturin*, which was to have been surrender'd to the *Swedes*; hang'd up the Governor; and impaled several Persons upon the Walls of the City; particularly he caused Mr. *Koningseck*, that was a Foreigner, and Brother to the famous *Polish* Envoy of that Name, to be first tormented, and then hang'd.

But notwithstanding this Disappointment, the King of *Sweden* would not hear of any Proposition made to him to retire. The *Cossacks* gather'd for a time in Parties, and assisted the King of *Sweden* with Provisions, &c. but the said Parties were afterwards dispersed and ruin'd by the *Czar's* Forces; and the King of *Sweden's* own Army lessen'd by several Actions, (tho' he still had the Victory where he himself was present;) till after having long endured the Extremities both of Hunger and Cold, several both of his Officers and Soldiers being frozen to death, and others having lost the Use of their Hands and Feet in the severe Winter that was at that time, were at length entirely ruin'd by the great Victory obtain'd at *Poltava*, *Anno* 1709; in which the King himself was wounded, his prime Minister Count *Piper*, his two Secretaries of State, and all his Generals, with his whole Army, were either kill'd, or taken Prisoners; except Major-General *Sparr*, and Major-General *Leger Croon*, who only with the King, and about 300 Persons more by the Assistance of

the

the aforesaid General (or Hetman) of the *Coffacks*, who knew the Countrey, with the utmost Difficulty swam their Horses over the *Neiper*, (or *Borysthenes*) and escaped to the City of *Bender*, in the Dominions of the *Turks*, whither afterwards some few other Persons made their Escape to him. The Particulars of which Action, having every where in *Europe* been made publick, I shall not go about here to relate.

By this signal Victory the *Czar* was made secure in his Dominions, and left to carry on his farther Conquests. Whereas had the King of *Sweden* beaten the *Czar*'s Army, his Design was to have went directly to *Mosco*, and to have endeavour'd to have dethroned the *Czar*, as he had before done King *Augustus*: And it is certain, that not only the *Coffacks*, but the *Russes* too, who were every where ripe for Rebellion, and who had before taken up Arms in several Places, and had been defeated, would, if the *Czar* had lost the Battel of *Poltava*, have made a general Revolt, in hopes of Relief to their Grievances complained of in the *Czar*'s Administration, and to be restored to their old Superstition and Ignorance, to be rid of the Foreigners whom they were always dissatisfy'd with, and to be eased of the Burthen of their Taxes, and drain of their People, occasion'd not only by the long War, but by the other publick Undertakings of the *Czar*: Such particularly as the erecting and fortifying of new Places on the Frontiers,

(whither

(whither they with their Families, Gentleme[n]
as well as Soldiers and Peasants, were oblig[ed]
upon the *Czar*'s Commands, to remove a[nd]
inhabit:) As also the building of Fleets, wi[th]
Works for making Rivers navigable, whi[ch]
they reckon'd they had no occasion for, a[nd]
which they nor their Fathers had nev[er]
known.

But Fortune having thus happily favou[red]
the *Czar* in the said Action, he thereupon r[e]
turn'd to *Mosco* in Triumph, making his E[n]
try with the chief of the Generals and Priso[n]
ers that he had taken; and among many oth[er]
things he had rich triumphal Arches built, a[nd]
splendid Fire-works made, on this Occasio[n]
and there was nothing but feasting, and [all]
manner of Demonstrations of Joy. By th[is]
so remarkable Turn of Fortune, it remain[ed]
for the *Czar* now to think of carrying on H[is]
Conquest into the Heart of *Sweden*, and t[o]
establish a Maritime Power in the *Baltick*.

Whereupon his Majesty was pleas'd to thin[k]
of employing me on that Side of the Coun[n]
trey, for making a Communication from th[e]
great River *Wolga*, by way of the *Lodiga* S[ea]
to *Peterburgh*; to bring things quite throug[h]
from the *Wolga*, which runs through th[e]
most plentiful part of *Russia*, to his said ne[w]
Favourite Town, by a free Water Carriage.

But I having been very long held out o[f]
my Arrears, and often expressed my Discon[n]
tent on that Account, I was utterly averse to
serve any farther without being first paid th[e]
full

all Money that was then due to me; and hearing that one of the Lords had, to my great Surprize, raised an Objection against my being paid my Arrears, by reason of my being so long without doing any Service in *Mosc.*, and because the Work for making a Communication between the *Wolga* and the *Don* was not finish'd; I therefore drew up the following Memorial, and first shew'd it to his Excellency Mr. *Whitworth*, who was then made Embassador Extraordinary to the *Czar*, and to Mr. *Goodfellow*, her Majesty's Consul, that they might see the ill Treatment I had met with; and when it was translated into the *Russ* Language, I deliver'd it to the forementioned Lord *Apraxin*, humbly desiring him to do me the Justice to represent it to the *Czar*: Which Representation I have order'd to be transcrib'd, and is as follows; but must first beg the Reader's Pardon, if he finds in it several Passages that I have taken some notice of before.

An Humble REPRESENTATION of th[e] hard Fortune and Discouragemen[ts] that the underwritten *John Perr[y]* hath met with, from the time o[f] his being entertained in *Englan[d]* to the present Year, 1710.

IN April 1698, an Agreement or Contra[ct] was verbally made with me in Englan[d] *for entring into his* Czarish *Majesty's Ser vice, by his Embassador the late Lord* Feo dore Allexyavich Gollovin, *for the Salary o[f]* 300 l. Sterl. *per Annum, besides a month[ly] Allowance, that was agreed to be paid m[e] sufficient for my Charges and Subsistence and that in case of my performing any extra ordinary Work relating to Rivers, Havens Molds, Docks, or Sluices, to have more over an extraordinary Reward given me t[o] my Content. I was thereupon sent directly forward from* England *to view and make [a] Report of the Work for making a Communi cation between the Rivers* Wolga *and th[e]* Don, *(that had been deserted by Colone[l]* Breckell;*) and according to his Majesty'[s] Orders I went forward thither, and sur vey'd it, and return'd the same Year back t[o]* Mosco, *with a Draught of what was neces sary to be done, and an Estimate of the same. Which being approv'd of and order'd to be ta*

ken

ken in hand by his Majesty, I required the Settlement of my Wages to be duly paid me every six Months, and that a farther Reward of 8000 Rubles should be given me when the Work should be perform'd.

Whereupon it was objected by my Lord Kneaz Burris Allexyeavitz Gollitzen, that a Letter had been writ to him from Holland by the aforesaid Embassador, that I should undertake the said Work without the Payment of my yearly Wages till it was perform'd; against which I therefore protested; and on March the 10th, 1699, deliver'd a Petition into his Czarish Majesty's own Hand, setting forth the Unreasonableness thereof, and that I could not consent to take the said Work in hand on any such Terms or Conditions, and therefore pray'd, that either I might be employ'd on some other Business, or have my Discharge given me.

To which his Czarish Majesty, in the Presence of Mr. Stiles, Mr. Lloyd, Mr. Crevett, and several other English Merchants, was pleased to give me repeated Assurances, and commanded me to rely upon his gracious Word, that the aforesaid Objection should have no Force against me; but that my full Wages, as aforesaid, should be yearly paid me, as well as monthly Subsistence Money; and a farther Reward to my Satisfaction more than the Sum abovemention'd, upon Performance of the Work: But by reason that Breckell when he had gather'd a Sum of Money

ney had deserted, as was objected by the Lord Gollitzen, his Majesty only required me to give Security not to do the like, and promised that I should receive my said Salary every six Months, before-hand, if I desired it.

Which gracious Promise I most chearfully embraced; but I being then a Stranger, and newly come into the Countrey, I could not reasonably expect, nor could I ask any Gentleman there to be bound for me in this Case. Yet I did not in the least doubt, but in a Year or two's time I should have been able to make such an Advance, and to have given such sufficient Proof of my Ability and Readiness for performing the Work, that would have quite removed all Scruple of my deserting so considerable and reputable a Service; and that by Consequence no Demur would be made in the Payment of my Salary, although no Security was given against Desertion.

But to my great Surprize, and unthought of Discouragement, when I came upon the Work I found the Men and Materials which I proposed for the doing of it not provided; my self and Mr. Luke Kenedy, my chief Assistant, treated in a very rough manner, shew'd the Gallows, and threaten'd to be hang'd by the aforesaid Lord Gollitzen, because I did not carry on the Work where I found Breckell had begun it, who had deserted it; and altho' he knew that upon my Representations in Mosco his Czarish Majesty had expressly order'd me to the contrary:

and

and afterwards when his Lordship, in hopes to find an occasion of an Objection against me, appointed Persons on purpose, and order'd a strict Measure and Examination to be taken of both Places; it was found (upon Computation) that there was above 20000 cubical Fathoms Russ Measure *, less Labour of digging work in the cutting of the Canal where I began it; besides a very great Advantage in the Necessity of placing the Sluices. But notwithstanding I gave full Satisfaction in this Point, I still found many other great Discouragements and Hindrances to the Work; and my Complaints, and repeated Demands in Writing given into the Precause † availing little: Therefore, February 17, 1700, I delivered to his Czarish Majesty himself a Petition, setting forth, that unless his Majesty would be graciously pleased to appoint me a Hearing, and examine himself into the whole Matter, I feared there was no hopes of my being ever able to perform the said Work.

Whereupon, after I had deliver'd my said Petition to his Majesty, I was the next Day order'd by the Lord Kneaz Burris Allexyavitz Gollitzen to give a new List into the Precause, and told that all things should be ful-

---

* Note, A Russ Fathom is 7 English Feet, and about the tenth part of an Inch.

† The Word Precause signifies the publick Office, where all Affairs, of what kind soever, relating to any Business, District, or Province, are examined and determined by Chancellors who are appointed thereto.

D   ly

by provided for the Work. I was glad to hear so encouraging a Promise, with fresh hopes that things would now go better on. But the second Summer having past away also in the same manner, the needful Men and Materials not given, and several parts of the Work lying unfinished, and subject thereby to Damage and Ruine by the Floods, particularly for want of Caulkers, which there was the greatest Necessity for; and finding still no likelihood of Redress upon my Complaints to the Lord Kneaz Burris Allexyavitz Gollitzen, nor in the Precause, I therefore thought my self in Duty bound, and again deliver'd into his Majesty's own Hand another Writing, dated the 23d Day of Jan. 1701, setting forth particularly, that all the digging Work that was done in two Summers might (by Computation and Measure) have been done in less than fifty Days, at the rate of 12 Men digging and carrying off but one cubical Fathom a Day, had the Number of labouring Men been given, and things carried on as I required. Also setting forth, that there still wanted several sorts of Timber, Caulkers, and other Artificers and Necessaries, without which it was impossible for any one Sluice ever to be completed: and which, to my very great Trouble and Discouragement, I had seen in two Years not provided. But that yet, notwithstanding all the Hindrances that I met with, if the needful Men and Materials were but

then

then fully given, which I had demanded in my first List, the Work that remained to be done might be depended to be finish'd in three or four Years time at the farthest.

Upon which I was informed, That now more strict Orders than ever were given, that all Necessaries whatsoever that I had demanded, and were wanting, should be duly provided; and I was commanded by his Majesty to prepare new Molds and Directions for the cutting of Timber, &c. which I carried and deliver'd into his Majesty's own Hands at his House at Brebazenski. But notwithstanding, at the latter End of this third Summer, I was in Writing inform'd by Kneaz Peter Evanwich Dashcoff[*], that the several Governors of the Towns, on all the Districts of the Wolga, whither Copies of the said Molds, and Directions for cutting the said Timber were sent, had taken Scalcoes or Attestations in Writing, under the Hands of the several Persons employ'd, that no such Timber was any where possible to be found.

Therefore I demanded a Company of Dragoons to go with me, that I might not be surprized by the Tartars, and went my self into the Woods, not two Days Journey from the Work, where in less than fourteen Days time I found very proper, well grown Tim-

---

[*] He was appointed General of the Army then covering the Work, and Governor of the Workmen.

ber enough for making the Gates, and finishing two Pair of Sluices; which Timber I shew'd to the Lord Apraxin, who happen'd to be at that time sent to supervise the Work; As also I represented to his Lordship, when he was upon the Spot, the great Want of Caulkers, and other Artificers and Necessaries, which to that Day were never given; nor the small Number of Smiths, Carpenters and Labourers continued in the Winter, which I had demanded in my first List. All which his Lordship took Cognizance of, and promised to represent to the Czar; and that he would be my Patron, and make a just Recommendation of my Endeavours to his Majesty.

On the 2^d of September 1701, I received an Order to leave Directions in Writing with one of my Assistants, whom I should choose to take care of the Work that was perform'd, and to come my self, with my other Assistants and Master Artificers that I had with me, to Mosco. And soon after the Beginning of the Year 1702, I was from thence order'd down to Veronize, where I made an extraordinary Work upon that River, for raising and letting off the Water at any time when ever required, for lifting his Majesty's Ships upon the Land to be re-fitted, that were then ready to sink as they lay in the River, for want of an effectual Method to repair them; which Work I finish'd in the Year 1703: And all his Czarish Majesty's *jesty's* Ships have accordingly been there since repaired that have required it. And after I finish'd this, I was employ'd in doing another Work for making the said River navigable for Ships of 80 Guns, the whole way from the City Veronize to the River Don; which I also perform'd as commanded, where the needful Men and Materials were given me to do it; though the Sluices are much larger, and the Floods in the Spring of the Year above ten times greater there than they are on the River Camishinka; and consequently the Works required to be made there with much greater Strength against greater Floods, and were far more difficult to perform.

In February 1706, after I had finished the said Works, I was ordered to Mosco; and on September *following I was sent down again upon the River* Don, *to survey a Place for making a Work to preserve his Majesty's Ships from Decay, and to return again to* Mosco *with the Report of the same*; where I have been ever since that time petitioning and soliciting for my Arrears to be given me, and to be employ'd on some other Business, or to have my Discharge, which is not given me, nor any part of my yearly Wages yet paid me, neither for the time I have served in the Cazans, nor the Admiraltitski Precause; only an Account has been formerly made out in the Admiraltitski Precause *for six Years Salary, at* 300 l. *per Annum, according to my Agreement*; but it was with this Injustice and Hardship, that all the monthly Subsistence Money that I had received for the said six Years should be deducted out of my said yearly Salary, and the same to be reckoned me but at a Russ Copeek for an English Penny, which according to the Course of Exchange at that time was at 38 per Cent. Loss to me: Not only so, but refusing also to pay me any part of the said Money, unless I would first set my Hand to agree to a new Contract, on such discouraging Conditions that were altogether unreasonable for me to comply with.

This is the true State of my Case, which I humbly pray may be justly consider'd: First, That it was no way my Fault that the Work in making a Communication between the Wolga and the Don was not long since performed, as has been shewn. And next, that no Objection at my coming into the Countrey was made against the immediate Payment of my annual Salary, but the abovesaid Scruple unjustly raised of my deserting, which now, after near 12 Years Proof of the Fidelity of my Service, I hope is sufficiently removed. And since his Czarish Majesty's Favour and Bounty is dayly extended to great Numbers of those that come from foreign Countreys to serve him, I humbly hope that I shall not be made an unhappy Instance of Misfortune and Ruine thereby: After having relied so many Years on his Czarish Majesty's gracious Promises

mises of my Wages made to me, and having spent the best of my Days, and faithfully exerted my utmost Judgment and Endeavours for his Majesty's Service, in all the Things wherein I have ever been commanded.

Mosco, Feb. 15. 1710. J. PERRY.

Having first given one Copy of this Representation to my Lord *Apraxin* as I have abovemention'd, I prepared another Copy thereof, and annex'd it to a short Petition, which I designed to have presented to the *Czar* himself, but I was persuaded by Prince *Mensicoff* (in whose Province the intended Work lay which I was next to be employ'd upon) not to deliver the same, but only to speak to his Majesty, without troubling him with any Writing, and that he would second me in my Desire; which he did accordingly, at a Place where I had the Honour, with a small Company, to dine with his Majesty that Day; and his Majesty was thereupon pleased graciously to promise me, that as soon as I had only been and made the Survey for the aforesaid Communication to *Petersburgh*, I should upon my Return assuredly have my full Arrears paid me, before he would desire me to take it in hand: Accordingly, relying on his Majesty's Word, since it was only to survey, and not to engage in the doing any new Work without my Money, I was willing to comply with his Majesty's Desire; which I

D 4 did,

did, as I thought, to oblige his Majesty, and when I had so favourable a Promise renew'd to me.

This intended Survey was in order to carry on a great and useful Design of the *Czar's*, as beforemention'd; his Majesty having for a long time had Intentions to bring the Trade from *Archangel*, and all the other Parts of his Countrey, to his said new favourite Town, situate at the Mouth of the *Neva*, which falls out of the *Lodiga* Lake into the *Baltick* Sea.

To which end, before I came from *Russia*, Storehouses were building for Merchants, and a great Number of Inhabitants already settled there; and though it be but a small part of what is designed in Variety of Undertakings, as particularly the Building of another new Town on *Richard's* Island, about 40 *Russ* Miles below the Mouth of the *Neva*, and 5 Miles from the Coast of *Ingermania*, which the *Czar* designs large enough for all his Nobility, Merchants, &c. with Canals through the Streets, like that of *Amsterdam*, and an artificial Haven both for his Navy and Merchant Shipping that are intended to trade thither; yet notwithstanding these his Majesty's new Designs of increasing his Strength and Commerce there, it will be found very difficult and burthensome to his People, without a free Communication be made to the more fertile Parts of his Countrey by Water; for by reason of the Tediousness of the Way, the

being

being obliged to wait for Floods and Rains at several shallow Places, and the Vessels and Floats being often dash'd and staved to pieces against the Rocks and Falls that are by the way, and the Goods often lost and spoiled; and by reason also of the very great Scarcity and Dearness of Forage for Horses where Land Carriage is required; Corn and other Provision of Burthen is usually at least 3 or 4 times the Price which the same is bought for between the Towns of *Rebna* and *Caffan*, the first of which is from *Petersburgh* near 1000 *Russ* Miles upon the said River *Wolga*: From which Side of the Countrey is brought also Oak Timber, and other Naval Stores for equipping out the *Czar*'s Fleets, the Charge of which is equally augmented by the Tediousness of the Carriage: So that the *Czar*'s Ships, which are now built of Oak at *Petersburgh*, though Mens Labour is abundantly cheaper, and that he has the Iron Work and Cordage out of his own Countrey, yet the Building of his Ships with Oak are as dear as to have them bought in *England*.

Therefore to remedy these Evils, his Majesty was pleased to send me three separate Ways quite through the Countrey, from the side of the *Lodiga* Sea to the *Wolga*, to trace the several Rivers, as they fall into each other, to the Places where, at the Heads or first Springs from whence they take their Rise, they come nearest, and are most commodious for a Communication to be made.

Accor-

Accordingly I proceeded and took the Defcent or Difference of Level, of the said several Rivers as they fall down into the *Wolga* on the one side of the Countrey, and discharge themselves into the *Lodiga* Sea on the other side of the Countrey; with such other Observations as were necessary to be made; and returned at the End of the Year 1710, to his Majesty, who was then at *Petersburg*, with the Draught and Report of the most proper Place, and the Time and Charge required for making the said Communication, by way of the Rivers *Koessha, Beila* Lake, and *Shacksna* on the one side of the Countrey, falling into the *Wolga*, (near the Town of *Rebna* aforesaid;) and by the way of the River *Whitigor*, the *Onega* Lake, and River *Swire*, falling into the *Lodiga* Sea on the other side of the Countrey; where there is required only the placing of twenty two Sluices, and the cutting of an easie Canal not three *English* Miles in Length: A Draught of which intended Communication, is shewn in the general Map hereunto annexed.

And for the sake of those who may have Curiosity in this Affair, I shall here add this short Abstract of the Survey which I made. First, That where I survey'd the Countrey by way of the River *Sass* and *Tiffin*, to the Top of the High-land within the Countrey, from whence an Arm of the *Tiffin* takes its first Rise; I found the same, the whole Way, with abundance of Falls descending into the *Lodiga*

Sea, in running 174 *Ruſs* Miles (winding as the Rivers take their Courſe) to be Difference of Level, 897 *Engliſh* Feet; and from the Top of the ſaid Highland, in running on the other Side of the Countrey, 420 Miles down the Rivers *Chacodoſhea* and *Molloga*, to the Place where the Mouth of the River *Shackſna* falls into the *Wolga*, I found the Deſcent to be by Obſervation 562 Feet.

Secondly, By way of the River *Emſta*, *Ilmena* Lake, and River *Volcoff* falling into the *Lodiga* Sea, I found the Deſcent in running 550 *Ruſs* Miles, to be 568 Foot; and on the other ſide of the Countrey, Southward, deſcending by way of the Rivers *Twere* and *Volga*, as far as the Mouth of the *Shackſna* aforeſaid, in running 720 *Ruſs* Miles, I found the Deſcent to be 233 Foot.

And in the third Place which I ſurvey'd, quite through the Countrey, by way of the River *Whitigor*, *Onega* Lake and River *Swire* falling into the *Lodiga* Sea; in the running of 278 *Ruſs* Miles, I found the Deſcent to be but 445 Feet from the Top of the higheſt Land where the Rivers come neareſt for a Canal to be cut; and the Deſcent down on the other ſide of the Countrey, in running 118 Miles, by way of the Rivers *Koefsha*, *Beila* Lake, and *Shackſna* falling into the *Wolga* at the ſame Place beforenamed, but 10 Foot.

This being much the loweſt or moſt level Part of the Countrey, attended with the leaſt

Falls

Falls, and requiring the least Number of Sluices to be made; and the Rivers *Swire* and *Shackna*, and good Part of the Rivers *Koefsh* and *Whitigor* being already navigable for small Vessels which pass the whole Year backward and forward, except only when the Rivers are frozen; I therefore recommended it to his *Czarish* Majesty, in my Report, as abundantly preferable for the making the said Communication that was intended.

But just before I arrived with the said Report, there came Advice, that the *Turks*, at the Instigation of the King of *Sweden*, had declared War on the other side of the Countrey, which put a new Face upon all Affairs. The Thoughts of the said Communication was then laid aside at once. The Lord *Apraxin* who was Admiral, with the other two Flag-Officers who were Foreigners, and most of the Captains and Seamen, were thereupon immediately sent to *Veronize*. Strong Detachments of the Army were ordered to march from all Parts, and new Levies immediately to be made. The Czar himself went first to *Mosco* to settle Matters with the Senate (whom he had created the Year before, composed of 9 *Boyars*;) and from thence he went directly to his Army, and I was left again to attend the uncertain Event of this new War.

But before his Majesty's Departure, as sudden as it was, I humbly renewed my Application to him for my Arrears, which he had
promised

promised me, as beforementioned; but could not obtain any more than only one Year's Salary, (reckoned at 300 *l. per Annum*) being only for the Time I was employed upon the said Survey, which was paid me by Prince *Menſicoff*, in whoſe Province the deſigned Work lay, and whoſe Command for that Reaſon I was then under; and I was put off for the Payment of my other Arrears, till the Return of the Lord *Apraxin*, who was gone to *Azoph*, with whom my former Accompts were ſtated, and out of whoſe Office I was to receive them.

The *Czar*'s Army, though the greateſt Part of them had between 2 and 3000 *Ruſs* Miles to march on this Occaſion, arrived on the Borders of *Moldavia*, with an Expedition that is ſcarce to be credited; where the *Czar* himſelf join'd them early in the Spring, and ſent a Manifeſto to the Inhabitants of *Valabia* and *Moldavia*, exhorting them to join and aſſiſt him, and that he would come on to the Banks of the *Danube*, and would redeem them from the *Turkiſh* Yoke, and eſtabliſh them in the free Enjoyment of their Religion, Liberties, and Privileges for ever.

Upon which they promiſed to take up Arms and join his Majeſty, who marched into their Countrey, and was got within ſix *German* Miles of the *Danube*, and had by an advance Party of Dragoons commanded by General *Renne*, ſurprized a ſmall Garriſon near the Mouth of the *Pruth*, where the

Turks

Turks had made a Magazine on this side of *Danube*. But the *Turks* at another Place above the Mouth of the *Pruth*, crossed the *Danube* with all their Army, before the *Czar* could come up to oppose their Passage as was designed to have been done. Whereupon the *Valachians* and *Moldavians* immediately went over to the *Turks*, and declared that they had only made Shew of joining with the *Czar*, who had march'd into their Countrey, and had been obliged to assist him with Provisions, &c. to save themselves from Contribution and Ruine, which otherwise they must have suffered. Only the *Hospodar* (or Prince) of *Moldavia*, with some few Persons of Note, who had acted sincerely in the *Czar*'s Interest, thought it best therefore to remain under his Protection; accordingly the said *Hospodar* continues to this Day in *Mosco*.

The *Czar*, when he drew near the *Danube*, was not only left by the *Valachians* and *Moldavians*, but the *Crim Tartars*, who had for some Days before appeared in Parties, so cut off both his Provision and Intelligence, that the *Turks* came upon him with more than three Times his Number before he had the least Advice that they were over the *Danube*.

The *Czar* upon this Surprize, retired with his Army towards the River *Pruth*, which was not far behind him, and where the *Turks* who had first appeared with a small Party in the Morning, came up in a full Body

Body in the Afternoon, and push'd on an Attack with all their Power: But the *Czar* having disposed his Army behind a Line of *Chevaux de Frize*, or Turn-pikes shod with Iron, he maintain'd so regular and strong a Fire, that the Enemy with all their Force could not break in upon them; and in the Evening, after between three or four Hours close Fire, they retired out of the Reach of the Artillery, which had done great Execution upon them, carrying off their Dead with them.

The *Czar*'s Army encouraged with Success thus far, after they had a little refreshed themselves, expecting another Charge, took up their Turn-pikes on Mens Shoulders, whom they relieved every half Hour, and marched the whole Night in order of Battel, keeping within Reach of the *Pruth*, that they might have Water for themselves and their Horses. The *Turkish* Cavalry came upon them again the next Day, and charged them in their March, which they still continued; but when the Enemy surrounded and came too close upon them, they were then obliged to set down their Turn-pikes and receive them in manner aforesaid; by means of which repeated Halts, the *Turkish* Infantry came up at length, and the whole Armies were that Day again furiously engaged for some Hours, till Night parted them as before.

This sort of running Fight not having been practised any where before in *Europe*, that I have

have heard of, I thought it would not be disagreeable to the Reader to relate the Circumstances of it; and it was done in a plain and open Countrey, without Inclosures, otherwise it had not been practicable.

The *Turks* in these two Days, according to the most impartial Accounts, lost between 10 and 12000 Men, with two or three Bashaw's; and the *Russ* about 7000 kill'd and wounded; among which were a Major-General, several Colonels, and many foreign Officers, particularly of those who commanded in the Artillery, which did singular Service on this Occasion. This Account I have had from several Gentlemen who were then present in the Action.

The *Turks* being weary, and discouraged by the vigorous Resistance which they found, began to call to Mind old Prophecies, and to think that Providence was against them. But the *Tartars*, among whom the King of *Sweden* (with the few *Swedes* he had with him) was in Person, having marched all the time on the other side of the River *Pruth*, to prevent the *Russes* crossing over, and killing many of them as they came to fetch Water; and the *Russes* finding themselves surrounded on all sides, without the least Prospect of any Retreat; and Provision for Man and Horse growing very scarce, by reason it had been cut off by the *Tartars* aforesaid, and that they had been obliged to quit most of their Waggons in their March;

as

as also not having sufficient Ammunition left with their Artillery, on which was their greatest Dependence, to hold out another Attack. A Trumpet, with an Officer, on the third Day, was sent into the *Turkish* Army to offer Conditions of Peace, before being reduced to the last Extremity. There was a great Enquiry made for Ducats thro' the *Russ* Army, which were said to be given to the *Grand Vizier* on this Occasion; and after about half a Day's treating, a Peace was concluded in the Field, and Hostages were exchanged; by which the *Czar* obliged himself to give up *Azoph* in the same Condition as it was in, in the Year 1696, when it was taken from the *Turks*, and to demolish *Taganroke*, a very strong Fortress built by the present *Czar*, on the *Palus Mæotis* (where Storehouses for his Navy, and the new Haven beforementioned was made;) as also to demolish two other small Towns built by the *Czar* on the Frontiers towards the *Nieper*, with some other Articles.

Thus the *Czar* by his expecting the Assistance of the *Valachians* and *Moldavians*, and by his marching so far from home, and not having secured any Place for a Retreat behind him, had like to have fallen exactly into the very same Misfortune which was the Ruine and Loss of the King of *Sweden*'s Army but two Year's before; only with this remarkable Difference, that the *Cossacks*, who had invited the King of *Sweden* into their

E Coun-

Countrey, as has been mentioned, after their main Design was broke, yet continued still in Parties, and acted long against the *Czar*; but the *Valachians* and *Moldavians* content to live under the Government of the *Turks*, never struck one Stroke for the Purchase of their Freedom and Privileges promised them by the *Czar*.

However disadvantageous the foresaid Conditions of Peace were to the *Czar*, there was by it an End put to the War the first Campaign, and the *Czar* left again to carry on his Conquests against the *Swedes*; who, tho' it was believed they had induced the *Turks* to this War, yet had no Article concluded for them. And the *Czar*'s Fleet on the side of *Azoph*, being rendred useless by the said Peace, Orders were given to leave off building any more Ships on that side; and the *Czar* himself, with all his maritime Officers and People, Builders and other Artificers, thereupon return'd to *Petersburgh*; where in the Beginning of the Year 1712, I was also ordered to attend his Majesty in order to be employed on the aforementioned Communication for Water-Carriage.

But when I arrived there, it began then again very much to be doubted, that a new War would break out with the *Turks*; for though *Azoph*, with the other Places agreed on, had been long delivered up, and in Possession of the *Turks*; yet upon the Complaints made by the King of *Sweden* against
the

the *Grand Vizier*, and by his Representations that much greater Advantages might easily have been obtained, and that he proposed to have delivered the *Czar* Prisoner, with his whole Army; wherein he was seconded by the *Cham* of *Tartary*; the *Vizier* who made the Peace, was deposed and sent into Banishment; the Articles, upon some Pretences relating to the *Tartars* and *Cossacks*, were refused to be ratified by the Sultan; the *Muscovite* Hostages strictly confined at their Houses, apart, and the Horse-Tail set up at the new *Grand Vizier*'s, the usual Signal for War.

Therefore the *Czar*, though he had sent new Instructions of Compliance to his Embassadors, and ordered his Army to be again in Readiness upon the *Ukraine*, until it should be known whether the Peace would be confirmed or not; he deferr'd his Orders of employing me on the aforementioned Communication, and was pleased to send me to survey some of the small Rivers which fall into the *Neva*, for the making a Work for floating his *Petersburgh* Fleet which began to decay upon the Land, to be repaired in manner as I had before done at *Veronize*.

Accordingly I went and pitched upon a Place at the Mouth of the River *Slavenka*, where the Ground was admirably good for that Purpose (having dug down 14 Foot below the Surface of the River, before any Sign of Water appeared;) and I was pleased

E 2   with

with the Thoughts of my being employed upon it; for it being at the Head of the *Baltick* Sea, where shipping come from all Parts, I believed it would have been of more Reputation to me, than that which I did at *Veronize*; when it would have been seen that the *Czar*'s Ships of 60 or 70 Guns, which are the biggest he has yet built there, should come directly out of the Sea, and by such a Work, without any Help of the Tide, (there being no Course of Ebb and Flood in that Sea) be raised on the Land to be rebuilt or refitted, like as in our Docks in *England*.

But before I had began it, in the Month of *May* 1712, a Courier arrived with the welcome News of the *Sultan*'s having at length ratified the Peace, and that the *Muscovite* Hostages were again set at Liberty. Whereupon his Majesty was pleased to tell me, that the said Work for refitting his Ships, should be then deferr'd, which might be done at another time; but that above all, it was first necessary to take in hand the forementioned Work, for a Communication to be made for Water-Carriage, that Stores and Provisions might be brought with greater Convenience; and soon after, his Majesty designing for *Pomerania* I was appointed to attend in the Senate (which was then call'd to *Petersburgh*) where the Matter of the said intended Communication was debated; and after the Draught and Report which I had made, was fully examined

ned, it was resolved, that ten thousand Men, with a proportionable Number of Artificers, &c. should be given for the Work, and I was commanded to give in a List of all the Materials requisite for the Performance, and to go immediately upon it. Upon which I delivered to his Majesty then in the Senate, a Petition for my Wages that were then in Arrears, setting forth the Agreement that had been made with me by his Embassador in *England*, and his Majesty's own repeated Promises to me for the Payment of them.

After my Petition was read in the Senate, it was referr'd, by the *Czar*'s Order, to my Lord *Apraxin*, who had long been my Enemy, and had hitherto obstructed my being paid; and who had, as beforementioned, injuriously suggested to the *Czar*, (which he still maintain'd) that my Design was only to get my Money and to leave his Service. Whereas his unjust Insinuations were the very Reverse of my Intentions; for my Design was to have married in the Countrey to a Woman for whom I had long had a great Esteem, and should have been content, for her sake, to have continued in the *Czar*'s Service, had my Money been justly paid me. But the said Lord only offered to give me 4000 Rubles in hand, which was but about a third Part of what was then due to me, with the bare Promise only of the rest; and that I should be farther particularly rewarded by the *Czar* when I had finished the said Communi-

E 3 cation;

cation; and that I should then have leave to go home, if I desired it: But that I must sign to serve his Majesty upon the aforesaid Work, upon the Receipt only of the said 4000 Rubles to be given me in hand, before I was to receive it: Which Offer, I presume, his Lordship did believe would have been a Temptation that I could not have resisted, knowing that he had long kept me out of my Pay, and that I was thereby in want of Money.

But I told his Lordship, that I had spent the best of my Days in their Service, and had been too much disappointed already to place any more Faith in Promises, therefore insisted upon all my Arrears being then given me in hand, and the establishing my Wages to be duly paid me every six Months for the future, as mentioned in my Petition; without which, I was resolved not to proceed any farther, and demanded my Discharge to be given me.

Whereupon his Lordship sent an Officer twice to me in the *Czar*'s Name, and threatned to force me upon the said Work; and would have done it upon his own Terms, had I not immediately put my self under the Protection of his Excellency Mr. *Whitworth*, her Majesty's Embassador extraordinary, then present at *Petersburgh*; who was pleased to represent my said Usage, amongst other Matters, to the Queen, and who being then coming out of the Countrey, brought me away with him under his Protection, without their giving me any Money, Pass, or Discharge.

Whereupon Mr. *Carchmin* (the *Czar*'s chief *Russ* Engineer, before spoken of) who was ordered to have been my Assistant upon the said Work, was sent forward upon it, without me, with some *Dutch* Artificers, and pretended to do it. But the Difficulties he apprehended in it, deterr'd him from taking it upon him; and I am since informed by some Gentlemen that lately came from *Russia*, that the said Work lies still undone without any Person to undertake it. As also I have been farther informed by the same Persons, that since I came out of the Countrey, the *Czar* has built Sheds over his Ships on the side of *Veronize*, to preserve them from Decay, but not in a dry Haven, according to that effectual Manner in which I proposed to have done it.

Mr. *Whitworth*, after he had taken me into his Protection, in a long Conference which he had with the Great Chancellor, Count *Gollofkin*, notified it to him in Form; and among other Instances of Injustice which he represented was done to her Majesty's Subjects, he was pleased to resent the ill Usage that I had received, in their not paying me my Arrears, and at the same time threatning to force me on farther Service: For which Reason he had taken me into his Protection. Three Days after this Conference, the aforesaid

said Lord *Apraxin* proposed to me, that if the Embaſſador would give it under his Hand, or his verbal Promiſe only, that I ſhould ſtay in the Countrey, that he would then give me Terms to my Content. But the Embaſſador having been pleaſed to inform me, that in his Report to the Queen, he had already ſent forward an Account of the ill Treatment I had met with; that I had put my ſelf under his Protection, and that he was bringing me away with him out of the Countrey: It was not then proper for me to deſire that Favour of him; nor was it then adviſeable for me to think of ſtaying any longer in that Service, after I had put my ſelf under his Protection, and by my publickly complaining, not only incenſed my Lord *Apraxin*, but ſeveral others of the Lords againſt me, who would ſome Time or other, certainly reach me with their Revenge; which is known by too many Inſtances, and which they find no Difficulty to do whenever they have a Mind to it.

Beſide, I was informed, that not only ſeveral of the Lords, but the *Czar* himſelf had let fall ſome Expreſſions of Reſentment againſt me; particularly at an Entertainment on board of a Man of War (called the *Poltava*) that was then launch'd, where his Majeſty began ſome Diſcourſe with one of the *Engliſh* Maſter-Builders, and laying his Hand on his Breaſt, ſaid to him, *That he loved him at his Heart, becauſe he was not like* Perry, *that he went where he was ordered, and did what he was commanded, and did not murmur and complain*; which made my Friends thereupon perſuade me, and fully confirm'd me in the Opinion, that it was then too late to think of my accepting of any Terms whatſoever.

Thus I have given an Account how I have paſt my Time, and been dealt withal in that Countrey; the Truth of which in every Part, is well known both to her late Majeſty's ſaid Embaſſador Extraordinary, who is now the King's Miniſter at *Ratisbon*, and to Mr. *Charles Goodfellow*, who was many Years her late Majeſty's Conſul and Agent-General in *Ruſſia*, and is now in *London*, as well as to many other Gentlemen who have been in *Ruſſia*.

A

Farther and more Particular

ACCOUNT

OF

RUSSIA.

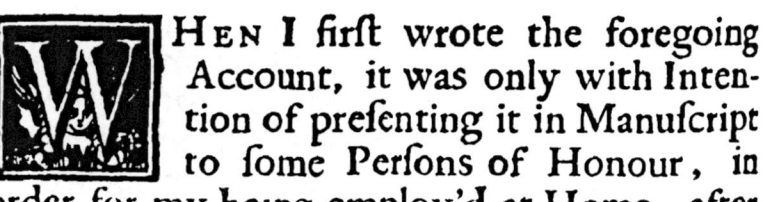

WHEN I firſt wrote the foregoing Account, it was only with Intention of preſenting it in Manuſcript to ſome Perſons of Honour, in order for my being employ'd at Home, after the Experience of ſo many Years that I have ſpent in foreign Service, where I have had both *Engliſh* and *Dutch* Maſter Artificers under

under my Command for making of Sluices; and where I have had all the Opportunities that could be desired for making such Experiments, as I found necessary; and not without some Hopes also that I may obtain an Order, that what her Majesty's aforesaid Embassador has mention'd in his Relations concerning me, now lying in the Secretary of States Office, may be examin'd, touching the Hardship done me, whenever it may be thought a proper Time for it; and that I may obtain the King's most gracious Orders to his Ministers to make some Instances for my being relieved, as to the Wages due to me, which was more than once tender'd to me in part, and according to my Accounts that have been made out in the publick Offices of the *Czar*, stop'd only on the hard and severe Conditions to force me to serve the *Czar*, as has been beforemention'd.

But after I had writ the foregoing Account, some Friends, to whom I shew'd it, persuaded me to make it publick as it then was, and blamed me for not having done it sooner at my first coming over to *England*, before I had offer'd my self to any Business: And some other Friends, with whom I had particularly often discoursed of the Manner and Customs of the People, and of the Reformations that the present *Czar* has made in his Countrey, have put me also upon writing the following Account of such remarkable Things that have occurr'd to my own Observation, and adding it hereto.

As

As I never had any Thoughts, when I was in *Russia*, that I should ever have written any thing of this kind, and therefore am not able to do it so full as I could wish; yet so far as I have written, I have taken care not in the least to deviate from the Truth; and I can be content all that I have writ should be read by the *Czar* himself, whom I shall ever personally honour and esteem; and should I believe, have served as long as I had lived, had it not been for the evil Offices of such of his *Boyars* who kept me out of my Pay, and set themselves directly against me, and against my Undertakings.

I have, with some Corrections, as far as accrues to my own Knowledge, hereto annex'd a general Map of the *Czar*'s Dominions, wherein I have pointed out the intended Communications before spoken of, and by a prick'd Line have shewn the Extent of the *Czar*'s Countrey, so far as inhabited by any People that pay Obedience to him; and by a double prick'd Line have shewn his late Conquest of the *Swedes*.

It is not, as I have before said, in my Power to make a full and perfect Representation of all the *Czar*'s Countrey and Affairs; nor is it my Intention to say much of that Part of his Dominions which borders upon *Europe*, and is already well enough known to the World: But shall only observe some few Things relating to the more remote Parts of the *Czar*'s Countrey, and of the Inhabitants

bor-

bordering to the Eastward of his Dominions, and then proceed to give a short Account of the *Czar*'s People, and of the Reformations that he has made amongst them.

I have often heard the *Czar* say, that he intends to send People on purpose to take a true Map of his Countrey, as soon as he has Peace and Leisure to apply his Mind to it; and that then he (who has the best Opportunity for it) will search out whether it be possible for Ships to pass by the way of *Nova Zembla* into the *Tartarian* Sea; or to find out some Port that falls into the *Tartarian* Sea to the Eastward of the River *Oby*, where he may build Ships, and send them, if practicable, to the Coast of *China*, *Japan*, &c. And if the said Sea, or at least some distance to the Eastward of *Nova Zembla*, be navigable, as 'tis believed, a Way or Passage for the carrying of Goods, at least, partly by Land, and partly by Water, may then be found from such Port where the *Czar* pitches upon to build his Ships; where the Time nor Price of the Carriage from thence cannot be much, to carry and bring Goods by the Conveniency of Sleds in the Winter, (which is the easiest Land Carriage in the World) to some other River or Port to the Westward of the River *Oby*, that may be found between *Archangel* and *Nova Zembla*; where Storehouses and a Factory may be settled, and whither *European* Ships may easily make short Voyages, and receive Goods this way from *China* and *Japan*, without crossing the Torrid Zone:

at

at least it will be much more practicable for the *Czar* this way, than the present Trade which he now maintains from *Mosco* to *Pekin*; that is the whole Way perform'd by Land Carriage, which requires many Horses and Men, and is both very tedious and chargeable.

The *Czar* also has Intentions to send Ships to search out the Eastermost Parts of the *Caspian* Sea, and establish there some Port to encourage a Trade with *Great Tartary*, who are a People that are known to inhabit most part of the Countrey between the *Caspian* Sea, and the Borders of *China*; and are famed for having conquer'd that Kingdom upwards of 70 Years since. They inhabit the best part of the temperate Climate, from the Latitude of about 38, and in some Places extend to the Latitude of 2 or 3 and 50 Degrees North, and their Countrey abounds with the Fruits of the Earth, Stores of Sheep and Cattle, and all things necessary for Life, except some small part that is reported to be desert. There are several large Rivers that run some of them several 100, and others I believe several 1000 *Russ* Miles through that Countrey, (if I may judge by the Extent of the Land) before they fall into the *Caspian* Sea, with which the *Russes*, who have been hitherto very dull Mariners, have had no Correspondence; but 'tis believed, that by proper Encouragement a Trade might be settled this Way, that would in time prove very advantageous:

vantageous: Of which I shall speak more in another Place.

I shall here return to give some Account of those People that inhabit that Tract of Land joining to *Nova Zembla*, and extending from the Borders of *Archangel* to the *Tartarian* Sea. The *Russes* injuriously call these People *Samoiedes*, (or a People that eat one another) though the Occasion is very unjust; for they live as friendly and neighbourly as other People; although by reason of their Necessity they are known at *Archangel* to eat sometimes the Intrails of Beasts, which they purchase of the Butchers, and the meanest of Food. They traffick to *Archangel* with Furs, Skins, and wooden Ware, with which the Shipping is supplied: But in other Places, on the Frontiers, they choose to have as little to do with the *Russes* as possible, because of their ill Usage, and Unfaithfulness to them. They are a People of a strong, swarthy Countenance, full Cheek-Bones, and short Noses, like some of the Eastern *Tartars*; and, as I am informed since my writing of these Papers, like the People that inhabit on the North Side, entring into the North-West Passage. They neither plough nor sow, for their Countrey is wholly too cold to ripen any Harvest; neither have they sufficient Food or Grass to breed up Cattel amongst them, but live principally on Deer and Bears, and other wild Beasts; on the Fowls of the Air, and on dry'd Fish, and Turnips for their Bread; only some few of them that live near the Borders of *Archangel*, purchase some small matter of Corn of the *Russes*, of whom they have learn'd to eat Bread.

They acknowledge Obedience to the *Czar*, but refuse to embrace the Christian Faith, in the superstitious Manner as the *Russes* represent it to them; and for the same Reason, as afterwards I shall have occasion to mention, the Christian Religion is refused even by many of those People who live immediately within the Districts of the *Czar*'s Government. I have discoursed with some of the said *Samoiedes*, who have told me, that they have no established Form of Religion, nor Order of Priesthood amongst them, but take their Rules of Life from such of their Elders who have lived justly, and acted righteously amongst them; and to whose Judgment they also submit in case of any Controversy between Man and Man, electing such Persons by common Consent. They believe that there is a God that rules the Sun and the Stars, and that blesses them with Health and Length of Days, according to the Equity and Justice of their Behaviour to each other.

The Countrey abounds in Deer, which feed upon a kind of Moss that is upon the Ground, and on the Trees in the Woods, with which they grow fat in the Winter. They are a particular sort of Deer, which God and Nature seems to have order'd on purpose for this frozen Countrey, and are abundantly serviceable

to

to the Natives in many respects. They do not much exceed the Height of our common Fallow Deer, but are more than twice as thick, with Legs of Strength proportionable to their Bodies, with a broad, thin, flat Hoof, which spreads so much, that they run over the Top of the frozen Snow without sinking into it, so as to hinder their Speed: And the Natives make use of them instead of Horses to draw their Sleds in the Winter Season, on all their necessary Occasions; for which purpose they make their Sleds also thin and light, to run any where over the Top of the Snow. But the *Russes*, with their Sleds and Horses, when the Snow is any thing deep upon the Ground, can draw no where as these People do out of the beaten Tract, or common Road, without being founder'd in the Snow. The Natives also have on occasion a long thin piece of Board which they tye fast to their Feet, with which they can run over the Top of the Snow, without sinking into it.

The said Deer serve the Natives also for their Rayment, as well as common Food. Their Skins are a very thick warm Fur, with which they cloath and defend themselves from the Severity of the Winter. Their Shirts are made of the Skins of young Deer, which being dress'd are soft, and warmer than Linen. Their Coat and Cap (Fur within and without) is made all of a piece, so that the Cold and the Snow cannot blow in at their Necks; and a Flap is made to button down upon their

F   Face

ly some few of them that live near the Borders of *Archangel,* purchase some small matter of Corn of the *Russes,* of whom they have learn'd to eat Bread.

They acknowledge Obedience to the *Czar,* but refuse to embrace the Christian Faith, in the superstitious Manner as the *Russes* represent it to them; and for the same Reason, as afterwards I shall have occasion to mention, the Christian Religion is refused even by many of those People who live immediately within the Districts of the *Czar*'s Government. I have discoursed with some of the said *Samoiedes,* who have told me, that they have no establish'd Form of Religion, nor Order of Priesthood amongst them, but take their Rules of Life from such of their Elders who have lived justly, and acted righteously amongst them; and to whose Judgment they also submit in case of any Controversy between Man and Man, electing such Persons by common Consent. They believe that there is a God that rules the Sun and the Stars, and that blesses them with Health and Length of Days, according to the Equity and Justice of their Behaviour to each other.

The Countrey abounds in Deer, which feed upon a kind of Moss that is upon the Ground, and on the Trees in the Woods, with which they grow fat in the Winter. They are a particular sort of Deer, which God and Nature seems to have order'd on purpose for this frozen Countrey, and are abundantly serviceable

to

to the Natives in many respects. They do not much exceed the Height of our common Fallow Deer, but are more than twice as thick, with Legs of Strength proportionable to their Bodies, with a broad, thin, flat Hoof, which spreads so much, that they run over the Top of the frozen Snow without sinking into it, so as to hinder their Speed: And the Natives make use of them instead of Horses to draw their Sleds in the Winter Season, on all their necessary Occasions; for which purpose they make their Sleds also thin and light, to run any where over the Top of the Snow. But the *Russes*, with their Sleds and Horses, when the Snow is any thing deep upon the Ground, can draw no where as these People do out of the beaten Tract, or common Road, without being founder'd in the Snow. The Natives also have on occasion a long thin piece of Board which they tye fast to their Feet, with which they can run over the Top of the Snow, without sinking into it.

The said Deer serve the Natives also for their Rayment, as well as common Food. Their Skins are a very thick warm Fur, with which they cloath and defend themselves from the Severity of the Winter. Their Shirts are made of the Skins of young Deer, which being dress'd are soft, and warmer than Linen. Their Coat and Cap (Fur within and without) is made all of a piece, so that the Cold and the Snow cannot blow in at their Necks; and a Flap is made to button down upon their

Face

Face upon occasion, with Holes only for their Eyes and their Nose, to breath and look out, when the Weather is severe. Their Boots or Shoes are made also of the same double Fur, with the two fleshy Sides sew'd together, the better to defend themselves from the Severity of the Cold, which lasts with them nine or ten Months in the Year; and the more Northern Parts are two or three Months wholly without the Sight of the Sun. Yet these People are content with their way of Life; and many of them that have been in *Russia*, and invited to continue there, chuse rather to return, and live and die where they have been born. So has God given every Nation to be content with their own Lot.

During the Severity of the Winter they live in Huts or Caves in the Ground, where a very little Fire keeps them warm. The Way of making their Huts, which is also practised by the *Russ* when they have occasion to winter or stay long in any Place where they have no Houses, is in the following Manner: They chuse some dry Bank or rising Ground, where they cut or dig down a Place a good Depth in the Ground, and face the Sides, and cover the Top with such sort of split Timber, or Balks, as come nearest at hand; and then ram the Sides, and cover the Top with a good Thickness of Earth; build Benches and Places round on the inside for Men to sleep on, and make a good Fire in the Middle, with a Hole at the Top to let out the Smoak. When there's there's occasion to light a Fire, and when the Fire is burnt out, they shut the Hole or Funnel for carrying off the Smoak; and these Caves or Huts will hold warm a long time. Which sort of Huts the *Russ* make in their Armies or Camps of Workmen, when they are not to stay long in a Place; but if they design them for the whole Winter, or any Duration of Time, they make then no Fireplace in the Middle, but instead of it an Oven at the farther End, in which they both dress their Victuals, and bake their Bread, (upon occasion) and when the Oven is shut to, and the Funnel stop'd, the Heat that is retained in the Sides of the Oven, &c. keeps the Cave to what Degree of Warmth soever is desired, with a very little Wood, heated but once, or at most but twice a Day. They usually make also an Out-Room or Shed at the Entrance of these Caves to break off the Cold, to chop Wood in, and lay things out of the way: And if they come to a Place where the Ground is frozen, they first make a Fire to thaw the Ground, according to the Dimensions the Hut is designed.

Had those *English* Seamen (who were formerly sent to seek out a Passage this way to *China*, and being taken with the Frost in the Attempt, were obliged to winter at *Nova Zembla*, and the next Year found dead in their Ships, with a melancholy Relation left by them in the Cabin in Writing, of their perishing with Cold, and the Miseries they endured, had they, I say) as soon as they found
themselves

themselves set fast in the Ice, (having their Day enough before them, and the Severity of the Winter not set in) immediately sent Men over the Ice directly to the first Land they could find, and in case of no Tract or Sign of any Natives to help them, (which perhaps so far Northward they might not have met with) had they built themselves such a Hut as before mention'd in the Ground, they might easily have brought their Provision from their Ship, and have dress'd it in the Hut; and in the time of moderate Weather and Moon-shine, (which they have there the greater share of in the Absence of the Sun) they might have had Opportunity to have gone out with their Guns, and have kill'd Deer, and pass'd the Winter with Safety and Pleasure: And in the Spring, when the Sun came on, and the Ice began to melt away, have taken themselves to their Ship again.

Some Men that I have discours'd with on this Subject, have here objected to me, that it would have been dangerous for Men to have left their Ship, and to have trusted themselves the whole Winter upon the Land, lest in so many Months they might have been devour'd by Bears and Wolves. The Notions and Stories that are told of this kind are wholly frivolous, and not to be regarded; for God has ordered, that such Beasts of Prey are always afraid and run away from Man, who is created Lord of all the Creatures: And it is certain, they never will set upon a Man,
unless

unless it be when they are first attack'd, and cannot make their Escape; or in the Spring of the Year when they have Young, and are severely put to it for Prey. But besides it is known, that the Bears lie still in Winter and suck their Paws, and are never supposed to be dangerous, but in the Cases aforesaid. And the *Russes*, though the Countrey is full of Wolves and Bears, travel every where alone through the Woods, more particularly in the Winter Season, when they constantly travel Night and Day upon Sleds; and yet there is seldom or never such a thing known, that a Man is attack'd or hurt by any wild Beast.

I have very often seen Bears and Wolves upon the Road, and have endeavour'd to shoot them, but they always run away from a Man. When I was employ'd at *Camishinka*, in my Journeys to and from *Mosco*, travelling over that part of the Countrey which the *Russ* call *Step*; where, by reason of the Incursions of the *Tartars*, there are no Houses for 50, in some Places a 100 or 200 *Russ* Miles: When we have been standing by the Side of a Wood where we have baited our Horses, and made a Fire in the Night, the Wolves have come in very great Numbers, and made a very hideous Howling and Noise round about us, and would no doubt have devoured our Horses, had they been alone. But when Men are with them, there is no Danger of it.

A wild Boar or a Bear, if you come close and fire upon them, will then make di-

F 3

rectly at you; and you must be sure of your Blow, or your Friends to stand by you: But a Wolf, when you shoot and not kill him, will run away like a Dog.

The Countrey of *Nova Zembla*, whither several *English* Ships have formerly been sent for finding out a Passage to the *Indies*, is known to be inhabited by the *Samoiedes* to several Degrees within the Frozen Zone; of which the *Czar*, as beforementioned, has Thoughts of sending Persons to try if there be any such Passage: But he is notwithstanding of Opinion that there is none; and says, That he believes his Countrey joins here to *America*, and that that Part of the World was first peopled this way, when there was not such vast Quantities of Ice, and the Cold had not so strongly possess'd the Parts near the Pole.

And it is not unreasonable to believe, that when the extreme Northern Parts were first inhabited, it was then more temperate and agreeable for Life, or Men would not have chosen, or even have been easily driven by any Necessity to inhabit so unfertile and uncouth a Climate. And it seems to be Demonstration, as Things in Nature appear, that in the Beginning, when God first made the World, there was then no Ice upon the Surface of the Waters; that there could with the severest Frost be no considerable Thickness made the first Year, and that what has in the Course of Time been since effected by the repeated Operations

rations of the Winter, has again, by the Power of six Months continued Sun, though in a very oblique Position, been in a great measure more or less, as the Winds have happen'd, still melted down again in the Summer: So that that vast Body of Ice which is now found several hundred Foot thick in many Places within the Frigid Zone, must have been the gradual Work of many thousand Years to effect. Especially if it be according to the Hypothesis of Doctor *Cheyne*, in his Philosophical Principles of Religion, that the Sun it self has abated the Force of its Heat, for which he has laid down his Reasons. This is my Opinion; and from thence may be concluded, that as the Body of Ice has in the Course of Time been gradually augmented; so the Cold, by Reflection from it, has been extended farther this Way than when the World was first created: But of this let every Man judge as he pleases. I shall only add a few Instances, to shew how the Inhabitants of the Northern Continent are at present affected by the different Operations of the Weather, according to the Power of Reflection, either from the Heat, or from the Cold.

The *English* Merchants, who travel every Year from the City of *Mosco* to *Archangel*, (which lies in the Latitude of 64, and have 21 Hours Sun in the midst of Summer) have told me, that it is common there to have the Weather sometimes so extremely hot that they go with open Breast, and can scarce bear

F 4 any

any Cloaths upon them when a gentle Breeze continues Southerly, which fouls on the Heat that is reflected from the Earth by the Sun Beams: But that when the Wind has suddenly shifted about to the Northward, which blows directly from off the Sea, the Air has been at once changed, and in an Hour or two's Time been so very cold, that they have been forc'd to put on their Furs to keep them warm; which extreme Difference of Weather often happens throughout the Summer, but they are more especially sensible of it in the Month of *June*, and the Beginning of *July*, when the Ice is perhaps still driving, or not long clear of the *White Sea*.

In the Year 1708, a Merchant Ship, (the Commander's Name I have now forgot,) in her Voyage from *England*, having passed the *North Cape*, and sailing round towards the *White Sea*, in the Middle of *June*, with warm Weather, and an agreeable Gale at S. S. W. accidentally run into a great Drift of broken Ice that was floating upon the Sea; and immediately they felt the Cold so severe from the Reflection of the Ice, that the Mens Teeth, by the sudden Change of the Air, chatter'd in their Heads as they walk'd upon the Deck; but sending Men up to the Top-Mast-Head to see how to get clear of the Ice again, they found the Air there to be (in comparison) warm at the same time, when by the immediate Reflection from the Ice, it was surprisingly cold upon the Deck; and after some
time

time, when by good Fortune and much Difficulty they got out again to Windward of the Ice, they then presently found themselves in warm Weather, as before. Also many other Ships in that Voyage running into the Ice, have met with the like Surprize.

Another Instance is also remarkable in *Archangel*, that in the Beginning of the Winter, in the Months of *September* and *October*, when the upper Crust of the Land is first frozen, and the Snow fallen upon the Ground to 3, 4, or perhaps 5 or 6 Degrees to the Southward of *Archangel*, and the Ice is not yet gather'd in the *White Sea*; then, as if the *Poles* had shifted their Stations, the Operations of the Winds have directly the contrary Effect of what is beforementioned; for then a Southerly Wind, which comes from off the Land, rolls on the Reflection of the Cold from the Snow, with which the Earth is cover'd as aforesaid, and makes it freeze hard in *Archangel*: But a Northerly Wind which comes directly from off the Sea, which is not yet frozen, nor the Cold has not taken place as aforesaid, is then sensibly warm, in comparison to a Southerly Wind that comes from off the Land. But at *Wolloda*, which is half way from *Archangel* to *Mosco*, and at *Mosco* it self, and all other Midland Parts, in the Depth of Winter, when once the Snow has spread the Continent to 10 or 15 Degrees farther on to the Southward, then it freezes equally hard, sometimes with one Wind, and sometimes

sometimes with another, but always most remarkably severe in clear still Weather, when there is little or no Wind to raise and mingle the Reflection from the Snow with the upper Air, the Frost has then the greater Power immediately on the Surface; and for the same Reason it is also that in the Summer time, when the Surface of the Earth is made warm by the Sun, still clear Weather, when there is no Wind to raise and mingle the Reflection with the upper Air, produces the Extremity of Heat

Another very remarkable Instance of the Extremes of Heat and Cold, as they take place, and the sudden and sensible Alteration of the Weather, is what the Inhabitants of the Continent farther to the Southward are affected with, who live near those high Mountains; that by reason of their height in the Atmosphere, are famed for being always covered with Snow. I will pass by the *Granada* Hills, and those of Mount *Ararat*, which are South from the *Caspian* Sea, and shall only mention those Mountains in *China*, about 20 or 30 Miles from the Cities of *Canton* and *Hyshem*; which, though within a Degree or a Degree and a half of the Torrid Zone, yet when the Winds blow any where from off those Hills, the People that border near them, are so affected with Cold, that they are forced to put on Furs to keep them warm; so that the wear of Furs is a great Fashion in *China*; and occasions, besides what

their

their own Countrey affords, a confiderable Demand of the fame from *Ruffia*, as will be fhewn hereafter. But on the other hand, whenever the Wind fhifts about to the South Weft, which blows from the plain Countrey, where the Power of the Sun takes place, and the Earth is made warm, the Inhabitants of the faid City and Province adjacent, are equally affected with the Excefs of Heat; and the like alfo happens in feveral other Places, by reafon of the high Mountains which run through that Countrey.

And in other Parts of *China*, efpecially in the Province of *Kittay*, (which is the Northern Part of the Empire) and towards the Eafternmoft Sea-Coaft, there a W. N W. and N W Wind, (which extends to them from towards the Point of *Nova Zembla*) blowing over Land in the Winter Seafon, after the Snow is once fpread upon the Face of the Continent, it then brings to them the fame Degree of Cold which an E. N E. or a N. E. Wind brings to the Weftern Shores of *Europe*; and an Eafterly Wind which blows directly to them from off the Sea, brings them more temperate Weather.

From which feveral Inftances, it is plain that Cold as well as Heat, where-ever it takes Power, gathers Force, and is extended on the Continent by Reflection; and which makes, that Iflands that are furrounded by the Sea, on which the Extremes neither of Heat nor Cold, cannot eafily take Place, by reafon of

the

the great Depth that either Quality muſt firſt be communicated to; are therefore always more temperate and happy in this Caſe than the Continent: For let it be at what Seaſon of the Year, and the Wind blow from which Quarter it will, neither the Cold nor the Heat can gather Strength paſſing croſs the Sea, but partaking of the Temperature of the Water, muſt loſe Part of its Force by the Way. Although it is nevertheleſs in ſome meaſure remarkable, that in the Height of Summer, from the latter End of *June* to the Middle of *Auguſt*, when the Heat has taken its full Power on the Continent, then an Eaſterly Wind brings more ſultry Hot, and a Weſterly Wind more cool Weather in *England*, as well as always the Reverſe of it in the Winter.

And the very ſame Extremities of Weather which happen to the Eaſtern Continent, [as particularly in the Latitude of *Moſco*, it's common to have the Froſts ſo ſevere, that the Birds as they fly in the Air fall down and die, and to have Men as they ſit on their Sleds come frozen to Death into the City, and even to have their Face or Hands, or Toes frozen as they paſs from one Place to another in the Streets and Suburbs of the City:] The ſame Circumſtances, if not more ſevere, in Places of the ſame Latitude, is well known to happen alſo to the Inhabitants of *America*; and were *England* ſituate as near to that Coaſt as it is to *Europe*, Weſterly Winds would be found as cold in the Winter there, as Easterly Winds are here. But were an Island in the same Latitude, situated half way between the two Shores, it is certain that the same would be much less subject to the Extremes of Heat and Cold, and consequently be more pleasant and agreeable for Life in this respect. As in *Ireland*, though farther to the Northward, yet being farther from the Continent, the Frosts are not so severe as in *England*.

But to go on with my intended Description of the *Czar's* Dominions: The next People who border to the Eastward of the forementioned *Samoieds*, beyond the great River *Oby*, and inhabit on the back side and to the N E. of *Siberia*, beyond the Mouth of *Oby*, all the way along the Coast of the *Tartarian* Sea, as far as *China*, have not yet any of them submitted themselves to the *Czar*, but have recourse to their Arms (which are Swords, Pikes, Bows and Arrows) and refuse to give Admittance to such People that have been sent from *Tobulsky** to search out the Countrey, and view the Sea-Coast, which is the Reason that the *Russes* as yet can give no Account of the *Tartarian* Sea; but relate that the said Inhabitants, with whom they have some Correspondence for Sables, &c. are something a more polite sort of People, but live much after the manner as the *Samoieds*.

---

* The capital City of the Kingdom of *Siberia*.

The Countrey of *Siberia* is the Place whither the *Czar* banishes capital Criminals and Offenders never to return. It was conquered by the *Russes* in the Time of *Evan Basfilavitz*; it extends in Breadth in some Places to the Latitude of 4 or 5 and 50 Degrees South, and extends beyond the *Troitzki* Monastery, which lies on the River *Tunguska* in the Latitude of 66 Degrees North, and in Length from the Borders of the River *Oby*, as far as the Head of the River *Argun* †, which is within a few Days Journey of the famous Wall of *China*; which (according to Father *le Comte*) was built about 1800 Years since, to defend them from the Incursions of the bordering *Tartars*, who have notwithstanding, about 70 Years since, made themselves Masters of the Countrey; and the *Chams* of *Great Tartary*, who are called the *Bogdoi Tartars*, continue Emperors of *China* to this Day.

The Conquest of *Siberia* was principally owing to the Conduct of one *Strugenooff*, a *Russ* Merchant, who had a vast Number of flat bottom'd Vessels (which the *Russes* still use;) some of them carrying near a 1000 Tun, which he constantly employ'd on the River *Wolga*, transporting Corn, Salt, Fish, and other small Goods of several sorts; and who had not only his Factors at all the great Towns upon the *Wolga* it self, but also at

---
† *The River Argun discharges it self into the great Sea directly East from China.*

several

several Places situate on the Eastern Rivers which fall into the River *Wolga*, and extended his Correspondence thereby with the People bordering on the River *Oby*, exchanging his Goods for the rich Furs of *Siberia*, black Foxes, Sables, Tigers, Martins, Beavers, &c. He encouraged the Natives, and by his Interest and good Understanding with the People in those Parts, first advanced the Design; and afterwards procured Forces from the *Czar*, amongst which were some of the *Donskoi Cossacks*, and in less than two Year's Time made an entire Conquest of the Countrey. The King was kill'd in the Action, and his Sons brought Prisoners to *Mosco*, and a Descendent of that Family (known by the Title of the *Sibersky Czarawich*, or Prince) is now in *Mosco*, where he has an Estate containing four or five small Villages allow'd him for a Maintenance, in some Proportion to that Character, and lives in good Esteem with the *Czar* and the Nobility.

The Kingdom of *Siberia*, and Provinces thereto belonging, is accounted the eighth Part of the *Czar*'s Dominions (as divided into Provinces about six Year's since,) and brings a considerable Revenue into the *Czar*'s Treasure, besides maintaining the Garisons in the Countrey, and sending constant Recruits to the *Czar*'s Army, particularly the *Sibersky* & *Tubollsky* Regiments both of Foot and Dragoons, are reckoned as good as any the *Czar* has,

has, excepting the Guards, which are Men chosen out of all Regiments.

Besides these Advantages, and the farther Prospect of extending the *Czar*'s Conquests quite on to the *Tartarian* Sea, when there shall be a Time for it, where the richest Furs are always found: By way of this Countrey, the *Russes* now carry on a beneficial Trade quite to *China*, there going every Year a considerable Carravan of Merchants that carry thither chiefly the rich Furs of *Siberia*, such as black Foxes, Sables, Tigers, Ermin, &c. with some small Goods also imported at *Archangel*, and return from *China*, Tea in great Jarrs, Damask Silks; with a sort also of Linen which is mixed with Cotton, which the *Russes* call *Kitay*, dyed some red, some blue, and other Colours, very much worn by the *Russ* Women. They make some Return also of Pearl and of Gold in Ingots from *China*. Besides the *Russes* themselves fish up Pearls in some of the Eastern Rivers bordering on the Dominions of *China*; between which and *Tobolsks*, in the way towards *China*, they have built several Towns and Places where the *Russes* keep Garrison. And I have been lately informed by Mr. *Solticoff*, the *Czar*'s Resident here, that since I came from *Russia*, there has been an Account sent to the *Czar*, from the Governor of *Siberia*, that the *Russes* have found upon a River that flows from the South-East Part of that Province, and falls into the *Caspian* Sea, a considerable Quantity

Quantity of Gold Duſt, which they hope will turn to good Account. There are alſo ſeveral Iron Works in *Siberia*, and the Iron that is brought from thence, is ſo much eſteemed for its Goodneſs, that it is ſold for a third Part better Price than any other Iron in *Ruſſia*: Alſo there is a ſort of Ivory brought from thence, being the Tooth of an amphibious Creature call'd a *Behemot*, uſually found on the River *Lama*, and about the Lakes in thoſe Parts. Farther, both the *Ruſs* Inhabitants and Natives of *Siberia*, hold mutual Correſpondence and good Underſtanding with the *Mungul*, the *Bratskoi*, the *Tungoeſe*, the *Bogdoi* and *Yousbeck Tartars*, who inhabit to the South of *Siberia*, as far as the Borders of *China*.

With ſome of theſe Eaſtern *Tartars* who border upon the *Czar*'s Territories, and own the Protection of the Emperor of *China*, the *Ruſſes* from *Siberia* carried on a War, and had built a Fort on the River *Yamour*, which they were in Poſſeſſion of ſince the preſent *Czar* came to the Crown. But in the Year 1691, the ſaid Fort was relinquiſhed to the *Chineſe*, the Bounds between each Countrey ſettled to be at the Head of the River *Argun*, and a Peace was accordingly concluded by the Negotiation of the forementioned Count *Gollovin*, who was the *Czar*'s Embaſſador here in *England*, and had been, before the *Czar*'s Travels, ſent into *China* for that purpoſe.

Also afterwards in the Year 1693, one Mr. *Isbrant*, a Native of *Denmark*, was again sent as Envoy or Embassador into *China*, by the present *Czar*, to confirm the said Peace, and settle Articles of Commerce with *China*; and in the Year 1694, an Envoy or Embassador to the *Czar* was sent from thence, and a mutual good Understanding is like to be continued.

The Countrey, all the way between *Siberia* and the *Caspian* Sea (Eastward of the River *Wolga*) is inhabited by the *Bucharsky*, the *Mungul* and the *Cullmick*, and several other particular *Hordes* of *Tartars*, who have their several *Aucoes*, or *Chams* apart. Many of them acknowledge one principal *Cham* as their Chief, who has his Residence at *Samarcand*, situated on a Branch of the *Oxus*, on the East side of the *Caspian* Sea; and derives his Pedigree, as 'tis said, from the Great *Tamerlane*. Some of these *Tartars*, particularly the *Cullmick*, own Protection from the *Czar*, and others live in good Amity with the *Russes*, and come every Year on the East side of the *Wolga*, and trade with the *Czar's* People. They are all of a Religion, not much differing from the *Mahometans*, only they eat Horse Flesh, and other Creatures which they like the Taste of, which the *Turks* and *Crim Tartars* refuse to do. All Informations agree that the whole way between the River *Wolga* and the Walls of *China*, the Countrey is interlined with Plains and Woods, with Lakes
and

and Rivers, some falling toward the *Caspian*, and others toward the *Tartarian* Sea, and is for the most part pleasant and fruitful.

The *Bogdoi*, *Tousbeck*, and *Bucharsky Tartars*, more towards *China*, live in Houses, and continue Winter and Summer in the same place; but the *Cullmick*, and several *Hordes* of Western *Tartars*, who border more towards the *Czar*'s Dominions, live in Tents, and move Northward and Southward, according to the Seasons of the Year, with their Flocks, their Herds, and their Wives and Families. They are generally of a swarthy Complexion, black Hair, low Noses, and broad Cheeks, with little or no Beard. I had Opportunity when I was at *Camishinka*, to observe much of their Way of Life, which is like that which *Moses* relates in the first Ages of the World; they neither plow nor sow, but move from Place to Place for fresh Pasture, and take the Fruits of the Earth as they find them. They keep Time with the Fowls of the Air, and move back Southward in the Winter to the Borders of the *Caspian* Sea; some of them going into the Latitude of 3 or 4 and 40 Degrees North, where there is little or no Snow that continues upon the Ground; and in the Beginning of the Year, as soon as the Snow melts away, and the Spring appears in its Verdure, they move on sometimes to the Latitude of 2 or 3 and 50 Degrees North, and some sooner and some later spread the Country in Parties, from 8 or 10, to 15, or sometimes

sometimes 20000 of them or more in a Body, and pitch their Tents in Streets and Lanes in the same regular Manner as in a Town or Village, and every one knows their due Place and Order; so that I have seen the Cows stop at their own Tents, when they drive them home to milk them.

As they go backward and forward, they usually come on the East side of the *Wolga* and stay 2 or 3 Weeks or more in a Place over-against those Towns where the *Russes* inhabit, and barter their Horses, Sheep * and Cattle, which they have in great abundance with the *Russians*, for Corn and Meal, for Copper and Iron, Kettles, Knives, Scissers &c. and take also some Cloth and Linen of the *Russes*

In moving their Camp and their Tents from Place to Place, as has been mentioned, the

---

* The Sheep of the Cullmucks, and all the other Tartars that I have seen come to the Banks of the Wolga, are very good Mutton, but of a quite different sort from any that have ever seen in other Parts of the World They have no Tail but a great broad Flap of firm hard Fat like that of the Brisket, which grows out of their Rump, and weighs usually about 6 or 8 Pounds, being near the same sort as the Turkish Sheep.

The Skin of the black Lamb (of which there are a great many among them) is usually sold for at least 2 or 3 Times the Price of the Lamb it self, being of a coal-black Colour, and a strong, small, smooth Curl, that wears with a beautiful Gloss upon it There are another sort of Lamb-skins which come from Persia, that are sold in Mosco, yet much dearer, which are of a perfect grey Colour, and of something smaller and finer Curl than the said Tartarian Lamb-Skins, and either the turning up of a Cap lined, or the outside of a Coat made of these Skins, is accounted a very rich Garment, and worn by the best Lords in Russia.

Wive

Wives and their Children are drawn on covered Machines fixed on two large Wheels of about 8 Foot diameter, and the Breadth is in proportion to the Height; so that they can easily ford over small Rivers; in which, as well as their Tents, they live like as in Houses; and Persons of Distinction have several of these for their Baggage and Retinue. They are drawn by Dromedaries, which is a large Beast bigger than a Camel, with two Humps on the Back, which serves as a Saddle for Men to ride on (there being just room enough for the largest Man to sit between the two Humps,) they have a Pace which is swift, easie and smooth, and these Creatures carry the Tents and Baggage of such who have not the forementioned Machines for it; they are taught to kneel down and to receive their Burden, tho' they do it (usually) with a grumbling sort of a Noise which they make.

With the Hair of these Dromedaries, the *Tartars* weave in the Fields a narrow Stuff the same as Camlet; and the *Russes*, who begin to leave off the Use of Caps, have in the present *Czar*'s Time, learn'd to make Hats, and use the said Dromedaries Hair for that purpose.

The *Cullmucks* have by Treaty, a small annual Pension allowed them by the *Czar*, which is paid them at *Astracan*, in Coin, and in Cloth, for which they are obliged to assist the *Czar* in his Wars, when he shall command them, not only against the *Turks* and *Tartars*,

Tartars, but his other Enemies; and tho' undisciplined, are a robust and warlike People, supposed to be of those ancient *Scythians*, who were so long famed for their War against the *Persians*. They have lately been useful to the *Czar* in his War with the *Swedes*, of which I shall speak more hereafter, when I shall mention the Regulations made in the *Czar*'s Army.

The common Tents, in which the *Cullmicks* and other forementioned *Tartars* live and move, with their Camps, from Place to Place, are made of small Lettice-Work, round like a Pidgeon-House, which they set up without Poles, and which when they strike, folds together in narrow Pannels. They cover them over with *Wylock*, which is a very light sort of Stuff, matted together like Felt or Hat-Work, but more loose and above half an Inch thick, which serves to keep out the Cold as well as Rain, as it lies shelving to carry it off. They are made with a Door to go in at, and a Hole at the Top to let out the Smoak, when they have occasion to make a Fire, which they make in the middle of the Tent, and when they go to sleep they lie round the Tent; the ordinary People on Beds, being a Peice of the *Wylock* abovementioned, only usually made double the Thickness of that with which the Tent is covered; and when the Door is shut too, and the Hole which is at the Top is covered, their Tent is as warm as a Stove: The same Tents are used also by Persons of Distinction;
only

only I have seen one of the *Aucoes* (or Chiefs) have his Bed made of *Persian* Silk, and his Tent richly lined with the same.

When I was employed at *Camishinka* on making the intended Communication between the *Wolga* and the *Don*, we had all the Summer long some or other *Hordes* of these *Tartars*, who came and pitched their Tents on the opposite side of the *Wolga*. They often came over the River, as well as the *Russes* went to them, to trade. They came many of them to see my Work, and were very curious in observing our Engines and Methods that we used. I had by this Means Opportunity of being civil to them, and they invited me and my Assistants over to their Camp, and asked us very proper Questions in Discourse concerning our Countrey and Place that we came from, and have made us very welcome amongst them

The next People that I shall take notice of, are the *Caban Tartars*, who are a very strong bodied, well proportioned People, black Hair and a swarthy Complexion, as generally are all the other *Tartars*. They inhabit to the Westward of the River *Wolga*, along the North-East Coast of the *Black-Sea*, and between that and the *Caspian* Sea, from whence they make frequent Incursions into the Out-Parts of *Russia*, plunder and fire Villages, and often carry off Cattel and Horses and People; by reason of which, there is a great Tract of Land on the West side of the *Wolga*, all
the

the way between the Town of *Saratoff* and the *Caspian* Sea, lies wholly uninhabited, save only the Islands about *Astracan*, and the People that live within the Towns of *Camishinka*, *Czaritza*, *Ischornico*, and *Terki*, the nearest of which are from 150 or 60, to above 200 Miles Distance from each other, (as the Road lies) where Garrisons are kept at each particular Place, and are always ready for an Alarm. And by reason of the Incursions of the said *Tartars*, the *Russes* do not plough and sow in these Parts (though the Land is extremely rich) but have every Year Corn brought down to them by the River *Wolga*, and the same Vessels go back laden with Fish and Rock-Salt, &c. of which the greatest Part of *Russia* is supplied from a Place 30 Miles below *Camishinka*: As also from *Astracan* there is returned every Year some small matter of rich Goods from *Persia* and *Armenia*, as wrought Silks, Calicoes, &c.

The said *Tartars* when they make their Incursions, it is usually in the Summer time, when there is Grass enough on the Ground; and each Man for Expedition sake takes two Horses, which they change as they ride, sometimes sitting upon one, and sometimes upon another. They always travel with Centinels at a convenient Distance from all Sides of their main Body, to prevent being discover'd, it being an uninhabited Country, as aforesaid, which the *Russes* call *Step*. They come with that Swiftness and Caution, that there seldom is any Advice of them; and immediately fall upon what Booty they can find, and do what Mischief they can, and then return again with the same Expedition as they came on, before the *Russes* can make any Head against them to cut off their Retreat: And those that happen to be taken, on either Side, are used very barbarously, with seldom or never any Redemption from their Slavery One of the Advantages therefore which was propos'd for making a Communication between the *Wolga* and the *Don*, was to have been a Barrier to prevent these *Tartars* from advancing farther into *Russia*.

Whilst I was employ'd at *Camishinka*, there was an Army every Year of 2000 Gentlemen on Horseback, being most part of them *Mordwa* and *Morzee Tartars*, immediate Subjects to the *Czar*, (of whom I shall have occasion to speak more hereafter) with 4000 Foot, and 12 Field-Pieces, who were sent to cover the Workmen from the Incursions of the said *Cabans*; and Guards and out Centinels were placed at several Miles Distance, on the Tops of Hills and proper Places, to prevent our being surprized: But notwithstanding all our Guards and Watches that have been placed, a Party of between 3 and 4000 of these *Tartars* once came just as it was Day in the Morning, without our having the least Advice of them, up to our very Camp; and when they found that the Alarm was taken, and our Cannon began to play upon them from our

our Lines, they immediately retired with the same Speed they came on, before our Men could mount or get in any Order to attack them, it requiring some time before they could come to their Horses; besides, that many of their Horses that were at some Distance without the Camp, were surprized and carried off by the Enemy. They carried off in all about 1400 Horses, some of which belonged to the Army, and others to the Workmen; with several People that were looking after the Horses where they were feeding in the Meadows, at some Distance from the Camp; there being no Inclosures in that Countrey.

The Countrey, all the way from *Camishinka* to *Terki*, as it is in the best Climate of the World, so it is for the most part extremely fertile and pleasant to inhabit. In the Spring of the Year, as soon as ever the Snow is off the Ground, which usually does not lye above two or three Months in these Parts, the warm Weather immediately afterwards takes place; and the Tulips, Roses, Lillies of the Valley, Pinks, Sweet-Williams, and several other Flowers and Herbs, spring up like a Garden, in very great Variety. Asparagus, the best I ever eat, grows so thick, that you may in some Places mow it down; and the common Grass in the Meadows is up to the Horses Belly. Liquorish, Almonds, and Cherries, the Fields are cover'd with; but the Trees are low, and the Fruit small. As also in Autumn appear ripe several sorts of Grain, and Fruits of the Earth, which by Cultivation might be much improved. There is great Variety of Birds, and Wild-Fowl in abundance of all sorts, both of Land and Water: As also small Fallow-Deer, Rayn-Deer, Elks, Wild-Boars, Wild-Horses, Wild-Sheep, of which I once eat part of one, that being chased by a Wolf, was taken by a Fisherman in his Boat on the River *Wolga*; it eat tenderer, and was much preferable to common Mutton. The Wool of this Sheep was very short and coarse, and good for little; but the Wild Horse Skin is a thick warm Fur, and is usually sold in *Mosco* for lining of ordinary Sled Decks, or Covers.

There is one thing more that I will mention: The Grass growing very rich in these Parts, as has been said, and being neither mow'd nor eat down by Cattel for want of Inhabitants, it remains as it grows up, dry upon the Ground; and oftentimes the *Russes*, and sometimes the *Tartars*, some or other of them, travelling in these deserted Parts, where they bait their Horses and rest by the way, usually light a Fire with Wood to dress their Victuals, and in a cold Season to lye round and keep themselves warm when they have occasion to sleep, as their manner is, laying such a piece of Wylock, as before-mention'd, which is their Saddle Cloth, under them for the Bed; the Cloth or Mantle, which is of the same, to cover them, and their Saddle under their Head, having several Days Travel between one Place and another; and some-

sometimes by accident, and sometimes on purpose, the said dry Grass is set on fire, and spreads and burns the Countrey with great Violence, which may be seen at a great Distance when the Flames are reflected on the Clouds in a dark Night, and in a Cloud of Smoak in the Day, by which Travellers avoid it. It runs on sometimes after the Fire is kindled on all the Points of the Compass, and does not usually stop till it comes to some River, or tall Wood; for where there happens to be low brush Wood, and tall Grass grows, there also the Fire runs on without being extinguish'd, sometimes for 20 or 40 Miles, or more. Also these Fires often happen on the East Side of the *Wolga*, and in many other Parts, which the *Russes* call *Step*, particularly on the West Side of the River *Don*, on the Way between *Veronize* and *Azoph*, bordering towards the *Crim-Tartars*; and usually burns most violent in the Spring, when it happens to be set on fire as soon as the Snow is off the Ground, and the Grass; by the Deadness of the Winter, is become throughly dry.

About 40 *Russ* Miles below the foremention'd Town of *Czaritsa*, which Word in the *Russ* Language signifies Queen, in the Latitude of 48 Degrees and 20 Minutes, there is to be seen the Ruins of a large City, call'd *Czaroff Gorod*, in a very pleasant Situation, and which is said to have been the ancient Residence of a *Scythian* King.

It

It is a thousand times to be lamented, that so rich and noble a Countrey, situated on the Side of the great River *Wolga*, which is perhaps the best stored with Fish of any River in the whole World, and where many small Rivers (not describ'd in the Map) fall into it, should now lye in a manner waste without Inhabitants, whilst the *Samoiedes*, before spoken of, pass their Days in Misery; and even many of the Northern *Russes* I have seen for want of Sun enough to ripen their Harvest, mingle Roots of Grass and Straw with their Corn to make Bread.

Therefore it will be worth the *Czar's* Thoughts to settle and cultivate a good Understanding with the said *Tartars*, and by giving them his Protection, improve and better people his Countrey to the Southward; as also by way of the *Wolga*, since he has fallen on the Thoughts of shipping and improving sailing Vessels for the Use of the *Caspian* Sea, which his Subjects before knew little of: He has an Opportunity to invite and settle, not only Trade and Commerce with *Persians* and *Armenians*, who are naturally a trading People, and with whom the *Russes* at present have some Correspondence, but also to settle a Trade with *Great Tartary* by means of the Rivers that extend that way, and the several other Countreys bordering on the *Caspian* Sea; which it is believed by our *English* Merchants, whom I have talk'd with in *Mosco* on this Subject, might in time prove a Means to vend

con-

considerable Quantities of *English* Cloth this way, as well as Linen, Corn, and other Things, the Product of the *Czar*'s Country, which they might, no doubt, in the Course of Time be brought to the Desire and Use of.

On the South Side of the *Caspian* Sea there are Apples, Pears, Pomgranates, Walnuts, Filbeards, Grapes, Peaches, Apricocks, &c in very great Plenty, and which grow wild in several Places. There is some Wine made on that Side, particularly in *Persia* and *Georgia*. I have often drank of it: It has a good Body, but does not hold good for any Time: But was it well made, it is believ'd it would be good; and a great deal, no doubt, might be vended to *Russia* in Exchange for other Manufactures.

The *Czar* has Thoughts of planting Vineyards, and improving the making of Wine on this Side the *Caspian* Sea, in *Terki* * and *Astracan*, where the Grapes, both red and white, are very large and good, and are brought from thence every Year to *Mosco*, with great Quantities of that delicious Fruit a Water Melon. Those of them which grow in the Countrey of *Astracan*, are said to exceed any in *Europe* by all that taste them. There are two Sorts; the Rind of both are of a lively green Colour; the Pulp of one is of a yellowish White, like the Colour of a Pine-Apple; and the other of a beautiful Rose

---
* *Terki lies in the Latitude of* 43½, *and Astracan in about* 46 *Degrees North.*

Colour, full of Juice, which has a very exquisite Taste, and cools as well as quenches Drought; and never surfeits that ever I could observe or hear of. But the *Russes*, who eat heartily of this as well as other Fruit, usually take a good Dram after it.

Each of these sort of Melons are commonly 10 or 12, and some of them 13 or 14 Inches diameter; but being set in *Mosco* (which some People do out of Curiosity) they will not grow to above 5 or 6 Inches diameter, and quite lose the Richness of their Taste. But they have of your common sort of Melons, which they eat with Sugar or Ginger in *Mosco* in great Abundance, as large and good as any in the World; the best sort of which are the *Bucharski*, which the *Russes* had by way of *Siberia* out of that Countrey; and of which sort the honourable Mr. *Whitworth*, at the time when he was her Majesty's Envoy Extraordinary, sent over some of the Seed to his Royal Highness Prince *George* of *Denmark*, and they are now in his Majesty's Gardens.

In the Year 1706, the *Czar* gave Orders to the late worthy Mr *Henry Stiles* Merchant in *Mosco*, to write for 10 or 12 Persons skill'd in the several Parts of Planting and making Wine, with Design to send them to settle at *Astracan*. But Mr *Stiles*'s Brother Mr. *Thomas Stiles*, (who is since also dead) return'd him for Answer from *London*, That he had wrote to his Correspondents in *Spain* and in *Portugal*, and they had treated with several Persons

for

for that Purpose; but hearing of the Rebellion that had happen'd in *Astracan* in the Year 1703, wherein all the Strangers that were in that City were cut to pieces in a revengeful manner, without sparing either Man, Woman, or Child (among which was one Captain *Myer*, and several other Foreigners that belong'd to some *Dutch* built Vessels which were appointed to go into the *Caspian* Sea;) no Person therefore, without very great Consideration, would engage in the Undertaking, to hire themselves to go to the said Countrey for making of Wines; and so that Design has lain cold ever since.

The said Rebels succeeded two Years in their Rebellion before they were conquer'd. After they had surprized and cut the Governor of *Astracan* in pieces, with most of the chief Officers of the Garrison, and all the Strangers that were found in that City as abovesaid, they then march'd to *Camishinka*, where the Garrison stood upon their Defence, and they were repulsed from thence. They went and besieged *Czaritza* also, but without Success; and afterwards they retired back again to *Astracan*, where the present Admiral's Brother *Peter Matfeaich Apraxin*, who was sent with an Army against them, retook *Astracan*, and put them all to the Sword, save some of the chief of them who were taken alive, and sent to *Mosco*, where they were put to the Torture, and after executed.

In the Year 1699, the King of *Georgia*, which is divided from *Persia* by the Mountains of *Ararat*, (where it is believ'd the Ark of *Noah* rested after the Deluge) and is one of the most pleasant and best inhabited Countries upon the Borders of the *Caspian* Sea, being driven out of his Country by his Subjects, came to *Russia* to implore the Protection of the *Czar*. And the first Summer that I was employ'd on making the Communication between the *Wolga* and the *Don*, he came to see my Work as he passed by. He was a tall well-looked Gentleman; whether in Complaisance or no, I cannot tell; but he wore a Beard like the *Russes*. I had the Honour to dine with him at the Governor's of the Town of *Camishinka*, who had Notice of his coming, and Orders to receive him according to the Dignity of his Character, as a Prince. And when he came to *Mosco* he was receiv'd with great Kindness by the *Czar*, and had the Revenue of several Villages appointed to him, to subsist with his Followers.

The *Czar* promis'd to re-establish this Prince in his Dominions; and in the Year 1702, there was 120 Sail of Vessels order'd to be built on the River *Wolga*, by *Dutch* Masters that were appointed for it, from 12 to 16 Guns, as 'twas said, with that Design. But there happening first the forementioned Rebellion in the *Czar's* own Country, with two others that follow'd, one in the Countrey of *Cazan*, and the other (which was most powerful) by the *Cossacks* on the *Don*, all within 3 Years one after another; and the War with *Sweden* pressing very hard at the same time upon the *Czar*, the said Vessels have since lain and rotted on the *Wolga*, without being sent on any Expedition.

The Prince, the Son of the said King of *Georgia*, immediately after he came into *Russia*, put himself into the *Czar*'s Army, where he was unfortunately taken Prisoner by the *Swedes* in the Battel of *Narva*, and died at *Stockholm* 4 Years since, known by the Name of the *Milletetsky Czaravich*, (or Prince.) And his Father, whom the *Russians* call'd the *Milletetsky Czar*, (*Czar* in the *Sclavonian* Language signifying King) died in *Mosco* about 20 Months since; whereby the pleasing Prospect which the *Czar* had in View of making a Conquest of *Georgia* when he should have had Opportunity for it, or at least of settling a Colony there, and obliging the Inhabitants to such Conditions of Contribution and Trade, as might have been of undoubted Advantage to his own Dominions, seems now to be wholly lost.

The *Caspian* Sea is much the largest Lake, and perhaps the best stored with excellent Fish of any Water in the World. The *Wolga*, which is one of the greatest Rivers that is discharg'd into that Sea, abounds with Bolluga, a Fish of about 8 or 10 Foot long, preferable to Sturgeon; of the Roe of which Fish
the

the *Ruſs* Caviar is made, which is admirable good; beyond what can be imagin'd, when it is firſt made: And when it is ſalted and preſſed for keeping, it is ſent abroad in great Quantities, and vended over all *Europe*, eſpecially in the Mediterranean Sea. The ſaid River *Wolga* abounds alſo with great Plenty of Sturgeon, Sterlet, Citera, Salmon, both red and white; Saudack, Pearch, Craw-Fiſh, Carp, Pike, Tench, and ſeveral other common River Fiſh; alſo with ſmall Turtle, (or Tortoiſes) which I have taken at *Camiſhinka*, and abound in the Southern Parts of the *Wolga*.

Sterlet is a ſmall Fiſh with a ſharp Noſe, of the ſame Nature as Sturgeon, but is ſomething yellower, and the Fat of it is in Taſte much preferable to Sturgeon. Citera is a Fiſh near as large, of the ſame Nature as Sturgeon, but is much whiter; eats admirably well dreſs'd any way, and is by *Engliſh* Men preferred to Sturgeon. All theſe abovenamed Fiſh cut and eat ſomething like Veal or Turtle; and have no Bone but the Back-Bone; and all eat very well cold, when ſouſed.

Saudack is a Fiſh neareſt in Likeneſs to a Whiting, but 6 or 8 times as large, (ſome of them) and the Fiſh firm like Cod; and which the *Engliſh* Men ſometimes, for Variety, ſalt a little, and eat with Butter and Eggs and Muſtard, like Cod. But of all the Fiſh which *Ruſſia* is allow'd to abound with, to me a white Salmon (which is not ſo luſcious as the red) is the ſweeteſt, and every way the moſt preferable to the Taste: But other Men praise the foremention'd Sterlet and Citera. The *Russians*, who have used the *Caspian* Sea, relate, that both the Lake it self, and all the Rivers that are discharged into it where they have been, abound with the same sort of Fish.

I have discoursed with several Masters of Vessels that have all their Life-time been employ'd in Voyages on the *Caspian* Sea, from *Astracan* to *Persia* and *Armenia*, in Vessels not fitted to ply to Windward, but only to run cross the Lake before the Wind, and have been driven sometimes where they never intended to go; and they have assured me that there are many other large Rivers that fall into that Sea which are not laid down in the Map: And considering that the said Sea, according to the best Accounts, is at least 150 Leagues in Length, and about 120 in Breadth, and situate in the Middle of so vast an Extent of Countrey, to the South, to the North, and to the East, there is no doubt but the same is the common Receptacle of many other great Rivers, and that the Quantity of Water that is discharged into this Sea must be very great. And since there is no known Out-let or Communication from thence with the grand Ocean, which all Men that have written any thing of that Sea have observed, it will be Matter worth Enquiry, what becomes of all these Waters. And that the Reader may the better judge of the Quantity of them, I will here lay

lay down my own Observations of the Quantity of Water which the *Wolga* alone discharges; which Observations I made as follows

About 3 Miles below the Town of *Camishinka*, in a narrow Place where the Stream runs free without any Eddy, and the Shore was bold on both Sides: First, I took the Current of the Stream, by an Observation which I made in several Places quite cross the River, and computing one Place with another, I reckon'd the Course of the Stream to be about 23 Fathom, or 138 *English* Feet in a Minute. Secondly, I sounded the River quite cross from Side to Side, and the mean Depth, reckoning one Place with another, I computed to be at least 17 Foot. Thirdly, the Breadth of the River, which I took by making an Observation with a Theodolet, I computed to be 5860 Foot, (Fractions not regarded;) and multiplying these 3 Sums, the Course of the Stream, with the Depth and Breadth of the River by each other, gives 13747560, the Number of cubical Feet that runs down the *Wolga* in the said time, and divide the said Sum total by 36, which is the Number of cubical Feet contained in a Tun of fresh Water, and the Quotient will be 381876 Tons of Water that runs down the River *Wolga* in one Minute of Time.

Which Computation was taken in the Month of *August* in the dryest Time of the Year, when the River was fallen several Fathom below the Top of the Banks; but if the vaſt Floods are conſidered which come down upon the melting of the Snows in the Spring of the Year, which ſwells the ſaid River uſually between 30 and 40 Foot *, and ſpreads and overflows the Countrey ſeveral Miles; and that I took the ſaid Obſervation not where the greateſt Quantity of Water is diſcharged, but (as the River runs) at leaſt 6 or 700 *Ruſs* Miles from the Mouth of the *Wolga*, where the Courſe of the Waters, by the Addition of many other ſmall Rivers, it is certain, muſt be much greater than the Place where I took my Obſervation.

Beſides it is remarkable, that the Courſe of the Floods which come down out of *Ruſſia*, and begin to ſwell the *Wolga* at *Aſtracan*, about the Middle, or towards the latter End of *April*, continue to a conſiderable Heighth above two Months, and are not wholly fallen at *Aſtracan* till about the laſt of *June*, or the Beginning of *July*, (occaſion'd by that great Length which the Floods from the Northern Snows, after they are melted, have to run :) which being conſidered, I believe that the Quantity of Waters diſcharged throughout the Year by the *Wolga* alone, may be at leaſt reckon'd one ſixth Part more, or 445522 Tons

---

* *When I was at* Camiſhinka *in the Year* 1700, *I obſerved the above ſaid River to ſwell near* 36 *Foot right up, and ſpread the Countrey between* 4 *and* 5 *Miles at* Camiſhinka; *but in other Places where the Banks are not ſo high, and the Land is more level, the Floods ſpread the Countrey, ſometimes* 15, 20, *or* 30 *Miles.*

in a Minute. And considering the Number of other Rivers, that from all Sides fall into the said Sea, and that some of them may be reckon'd to run through well nigh as great an Extent of Countrey as the River *Wolga*; all the Waters and Floods that are discharged into the said Sea, I believe may, by a modest Computation, be reckon'd at least three times as much as is discharged by the River *Wolga* alone, or 1336566 Tons of Water in a Minute, besides the constant Rains that may be reckon'd to fall into the said Sea; and yet there is no known Out-let and Communication with the grand Ocean for the Discharge of these Waters, as I said before.

In the Year 1699, the foremention'd Prince, or *Kneaz Gollitzen*, coming down to *Camishinka*, to see the Work that I was employ'd in for making a Communication on that Side of the Countrey, he was pleased (in a small *Dutch* built Vessel that was launch'd the same Year) to send one *Sheltrup*, who was of the *Danish* Nation (and one of my Assistants on the said Work) to go and survey the *Caspian* Sea, and to take a true Map of all the Rivers, Coast, &c. I directed him to take the Opportunity of fair Weather, and to run cross the said Sea in two or three Places, and found the Depth; and in case of finding that he had not Line enough in any Place, (for which he took a 1000 Fathom with him) when he had the Opportunity of still Weather, to let down a large Stone, with a Ball of Cork of 8 or 10

Inches diameter, flung and hook'd with a very short Hook to the Stone, so that as soon as ever the Stone should touch the Ground, the Ball of Cork should unhook and come directly up again to the Surface of the Water; and by computing the Time of the Stones sinking, and the Corks rising up again for a 100 Fathoms, it would be easy thereby to account how many Fathoms it would be from the time of letting go a Stone, and the Corks coming up to the Surface of the Water again, in any place whatsoever; whereby a tolerable Judgment, at least, might be made of the Depth of the said Sea, in case of not having Line enough for it, which would have been of very good Satisfaction, touching the Notion of a subterraneous Passage supposed by some Men. But this Gentleman unfortunately never return'd again to give any Account thereof.

Going in his Boat to view the Entrance of a River, in a Bay on the South side of that Sea, he was taken by the Natives (Subjects of the King of *Persia*) who strip'd him of his Cloaths and Instruments, and carried him up to a small Town upon the same River, and put him in Prison; where he was taken with a violent Fever, and died in a few Days. Notice was given of him as soon as he was taken, to the Court of *Persia*, and a Messenger was thereupon sent Express with Cloaths and Necessaries, to have carried him to *Ispahan*, but they came too late for it. A *Russ* Servant

Servant that lived with him, was carried to *Ispahan*, where he was very civilly used, and after having been examined touching his Master's Voyage (which he knew but little of) he was sent back to *Russia*, with a Guide to the Place where he took Vessel, and his Charges born him. At his Return, which was the Year after, he came and related this Account to me.

Had this Gentleman not been lost, I should have been able to have given a better Account of that Sea in many Respects; however, according to the Enquiry that I have since made, it has by several Persons been affirmed to me, that the Waters do not always continue at the same height, but swell and decrease according to the different Seasons of the Year, and according as it happens to be a hot and dry, or cold and wet Summer. There are Low-lands and Places, which some Years are overflowed, and other Years not; and the Waters in that Sea, are known to be usually lowest in the Months of *August* and *September*; and in the Winter Season, when all the Northern Rivers are frozen up, and no Rain to the Northward falls on the Ground for 5 or 6 Months, then the Water swells and grows high in the *Caspian* Sea, more than what it is at other times. And the very same Circumstances I have my self observed in several other lesser Lakes that have had their Feeders fall into them, on which I shall not enlarge; the Testimonies abovementioned,

Inches diameter, flung and hook'd with a very short Hook to the Stone, so that as soon as ever the Stone should touch the Ground, the Ball of Cork should unhook and come directly up again to the Surface of the Water; and by computing the Time of the Stones sinking, and the Corks rising up again for a 100 Fathoms, it would be easy thereby to account how many Fathoms it would be from the time of letting go a Stone, and the Corks coming up to the Surface of the Water again, in any place whatsoever; whereby a tolerable Judgment, at least, might be made of the Depth of the said Sea, in case of not having Line enough for it, which would have been of very good Satisfaction, touching the Notion of a subterraneous Passage supposed by some Men. But this Gentleman unfortunately never return'd again to give any Account thereof.

Going in his Boat to view the Entrance of a River, in a Bay on the South side of that Sea, he was taken by the Natives (Subjects of the King of *Persia*) who strip'd him of his Cloaths and Instruments, and carried him up to a small Town upon the same River, and put him in Prison; where he was taken with a violent Fever, and died in a few Days. Notice was given of him as soon as he was taken, to the Court of *Persia*, and a Messenger was thereupon sent Express with Cloaths and Necessaries, to have carried him to *Ispahan*, but they came too late for it. A *Russ* Servant

Servant that lived with him, was carried to *Ispahan*, where he was very civilly used, and after having been examined touching his Master's Voyage (which he knew but little of) he was sent back to *Russia*, with a Guide to the Place where he took Vessel, and his Charges born him. At his Return, which was the Year after, he came and related this Account to me.

Had this Gentleman not been lost, I should have been able to have given a better Account of that Sea in many Respects; however, according to the Enquiry that I have since made, it has by several Persons been affirmed to me, that the Waters do not always continue at the same height, but swell and decrease according to the different Seasons of the Year, and according as it happens to be a hot and dry, or cold and wet Summer There are Low-lands and Places, which some Years are overflowed, and other Years not; and the Waters in that Sea, are known to be usually lowest in the Months of *August* and *September*; and in the Winter Season, when all the Northern Rivers are frozen up, and no Rain to the Northward falls on the Ground for 5 or 6 Months, then the Water swells and grows high in the *Caspian* Sea, more than what it is at other times. And the very same Circumstances I have my self observed in several other lesser Lakes that have had their Feeders fall into them, on which I shall not enlarge; the Testimonies abovementioned, ed, I take to be sufficient Proof, that the *Caspian* Lake, or Sea, has no subterranean Passage or Communication with the grand Ocean; and consequently there is no other Way in the World whereby to account for the Discharge of the Waters that run into the said Sea, but by the Power of the Exhalation of the Sun and the Force of the Winds, according to Mr. Professor *Halley*'s most approved Solution of the Waters which fall into the Mediterranean Sea; which he has done by very curious and exact Experiments made of the constant Evaporation of Waters, laid before the Royal Society; to which I refer the Reader in the Philosophical Transactions for the Year 1687, N°. 189, and N°. 212. I I shall only beg leave to observe, that in making his Computation of the Waters which are discharged by several Rivers, which fall into the Mediterranean, he supposes them to be 90 Times as much as the Waters (abstracted from the Tides) which are discharged by the Course of the *Thames* into the *Brittish* Seas. But if the River *Nile* may be compared to the *Wolga*, and if I may judge by the Extent of the Countrey through which the Rivers *Don* and *Nieper* (or *Tanais* and *Borysthenes*) take their Courses, the least of which running near 2000 *Russ* Miles, and having both of them very numerous, large Rivers which fall into them, before they disembogue themselves, one into the *Palus Mæotis*, and the other into the *Black Sea*: I

humbly

humbly believe that the Quantity of Waters discharged by the several Rivers, into the Mediterranean, are much greater than the Allowance that he has given for it; not but that the Current which sets in at the Streights Mouth, where it is reckoned near 20 Miles broad, and no Depth said to be found (that ever I heard of) and therefore no Dimensions can be taken of it, is otherwise sufficient abundantly to answer the full Computation that he has made of the Quantity of Waters that are evaporated throughout the Year

But farther, because the Waters which constantly set in both here, and in the *Caspian* Sea, have been strongly supposed by some Men, to be discharged into the grand Ocean by subterraneous Passages, I will crave leave to affirm on this Occasion, particularly of the Mediterranean, that if there were supposed any subterraneous Passage, or other Communication whatsoever with the main Ocean, besides that of the Streights Mouth, the Water would also always set in, and not out at such Passage or Passages. For saving the Influence of the Winds, and the Attraction of the Sun and Moon, all the Waters in the World equally press to, and strive to be equally distant from the Center of the Earth, with one common Tendency to make the Surface equal from which side soever there is any Pressure or Communication; and was not the Surface lower or nearer the Centre of the Globe

Globe within, than it is without the Streights Mouth, it would be a thing impossible in Nature, for the Water to set in there; for where there is no Descent, there can be no Current; and as the Waters always run down from the highest Place to fill up the lowest, so likewise if there was any other Passage or Communication from the said Sea with the Body of the Ocean, the same Cause, by the Necessity of Nature, must have the same Effect.

As for Example, let a Communication be supposed to be made between three Ponds that are at some Distance from each other, whether by a Canal above, or by laying Pipes underneath, and the same Tendency will be from each of these Ponds, to keep the Surface always equal; and let but the least Water be drawn or taken out, or the Surface by any Means whatsoever be in the least abated, and the Water will immediately equally press in from both the other two, to supply that which is lowest: So that the common Notion which some Men have entertained touching a subterraneous Passage, to account for the Waters that continually run into the Mediterranean, is directly against Nature, and against Reason

And farther, touching what the learned Mr. Professor *Halley* has proved, with regard to the Nature and Power of Exhalation from the Heat of the Sun, I will here lay down two or three Instances of some Observations I have made in *Russia*, and which must more or less have been observed by all Persons who have lived any Time there, or in any of those Northern Countries where the Frosts are severe, and where Stoves are made use of to keep the Rooms warm in the Winter Season; amounting to the same Truth, but carrying with it a farther Appearance than the Experiments which Mr. *Halley* has made, and which I believe may not be unacceptable to the Reader here to relate.

The said Stoves which are made use of, are a sort of tall Ovens that are built up within the inside of a Room, artificially contrived to keep in the Heat, so that with an armful of Wood set on fire, usually but once, or in the Time of the severest Weather, but twice a-Day, you may sweat in them, or be kept to what Degree of Heat soever is desired, there being always a good Thickness of Earth laid above upon the Upper Floor for keeping in the Heat, and the Doors and Windows being made perfectly close, without any Chimney in the Room, or the least Passage for the Circulation of the Air, which would carry off the Heat with it. And what is extraordinary to be observed in these Rooms thus contrived, is, that when they are washed, (and the Stoves being then usually heated rather more than ordinary to dry the Rooms the sooner) the Water with which the Room has been washed and is left wet, by the Heat of the Room evaporates into the Air, and is immediately drawn, or flies to the Windows,

where,

where, when the Frost is not very strong, it settles on the Glass and trickles down in Puddles at the Bottom of the Window; but if the Frost be strong without Doors, it then freezes fast to the Glass, and remains a white, spungy Frost, almost as solid as Ice upon the Windows; and always the greater the Heat is within, and the stronger the Frost is without, the quicker this Operation is made; and if the Wet be repeated in the Room (which I have purposely done to try the Experiment) the Frost will soon become half a Quarter of an Inch thick upon the Windows. Or if you take half an Inch deep of Water in the Bottom of a Tub, and set it near the Stove in a warm Room, it will soon be drawn out of the Tub, and be attended with the same Effect.

Another Instance, is this: Take a Tankard of cold Beer, or a Bottle with cold Liquor, out of a Cellar that's cold, and bring it into one of these warm Rooms, especially if not long after washed, or if much Company be in the Room, which occasions a Moisture with their Breath, and set the Tankard or Bottle upon the Table, and within a few Minutes after, the Dew will settle in Drops, and trickle down off the sides of the Bottle or Tankard: But when some time after the Bottle or Tankard has been in the Room, it begins to grow warm by the Heat, the Effect then ceases, and no more Moisture settles or comes to it. Also if you are upon the Road in the

Winter-time, and take a Pair of Pistols out of your Sled, and bring them in your Hand into a warm Room, a strong Dew in Drops of Water, will immediately settle upon them; so that you must take Care to wipe them dry after they have lain a little while in the Room, or they will rust aud be spoiled. Or if you draw your Sword out of the Scabbard, it will have the same Effect: So that in all these Instances, it is evident, that either the Moisture of it self, as it circulates in the Air, flies off towards the Cold, or that the Cold attracts and draws it out of the Air in a close Room heated by a Stove, and the Door kept shut in manner aforesaid. But if there be a Fire or Chimney made in the Room, then the Moisture goes off with the Circulation of the Air, and has not the same Effect. One Observation I made when I was at *Veronize*, having Liberty to build a House to my own Mind at the *Czar*'s Charge: Upon my Works there, I made one handsome Room for the Reception of his Majesty when he came down, and in this Room I built a Chimney adjoining to the Stove, on purpose for making of a Fire after the *English* Fashion, having a good many of our Countrey Men in that Place. But whenever this Room was wash'd, and the Stove made warm at the same time, as well as a Fire made in the Chimney, the Moisture that then dry'd up from off the Floor, (which was as soon and effectual as at other Times) circulated with

the

the Air that went up out of the Chimney, and did not in any Degree settle upon the Windows, nor in Drops upon any thing brought cold into the Room, like as in either of the Cases beforemention'd

The first of which Instances of the Waters evaporating, and being dry'd up from off the Floor of a close Room heated by a Stove, and passing from thence to the Windows, I take to be the most clear and convincing, to prove the Nature of Exhalation, or the Evaporation of Waters by the Heat of the Sun; and that none of those Waters which we see daily dry'd up, in any Case whatsoever, are lost or destroy'd, but only shift and change their Station. But how the Wet from off the Floor of a warm Room, in manner as has been said, is immediately drawn or carried, not to the Top or Sides of the Room, but directly to whatsoever is brought cold into the Room; and more remarkably to the Windows, where it either freezes fast, or may be taken up again where it runs down at the Bottom of the Windows, in the same Body of Water; that is, how the Moisture is raised, or the Air attracts and draws it immediately from off the Surface of any thing that's made warm, more especially from whatsoever is warmer than it self: And afterwards, how the same Moisture circulates in the Air, and is drawn or carry'd directly to any thing that's cold, and there sticks fast, how this, I say, is perform'd; whether it be that the Cold attracts and draws
the

the Moisture out of the warm Air, or whether it be that the Heat only repels and throws off the Moisture towards the Cold, or that both these Causes mutually assist in the said Operation, I shall not take upon me to determine; only here fix my Opinion, that after the very same manner, all the Waters that we see daily dry'd up from off the Face of the Earth, and which by the Power of the Sun, and Force of the Winds, &c. are in Particles, imperceptible to the naked Eye*, continually forced from off the Surface of the Seas, Rivers, Ponds, &c. are in like manner raised and carried to the middle Part of the Amosphere (when not intercepted by Clouds by the Way) to that Height where the Air is too thin and subtile to bear them any higher, where being frozen and expanded by the Severity of the Cold, the bounded Particles striking in infinite Numbers against each other, are turn'd into thin Flakes of Snow, which floating at the said Heighth in the Atmosphere, are by their own Tendency, to attract each other, and by the Pressure of the Winds driven and roll'd into Clouds, until at length they acquire such a solid Body, that they are again by Earth and Sea attracted, (or in the common Ac-

---

* *But by letting the Rays of the Sun into a dark Room where Water is placed, and viewed through a Microscope, these Particles may be seen constantly to rise from off the Surface of the Water in greater or less Degree, and the Particles more gross or more fine, according to the Temperature of the Air and the Water.*

ceptation)

ceptation) fall off by Weight from the laden Clouds, and come down in the same Flakes of Snow compress'd, or as they meet with Heat are turn'd into Drops of Rain by the Way.

For the clearer Apprehension of which, I shall observe, that at the first rising of the Dews above to that Heighth in the Atmosphere where they first appear, when turned into Particles of Snow, its certain that they are then extremely light (much lighter than the Air which has buoy'd them up) and that those Flakes of Snow which afterwards come down through the lower Air, and fall to the Ground, must have been compress'd and become more heavy before they fall; and that all the Particles of Dew that compose a single Flake of Snow, at their first being conjoin'd or form'd into Clouds, are then loose and expanded, and sit easie and light upon the Atmosphere. We see sometimes in fair Weather, those thin Clouds which are first form'd, appear white, and move high in the Atmosphere, and the Sun and Moon shines easily through them; whilst we observe at the same time, those below are gathered, one Flake upon another, till they darken and shade the Light of the Sun; and as they are more laden and have usually more Wind in them, as a laden Ship presses hard upon the Water, so they press hard upon the Atmosphere, till they come near the Earth and disburthen themselves again.

And

And that all the Particles of Water that are exhaled and forced from off the Face of the Globe, are first carried to such a Heighth as has been mentioned, and there made Snow before they come down, I shall offer some few Reasons to prove.

The *First* is, that we see in *England*, that there never does fall any thing from the Clouds but Snow in the Winter-Season, when the Air is so cold that it cannot melt in coming down.

Secondly, That in the hottest Countries in the World, the High-land and Tops of great Mountains, are always covered with Snow. And,

Thirdly, As there never does, nor can fall any Rain, where it actually freezes at the same Time; so there never was since the Creation of the World, any one Flake of Snow seen to fall any where in or near the Torrid Zone, excepting upon or near the Tops of those remarkable Mountains, that by reason of their Heighth in the Atmosphere, are always invi-ron'd with Cold. Particularly I have several times observed at *Teneriff*, that when it has rain'd hard in the Road, (where the Ships ride) and in all the low Parts of the Island, the Bottom of the Body of the *Peek* has been immediately covered over with Snow, and which in a few Hours after, having fair Weather, has been melted away again, when higher up upon the *Peek*, it has still remained white; which must have been observed by every Man elfe as well as my felf. As alfo it is well known, that at the Town of *Oratavia*, where the greateft Part of our *Englifh* Ships load; that though there never was known the leaft Degree of Froft, nor the leaft Flake of Snow feen to fall any where below near the faid Town, yet the whole Year through, there is Ice brought down from the Body of the *Peek*, and fold by the Pound to Gentlemen in the Town for cooling their Wines; and that upon that Ifland (as well as many other Places in the World) in the moft fultry Seafon of the Year, if you go higher up upon the Body of the Ifland, you may chufe your Temperature of Weather, and live as cool as you pleafe.

Fourthly, I take it, that a Cloud can be compofed of nothing that is more folid or of any other Nature, than the frozen Atoms, which I have defcribed to be the inevitable Effect of the Dews being exhaled and raifed to that Height, where by Reafon of the Rarefaction, and Subtilenefs of the Air, and the Reflection of the Sun-Beams not extending their Force, it inceffantly freezes: And I take it to be certain, that thofe Particles of frozen Vapours or Dews, which compofe every individual Flake of Snow, are (at what Height foever they move) intermix'd with and buoy'd up in the Air, in the fame manner as a Faggot is in the Water; for it would otherwife be a thing impoffible for fuch a Quantity of Water, or Body of Snow, of which a Cloud is

compofed

composed, to keep up in the Atmosphere, did not the Air fill the whole, and support every individual Particle, in the same Nature as if each were loose and separate by it self, till laden one Flake of Snow upon another, and coming down nearer to the Earth, where the Air is more warm: When they begin in the least to thaw, they become more heavy and depressed, and fall off from the Clouds in the Form that we see come to the Ground, or as has been said, are turn'd into Drops of Rain by the way.

Fifthly, It is always to be observ'd, that in hot Countries, and in hot Weather, this Operation of falling off from the Clouds, is quicker perform'd; that is, the warm Air then extending farther from the Surface of the Earth or Sea, the Clouds do then never come near so low to disburthen themselves as in the Winter.

But if it happens, as it does sometimes on the Sea (which as it is less porous, attracts more than the Land *, and in still Weather, the Reflection of the Sun-Beams, like as from a Looking-Glass, being stronger upon the Water than upon the Land) when a Cloud comes so near as to be mingled with the warm Air, I take it to occasion that which the Seamen

---

* *A Gun loaden with the same Quantity of Powder, and the same Weight of Ball, or the same Weight of Small-Shot, and fix'd exactly to the same Level, and discharged at a Mark, the Shot will always fall lower when shot a-cross the Water, than when shot a-cross the Land.*

call a Spout †, or Water-fall, when all the lower Part of a Cloud is melted, and comes down in a few Minutes, appearing like a Funnel, broad at Top and narrow below; for as a large Flake of Snow coming into warm Air, gives and melts, and is by Attraction drawn into a single Drop; so a greater Quantity of Snow coming suddenly into warm Air, attracts it self in its Fall, and becomes a solid Body in coming down. We see also, especially in or near the Torrid Zone, that in hot, still Weather, the Showers are strong, and the Drops are prodigious large, when only a Shower happens, or the Rain first begins to fall. But again, when it has rained for some Time, and the Air is thereby become cool, by being mingled with and melting so much Snow, in coming down, the Drops then become considerably less: And in colder Coun-

---

† *It has been the vulgar Opinion of Seamen, that the Water is attracted and drawn out of the Sea up into the Clouds, by such Spouts; wherewith they argue, that the Clouds are constantly furnished with Rain to water the Earth, or at least will have this to be one Cause of it. But this Notion will soon appear to have no Validity in it, by considering, among a great many others, only these two Things. First, That it is impossible in Nature for a Body that is infinitely light, such as are the Particles of Snow which float merely loose in the Air, to draw up a heavy and solid Body of Water in a Spout to them; as will hereafter appear, in shewing the Nature of the Atmosphere. And Secondly, That even were this supposed possible, yet such a Body of Water (of which Ships that have been near, affirm a Spout is composed) could not keep up a Moment in the Air, without being impartibly expanded and turned into frozen Atoms, as I have described. But how such an Operation can be supposed (as some Men will still have it) must therefore be explained before it can be believed.*

tries

tries, and in the Winter Season, we see the Clouds fly low, and the Rain is then usually missling and small.

Another thing observable in the Northern Latitudes, and particularly in *England*, is that even in the Height of Summer, if the Clouds by a steady Gale happen to be driven long over our Heads, when they are not so laden as to disburthen themselves; the Air in such Case grows sensibly cold in respect of what it is at other Times; which happens not only by the Sun's being shaded from the Earth, but from the continued Reflection of Cold from the Snow that *is* in the Clouds; and the Warmth that is in the Air, extending then not far from the Earth, the Clouds must either come lower down and be more black and laden, or be clear for a while, and the warm Air again take place before it usually rains.

Sixthly, In the hottest Countries and the hottest Weather, where the Exhalations are always greatest when the Sun goes down, and the Power of the cause in a great measure ceases, which has raised those large Quantities of Dews that were on their Way toward the Top or foresaid Height of the Atmosphere, though the Particles are so imperceptibly fine that they cannot be discern'd, yet not being carried high enough to be frozen, and expanded by the Cold, and the Air not strong enough to keep them up in that Body they were raised without it; they return with their own Weight, and fall down again upon the Earth, the heaviest and greatest Part of them; more especially when there happens to be little or no Wind.

A most evincing Instance of the same Nature happen'd at the Time of the late great Eclipse, which my self and several other Persons standing upon the Leads on the Top of a House in the City of *London*, observed. It being then a clear still Morning, it was remarkable, that just before the Heat of the Sun was totally shaded from the Earth, the Dews which then fell, came down like a Mist, and were easily discern'd by the naked Eye; and I take it to be certain, that the Cold which was very sensibly felt at that Time, proceeded not so much from the Cause of the Want of the Sun, which is equally the same in the Night, as that the Dews with which the Air below was filled at that Time, fell from a considerable Height, where they had been chill'd by the Cold, and which was the Occasion that made them appear something of a whitish Colour, and which (with their being joined, and sticking many Particles to each other) became thereby discernible to the naked Eye.

In *Russia*, when the Rivers and all the Face of the Earth has been frozen and spread over with Snow in the Time of very hard Frost, and still clear Weather, those Particles of Moisture which then come into the Air, and cannot easily be exhaled, or raised to the usual

usual Height in the Atmosphere without the Heat of the Sun; as for Instance, such as are continually thrown off into the Air by Perspiration through the Skin, or those more gross, by the Breath of all living Creatures, by the opening of a Door of a close Room heated by a Stove, when the moist Air that is in the Room may be seen, (especially where there is no Shed or outward Room to break off the Cold) strike out like a Cloud or Fog at the Door, and freeze in an instant, and by all other Instances which occasion the Evaporations of Moisture by the Operations of Fire; as also by the Particles of Moisture arising from all Springs and Water Falls, and open Places of Streams and Rivers, which when it freezes hard are always seen with a strong Fog arising from them: In this, or in what other Occasions soever the Particles of Moisture that come into the Air are instantly expanded by the Severity of the Frost; and the Air being then without that Strength of Elasticity or Buoyantness that is occasion'd by the Heat of the Sun, (as particularly appears in the Instance of the Falling of Dews beforemention'd) there neither is then the usual Tendency to raise such Particles above in the Atmosphere to be form'd into Clouds as in warm Weather; nor can they, being frozen, easily fall to the Ground, but float about upon the Surface of the Globe, till the whole Air is fill'd with frozen Atoms, which may be seen sparkle and glitter in the Rays of the

Sun

Sun striking through them in a fair Day, when the Sky looks blue and clear towards the Zenith (where there is less Interception of the Sight by such Atoms) but occasions it at the same time to be extraordinary hazie, to 10 or 15 Degrees above the Horizon*; which seems to magnify the Diameter of the Sun, and makes it look half as big again as at another time. In like nature as we see sometimes the Sun or Moon, by reason of the Thickness of the Air that lies near the Surface of the Earth, looks bigger at rising or setting, though then near the Semi-diameter of the Earth farther Distance from us than when in the Meridian.

And now I have made Mention of this sort of hazie Weather, it puts me in mind also of what is usually observed by Seamen in their Voyages. In the Time of the greatest Heats, when there is little Wind, and perhaps scarce a Cloud to be seen in the Sky, it is then very rare to find a clear Horizon, when there's occasion to take an Observation of the Height of the Sun at Noon; which I take to be occasion'd by the extraordinary Exhalation of the Waters at such a time, which so thickens the Air, that the Horizon cannot rightly be distinguish'd; and that neither a Ship at any considerable Distance in the Sea,

---

* In which Countrey (in the Winter Season) the Sun, when in the Meridian, appears but very low above the Horizon, Mosco it self being four Degrees to the Northward of the City of London.

nor the Land cannot far be discover'd at such time; which is the Reason that for that purpose Men are usually sent to the Top-Mast-Head to look out in the Morning, and in the Evening, when the Air is abundantly more serene and clear.

Lastly, That those Particles of Dew that are raised to the Heighth in the Atmosphere, as has been described, are certainly expanded and made lighter than when first raised from the Surface, will appear, by considering the Nature of solid Ice: That a Vessel or Bottle fill'd with Water, the Water when it freezes expands and breaks the Vessel: And that a Foot or an Inch square of solid Ice (when it freezes hard) is about one seventh part higher than the same cubical Body of Water that is not frozen. And as this Experiment will hold good in a Foot or an Inch of Ice, so I take it to be as undeniable, that the same Rule will hold good in a Drop, or in a Particle of Water that is frozen, *viz.* that the same becomes one seventh part lighter than when it is not frozen.

These several Instances which I have laid down, have to me been sufficiently convincing that the Dews are raised, and the Clouds form'd of Snow, as aforesaid; and that the Cold that is above in the Atmosphere, as well as the Heat that is reflected from the Earth, both equally contribute to, and are equally necessary for the Work that has been described. That that Region above, where
the

the Cold always resides, is as the great Alembick of the World, (if I may so speak) whither all the Dews that are raised by the Heat of the Sun are continually carried; and that nothing but the Nature of the Cold, which immediately expands those Dews and Vapours that are raised, could otherwise by any means possibly give the necessary Qualification for the Clouds to keep up in the Air, and to be carried about the Globe, whither God in his Providence disposes them to water the Earth.

It was not at all in my Thoughts to have taken upon me to have treated on this Subject when I first began to write these Papers, which I design'd more strictly to have related only to the *Czar*'s Countrey; but the Mention of the *Caspian* Sea, when I came to speak of it, has engaged me farther than I intended: And though my Knowledge in the Mathematicks I must confess is but very little, yet by reason of the particular Observations which I have had the Opportunity to make, I hope I shall be more favourably pardon'd, and my Faults herein be the more easily forgiven.

And because some Men that may perhaps come to read this Discourse may not rightly comprehend the Nature and Extent of the Atmosphere, I believe it may not be amiss for me therefore farther to mention, that (according to the modern great Astronomers) that which is call'd the Atmosphere is a fluid Body of Air created by God, that always presses

upon,

upon, and attends the Earth in her annual and diurnal Motions, and sits like a thin Shell upon the Surface of the Globe, not above 40 or 45 Miles thick*: The lowermost part next the Earth more strong and buoyant, and the upper part more expanded, wearing off more thin and rarified; beyond which to infinity of Space, and to every Point that Thought can be extended to, there is nothing but an inexpressible, mighty, boundless *Vacuum*, without any Particle of Matter, or Breath of Air, excepting what belongs to other created Bodies, that 'tis believ'd have also their Atmospheres about them. That a Man or a Bird, (capacitated by God and Nature to live here) werethey carried but just above or without the Bounds of our Atmosphere, must instantly die for want of Air, as a Fish dies for want of Water, but abundantly more quick and sudden, as is experimented by the Use of the Air-Pump. Put a Bird into a large glass Receiver, and pump the Air out, and the Bird (or other Creature) instantly falls down and dies. And it is upon this Body of the Atmosphere, by which all Creatures move, without which even Trees and Vegetables

---

* *According to the Experiments that have been made, and the Judgment of several great Astronomers, others have reckon'd it not above 5 or 6 Miles distant from the Earth But let this be as it will, this is certain, that the highest Clouds that are visible to the Eye are not above two Miles distant from the Earth, beyond which the Air is so fluid and expanded, that it is impossible for any Particle of Matter belonging to the Globe to take rest or be born up upon it much farther*

would

would cease to grow, and which is the Spirit and Life of this World, that the Particles of Dew which are exhaled by the Sun, being expanded and made light, rest; and that the Clouds are carried about the Globe, in manner as has been describ'd; the Birds are born up when they spread their Wings; and that those small Atoms which are rubb'd from off every thing that is touch'd or moved, which in the Sun Beams (let into a dark Room) we see roul and circulate in the Air do easily keep up, though derived from the same Matter, that in a Lump would fall to the Ground.

Even Gold, which is the heaviest of all Metals, when beaten into thin Leaf, and fine Dust of Stone and Steel, though the Particles are so gross that they are easily visible to the Eye, yet with the least Breath of Wind they are raised in the Air; and when stirr'd in a Glass of Liquor float about, and do not presently sink to the Bottom. And for the same Reason that whatsoever of any solid Species, as it is of greater or less Weight, and as the Particles are more or less divided, sinks slower or quicker in the Water, so also it has the same Effect in the Air, according as the Superficies and Weight of the Species bears Proportion with that of the Atmosphere. A piece of Cork cannot be thrown so far with a Man's Hand as a Stone, and a Wod out of the Mouth of a Cannon is soon stop'd and falls to the Ground, when a Shot that is discharged by the same Force of Powder is carried to a greater Distance. A Musket-Ball in one entire piece of Lead is thrown a long way; when the same Weight of the very same Species, divided into small Shot, cannot fly a third part so far: So likewise any thing let fall from any Heighth in the Air, acquires more or less Velocity, and comes slower or quicker to the Ground, only as in Proportion to the Weight, one more than the other meets with the Resistance of the Air by the way.

A most surprizing and convincing Experiment of which is this: Pump the Air out of a large glass Tube, or other Receiver, as beforemention'd, and let go a Musket-Ball and a Feather together, and they will both come alike to the Ground, or Bottom of the Receiver: And for the same Reason also, were a Tube fix'd to the Top of the Atmosphere, or Heighth of the highest Clouds, and the Air pump'd out, the lightest Particle of Snow, or Atom of Dust, let go from the Top of it, would fall like Lead to the Ground. From which several Instances it may be concluded; First, that the Gravity or common Tendency towards the main Body is so great, that take away the Resistance of the Air, and every thing from all Sides of the Globe would fall directly to the Centre. From whence it is plain, that no one Particle of Moisture, or Atom of Dust, can (without the interposing Power of God) fly off beyond the Bounds of the Atmosphere, or be lost from our Globe

for

for ever. Secondly, That as it is in the Nature of Water and other Liquids, that nothing can possibly keep up or float upon them, but what is lighter than their own Body; nor sink, but what are heavier: So also it is in the Air, nothing but what is equal to or lighter than it self, can (without the Force of some immediate Power) possibly keep up in the Atmosphere; and consequently that the Circulation of Dews, and Course of Rains, can be perform'd in no other manner than what has been described: And on this Occasion it is worthy to be observed, that the wonderful Wisdom of God can never enough be consider'd: First, that he has so created the Temperature of the Atmosphere, more strong and buoyant below, and more subtile and rarified above, that thereby the Clouds are kept up and bounded to a certain convenient Height above us, and do not come near to brush the Tops of Trees and Houses, and to strike us with sudden Cold at any time. And secondly, that he has so exactly temper'd the mutual Operations of the Heat and the Cold, and so regulated the Nature of Air and Water, that the Quantity of Rains are constantly the same; and never too much, nor too little, to replenish the Earth.

For if this general Rule or Principle be granted, that the same Cause must produce the same Effect, and that the Earth constantly performs her Revolutions at the same Time, and at the same Distance, then the same Heat

of

of the Sun, the grand Agent, which shines just upon half, or rather (by refracting her Rays through the Atmosphere) upon more than half the World every Moment since the Creation, the Quantity of Waters exhaled must from the same Cause be always the same, take the World in general; though God, by the interposition of his Providence, so directs the Winds and the Clouds, that sometimes one Place has more, and another less Rain.

Upon what has been laid down touching the ordinary Course of Dews, and Vapours being raised in Particles imperceptible, also of the Nature of the Atmosphere, that nothing but what is equal or lighter than the Air can possibly be kept up in it; I farther therefore believe it may be proper to say something on the two following Points:

First, Of the Occasion of Fogs, which are visibly seen to float about upon the Surface of the Earth, and in a greater Measure upon the Water; as also they are known sometimes to hang upon the Tops or Sides of Mountains, that are not so high in the Atmosphere as to be wholly possess'd with Frost, or cover'd with Snow.

Secondly, How Hail, which is a solid Body, (notwithstanding what has been said of the Atmosphere) is form'd above in the Air, from whence we see it fall; and after what manner, and how long it is made before it comes down.

K And

And first of Fogs: It is usually observ'd, particularly in *England*, that they happen principally in the Autumn and Winter, or that part of the Year when the Heat declines; and not in the Spring, or the Height of the Summer, when the Heat increases; which Circumstance I take to be a plain Evidence of the Occasion of them: That after the Sun has made its strongest Impressions of Heat on this Side the Globe, and returns again towards the South Pole, the Air, as the Sun passes the Equinox, begins to be more cold than the Earth, especially in the Night; and more particularly, and to a greater Degree becomes in proportion colder than the Sea, which by reason of the Heats being communicated to a greater Depth from its Surface, cannot soon change its Quality. And when the Air is thus (by the Declension of the Sun) become cold, and the Sea and Earth continues yet warm in proportion to it, (especially the Sea) I take it to be the grand Cause which gives the Growth and Rise to Fogs; as particularly is more remarkable on the Coast of *Ireland*, which is more bordering on the Depth of the main Ocean, and consequently the Water more warm in the Winter Season. It is always noted by Seamen, that the Fogs are stronger there than on the Coast of *England*, in the *British* Channel.

The Occasion of which I take to be in the same manner as I have already described in the Case of Fogs and Damps arising in the

Time of hard Frosts from Springs, Water Falls, and open Places of Rivers, when it is usually said, as of Cellars, &c. that they are warm; and so it is indeed in respect to the Air at that Time: But then it would be a very gross Mistake (where the Air has the least Communication or Penetration) to imagine, that they or the Sea are warmer, or near so warm in the Winter as in the Summer: But of this here needs no more to my Purpose. It will be enough to have it granted, that the Sea, or other open Waters, are at such time apparently warmer than the Air; and the two different Qualities of Cold and Heat always striving, if I may so express it; to mingle together; and become of one Temperature. And in this Case, the greater the Difference is between the Temperature of the Air and the Water, with the more strong Tendency the Heat that has been received from the Sun pressing back through the Surface of either the Earth or the Water; the more plentifully it throws off the Particles of Moisture along with it; especially from the Water, where the deepest Impression of Heat has been made. Which also, as has been observed in the particular Instance of a warm Room, and in the great and general Case of the Dews being carried to the middle Region of the Atmosphere, the Cold (as I take it) with mutual Force attracts, and draws the Particles of Moisture to it self, where-ever they are loose in the Air: And in this Case, the stronger the Occasion of the Dews and Vapours being raised, that is, the greater Difference there is between the Temperature of the Heat and Cold, consequently the more gross are the Particles; and being of equal Weight with the lower Air, (which wants of its usual Elasticity at such time) cannot possibly rise higher, but in a continued Succession of Particles, as they rise from off the Surface, either of the Earth or the Sea, striking against each other, form a thick Body, become visible and float about near the Surface of the Earth, until the Power of the Sun takes place to warm and give a new Spring to the Air, and to dissipate and raise them to the lighter and more rarified Regions above. As is usually seen in fair Weather when the Sun gets up in the Morning; but if it be cloudy and cold, with little Wind, then the Fogs hang about the Earth, and continue sometimes without being clear for several Days and Nights together. Which is very common to happen in Places near the Sea, and other great Waters; but farther on upon the Continent, as particularly in the Situation of *Mosco*, there the Air is more serene, and a Fog is very rarely known.

Farther likewise it is remarkable in hot Countries, and in hot Weather, that in all the Parts of the World, at the Tops or Sides of such Mountains which do neither lye so high in the Atmosphere as to be affected with the Severity of Cold that is above, nor with the Heat that takes place, and exhales the Dews and Vapours from below, but where the Air is at such a Temperature and Degree of Elasticity as is just before described, in the Occasion of Fogs: For instance, at the Top of the Peek of *Teneriff*, where the Snow always lies, (on one side or other) there the Air is too thin and subtile to bear up such heavy Particles, and impossible for a Fog ever to be form'd. But lower down, at the Bottom of the Body of the Peek, and at the Top or upper part of that, and several other of the *Canary* Islands, between the Excess of Heat below, and the Extremity of Cold that possesses the higher Regions of the Air, a Fog in still Weather is immediately seen to take place.

To come nearer home; upon the high Land in the Principality of *Wales*, and upon the Hills to the Southward of the City of *Dublin*, though not to be compared to the Height of the Hills beforemention'd, yet the Air being much colder there than it is in the Valleys, the Particles of Moisture that are exhaled and circulate in the warm Air from below, are in the same manner as I have mention'd in the Case of a warm Room, drawn and carried to the cold Air that hovers at the Top of such Mountains; where, especially in still Weather, or with a gentle Breeze, such Air being not buoyant enough to raise them higher, they strike against each other till they thicken and become a Fog, (or that which is usually esteem'd and looks like Clouds) hang ing at a Distance, until either at some Times they are dissipated by the Power of the Sun, and at other Times driven from thence by the Force of the Winds.

Thus I have laid down my Opinion of Fogs in general; of which whether what I have described be the true Cause or not, I will humbly submit to better Judgment: But this I am sure, that the Circumstances in each of the Cases that I have mention'd agree, and that the Effect (at least the Appearance of it) is always true.

Secondly, touching the Occasion of Hail: That notwithstanding what has been said of the Nature of Dews and Rains, and of the Insufficiency of the Air to bear up any thing but what is at least equal to or lighter than it self, and that the upper part of the Air is abundantly the lightest; yet we see that Hail, however it is form'd, and however held or kept up in the Air, is a condense and solid Body, and falls from a great Height, directly from the Clouds, when it comes down

Of the Nature and Cause of which I will not go about to enlarge; but only shall lay down this one Circumstance, *viz.* that Hail is always, or at least very often, found to fall immediately after Lightning in some Place or other, either directly under, or not far from the Place where the Lightning happens to be strongest. And usually in the hottest Weather, and the strongest Lightning, the greater the Stones of Hail are seen to fall; this
there-

therefore I make no Scruple to believe is one Occasion of it; that the Lightning which is known to have a prodigious Force in other Cases, flashing in Veins through the Clouds, at once melts and contracts the Snow into Drops, or more irregular Forms of Water, and which as Water thrown into the Air in the time of severe Frost, which I have seen in *Russia* freeze before it comes to the Ground; so likewise such Water, melted by Flashes of Lightning, instantly freezes as it falls, if the Lightning happens to strike thro' the middle or upper part of a Cloud that flies high, where the Frost is always severe; and falling through the Parts and Flakes of Snow that are below the Place where it was first melted, gathers and freezes fresh Particles of Snow to it by the way, which, as I take it, causes that Roughness which we see when the Hail comes to the Ground. But if the Lightning happens to strike through the lower parts of a Cloud only, then it produces, as we usually see immediately after strong Thunder and Lightning, strong Showers of Rain; at other Times it falls both Rain and Hail together.

And one thing farther is generally remarkable, that these sort of Showers, particularly those of Hail, do not spread or extend to any great Distance, and often are known not to fall upon the Earth a quarter of a Mile in Breadth.

Thus I have run through the several Points of this Subject, which, I had not the least Intention of taking upon me when I first began to write these Papers: But when I came to give an Account of the *Caspian* Sea, which has been treated of, more or less, by all who have written any thing of that Part of the Countrey, I believed that the Mention of the Calculation which I made of the Waters which run down the *Wolga*, might be agreeable to the Curiosity of some Persons, as well as it was to my own: As also that the Observations which I made of the Waters being dry'd up in a close Room, heated by a Stove, might generally be as acceptable: and what I have farther enlarg'd thereon, after I found my self engaged in it, in endeavouring to make it clear, I hope may not be thought improper on such an Occasion, and shall wholly submit the same to such Gentlemen of Knowledge in the Mathematicks, on the Principles of whose modern great Improvements and Experiments, I have laid down what I have humbly offered, according to the particular Observations which I have made in my Travels in the World.

And to go on now again with my intended Relation of the *Czar*'s Countrey: The next People that I shall give an Account of are the *Crim-Tartars*, who border on the *Black Sea*, and on whom the *Czar* has the most

Thoughts of extending his Southern Conquests.

They are in Possession of a very fruitful and pleasant Countrey, which is almost as an Island surrounded, partly with the Waters of the *Black Sea*, and partly with those of the *Palus Mæotis*, situated from the Latitude of 44 ½, to 46 ½ Degrees North, which is properly the *Crim*'s: And they have also a good Tract of Countrey farther to the Northward, and to the Westward, as far as the Mouth of the *Neiper*. These *Tartars* have been many hundred Years in strict Alliance with the *Turks*; and in case of any Failure of the *Ottoman* Male Line, the *Cham* of this *Crim-Tartary* is to succeed to the Crown of the *Turkish* Empire. It was the *Cham* of these *Tartars* who, being jealous of the *Czar*'s growing Power, joined with the King of *Sweden* in making Instances (as 'tis said) for the *Ottoman*'s to declare their late War against the *Muscovites*; by which the *Czar* has not only been obliged to give up *Azoph*, and the strong Places on that Side, but by Pretensions since made, the *Czar* has (as 'tis said) been obliged, or at least strong Instances were made by the *Turks*, that the *Czar* should pay to the said *Tartars* the Sum of 100000 Ducates *per Annum*, which the *Muscovites* had formerly been obliged to pay them, till about 26 Years since (as I have had the Relation given me;) at which time the *Turks*, being equally engaged
with

with the *Germans*, the *Poles* and the *Venetians*, the said *Tartars* were not only obliged to quit their Pretensions, but the *Czar*'s Army, being then victorious, advanced so far into their Countrey, that it was judged that an entire Conquest might easily have then been made. The Neglect of improving this Success of the *Czar*'s Army, at that Time, was thus occasion'd:

Duke *Gollitzen*, nearly related to the forementioned *Gollitzen*, (under whose Command I served at *Camishinka*) who was *Generalissimo* of the *Czar*'s Forces at that Time, and had got with a powerful Army within the Neck of Land that leads into their Countrey, being tempted by a great Sum of Ducats of Gold, which they brought to him in Barrels (amongst which, as 'tis said, there were many Counters) he concluded Conditions of Peace in the Field, and withdrew his Army. For which, and his being charged with adhering to the Princess *Sophia*, (of whom I shall speak more hereafter) he was sent into Banishment with the Allowance of only Six-pence a Day during his Life, and his Estate wholly confiscated to the *Czar*.

The said *Tartars*, after the Peace that was concluded with the Christian Princes at *Carlowitz*, 1699, have since fortified several Places on the Frontiers, the better to secure themselves against future Danger. The *Turks* also upon Conclusion of the said Peace, whereby they were obliged to leave *Azoph* in the
Hands

Hands of the *Czar*, which he had taken from them, *Anno* 1696, to prevent the Progress and Establishment of the *Czar*'s Naval Power in the *Black Sea*, have since run out very strong Works on each side the Streights of *Kertzi*, (or *Caffa*) to command the Passage between the *Palus Mæotis* and the *Black Sea*, as described in the Map hereunto annexed. In the doing of which Work, they say, that *Breckell* was employed, who had deserted the making the Communication at *Camishinka*, and had changed his Name, to put himself into the Service of the *Turks*.

The said *Tartars* were formerly victorious against the *Russes*. They have often penetrated into the Heart of *Russia*, and in *Anno* 1671, they burnt the City of *Mosco*, and by the Articles of Peace that were concluded in the Time of the *Czar*'s Predecessors, the *Russes* were obliged to submit to very scandalous Terms; not only to be tributary to the said *Tartars*, but even to have it inserted in their Articles, that the *Czar*'s of *Russia* should hold the Stirrup to the Great *Cham*, in case of their happening to meet together. But if the Princes of Christendom should again be jointly engaged in a War with the *Turks*, and the *Czar* be disengaged but a little Time from his present War with the *Swedes*, the *Crim* will then certainly be a bloody Seat of War, and the *Czar* will revenge these Indignities, with exerting his utmost for the

Con-

Conquest of it, thereby to make his Way into the *Black* Sea.

I have often heard the *Czar* say, when he was building of his Ships, and preparing Magazines on that side, particularly on the Occasion of the Proposal which I made for preserving his Ships from Decay that were then preparing against the *Turks*; that he hoped, in case he lived, that it would not be many Years before he should make himself Master of *Kertzi*, and have that the Place of laying up, and Rendezvous for his Navy: There being on the Bar of *Azoph*, commonly not above 7 Foot Draught of Water, unless in Force of Weather, when the Wind is at S. W. Nor did there prove to be so much as 7 Foot at the aforesaid Haven that was intended to be made at *Taganroke*; whereas at *Kertzi*, there is Water enough for the biggest Ships the *Czar* can propose to build, and where may easily be made good Security for the greatest Navy in the World.

The Views which the *Czar* has, and the Success that he promises himself one time or other to obtain on this side, is, that he will either by Force or Consent, oblige the *Turks* upon paying them Tribute, (as is used in the Sound) to let him trade with his Ships into the Mediterranean, thereby to vend Naval Stores, and other Manufactures of his Countrey, for the Inlargement of his Trade, and enriching of his People this Way.

These

These are the great Designs of the *Czar*, for which his Countrey is happily and most advantageously situated, and in which he pleases himself with the Thoughts of going beyond the Steps of his Fathers, to have Ships on all sides of his Countrey, and Trade equally carried on by his own Subjects to the *Baltick*, the *White Sea*, the *Caspian Sea*, and to the Mediterranean through the *Black Sea*; as well as to search out also if it be practicable to send Ships, by way of the *Tartarian Sea*, to the *Indies*, as has been before-mentioned.

The Occasion of his first falling upon the Thoughts of Shipping, and of his travelling to inspect the Improvements of other Countries, was owing chiefly to his early Genius and Curiosity to enquire into the Reason and Causes of Things; which Method in his common Conversation, he still uses with indefatigable Application in the minutest Things. And next was also owing to an Accident that happened, which led him to a Liking and Pleasure in Conversation with Foreigners.

In the Time of the former *Czars* of *Muscovy*, no common Person or Stranger, was to come near their Persons: It was to detract from the Lustre of their Greatness; they were not to be seen by vulgar Eyes; but when the *Czar*, or next Princes of the Blood, rode through the Streets of the City, Officers were appointed to go before to make
the

Conquest of it, thereby to make his Way into the *Black* Sea.

I have often heard the *Czar* say, when he was building of his Ships, and preparing Magazines on that side, particularly on the Occasion of the Proposal which I made for preserving his Ships from Decay that were then preparing against the *Turks*; that he hoped, in case he lived, that it would not be many Years before he should make himself Master of *Kertzi*, and have that the Place of laying up, and Rendezvous for his Navy: There being on the Bar of *Azoph*, commonly not above 7 Foot Draught of Water, unless in Force of Weather, when the Wind is at S. W. Nor did there prove to be so much as 7 Foot at the aforesaid Haven that was intended to be made at *Taganroke*; whereas at *Kertzi*, there is Water enough for the biggest Ships the *Czar* can propose to build, and where may easily be made good Security for the greatest Navy in the World.

The Views which the *Czar* has, and the Success that he promises himself one time or other to obtain on this side, is, that he will either by Force or Consent, oblige the *Turks* upon paying them Tribute, (as is used in the Sound) to let him trade with his Ships into the Mediterranean, thereby to vend Naval Stores, and other Manufactures of his Countrey, for the Inlargement of his Trade, and enriching of his People this Way.

These

These are the great Designs of the *Czar*, for which his Countrey is happily and most advantageously situated, and in which he pleases himself with the Thoughts of going beyond the Steps of his Fathers, to have Ships on all sides of his Countrey, and Trade equally carried on by his own Subjects to the *Baltick*, the *White Sea*, the *Caspian Sea*, and to the Mediterranean through the *Black Sea*; as well as to search out also if it be practicable to send Ships, by way of the *Tartarian Sea*, to the *Indies*, as has been before-mentioned.

The Occasion of his first falling upon the Thoughts of Shipping, and of his travelling to inspect the Improvements of other Countries, was owing chiefly to his early Genius and Curiosity to enquire into the Reason and Causes of Things; which Method in his common Conversation, he still uses with indefatigable Application in the minutest Things. And next was also owing to an Accident that happened, which led him to a Liking and Pleasure in Conversation with Foreigners.

In the Time of the former *Czars* of *Muscovy*, no common Person or Stranger, was to come near their Persons: It was to detract from the Lustre of their Greatness; they were not to be seen by vulgar Eyes; but when the *Czar*, or next Princes of the Blood, rode through the Streets of the City, Officers were appointed to go before to make

the

the Common People get out of the Way, or to fall down with their Faces to the Earth. The old *Boyars* did this on purpose, or at least it is certain that it had this Effect, that they kept thereby the Government of Things intirely in their own Hands, and ruled the former *Czars* by whatsoever superstitious and biggotted Schemes and Notions they had a Mind to; establishing this for a Rule, That as it was not proper for sinful Men to apply themselves directly to God, but to approach him by the Way of his Saints: So also it was Presumption on Earth to think of coming any Way to the *Czar*, but by addressing his *Boyars*. Which Maxim (notwithstanding all the Steps the present *Czar* has taken) is still in some measure kept up in that Countrey: For since my Time, there has been an Order made, and Publication given of it, That in Case of any Grievance whatsoever, no Man shall presume to apply himself, or deliver any Petition directly to the *Czar* himself, but that they shall first apply themselves by Petition to the proper *Boyar* or Officer in the *Precause*, (or Court) before whom such Complaint is cognizable: That every Person shall be at Liberty to give in two several Petitions, and that if thereupon no Redress be given to the Petitioner, they may, if they think fit, then Petition the *Czar* himself; but 'tis under this severe Penalty, That whosoever, upon Examination before the *Czar*, shall be found to be in the Wrong, either the *Boyar* or Petitioner, shall suffer Death;

Death; which Order has carried such a Terror with it, that since the making of it, I never heard of any one Person, even in Cases of the most notorious Injustice, that ever dared to attempt to petition the *Czar*, but have thought it better to sit down content; well knowing, that whoever goes about to struggle with any superior Power, is sure to suffer by it; there being no Juries in that Countrey, nor Counsel admitted to plead as in *England*, but the Will of the Judge, pretending to take some Statute for his Guide, decides the Law as he pleases.

The present *Czar*'s Father, *Allexyea Micchalovitz*, at his Death left two Sons, *Feodor* and *Evan*, with one Daughter named *Sophia*, by a first Wife, and the present *Czar* by a second Wife: *Feodor*, the eldest Brother, died, after having reigned only six Years. But before his Death, appointed his youngest Brother *Peter* (by a second Wife) his Successor to the Throne, judging his Brother *Evan*, by reason of the Weakness of his Eyes, and the Infirmness of his Constitution, unfit for the Government; and accordingly the youngest Brother, *Peter*, was proclaimed *Czar*, being then not above 12 Year's of Age. But the Princess *Sophia*, a handsom young Lady, then upwards of 23, and who had born Part in the Regency during her Brother *Feodor*'s Minority, being now chagrined to see *Evan*, her Brother by first Marriage, excluded from the Succession to the Throne, having engaged the General

neral of the *Streletzes*, with many of the Chief of the Nobility and Clergy on her side, it was resolved to put the Crown upon her Brother's, or rather jointly upon her own Head. To effect this Design, and to work upon the Minds of the Populace, a Report was industriously spread, that the eldest Brother, *Czar Feodor*, had been deprived of his Life by the Physicians, at the Instigation of some of the chief Men at the Helm, whose Names were artfully whispered about; and the more strongly to exasperate and draw the *Streletzes* into their Party, (who were established Forces, like as the *Janizaries* to the *Turks*) it was rumour'd, that a Design was form'd at the Court, to have mixed Poyson with the Brandy and Beer that was to be given them at the forementioned *Czar Feodor*'s Funeral. And the General, with many of the chief Officers, who were generally of the younger Brothers of the chief Families in *Russia*, being before engaged in the Design, and the Army thus enraged against the Court, they began first with the Murther of the two Physicians that had administred Physick to the deceased *Czar*; cut in Peices several of the chief Officers of the Crown who were pointed out for Destruction, and threw others from the Balcony of the Royal Palace, upon the Soldiers Pikes, who stood underneath for that purpose, with their Pikes planted upright to receive them; committed many other Violences, and put the City every where in an Uproar,

Uproar, till after some Days their Fury was ceased, and *Evan* was proclaim'd *Czar* in Conjunction with his Brother *Peter Alexyavich*.

In the Height of this Tumult, Prince *Burris Allexavich Gollitzen* took the present *Czar* in his Arms, and carried him to *Troitsky* Monastery, a strong Place 60 *Russ* Miles from *Mosco*, to secure his Person till this Rage was over; which ended in the General's being drawn into an Ambuscade near *Troitsky* Monastery, where he was taken, and afterwards carried Prisoner to the *Czar*, and his Head taken off in the said Monastery. The Princess *Sophia* also was seized and carried into a Convent near *Mosco*, where she remained strictly confined till she died, which is about 4 Years since. Many of the *Streletzes* who were found the Ring-leaders of this Rebellion, were destroyed, they and their Families, and their Houses razed to the Ground. This Rebellion happened in the Year 1683, and about 11 Years after, the aforesaid *Evan*, who by reason of his Incapacity, had born but little Sway in the Government with his Brother, died, and was interr'd privately in the Church where all the Bodies of the Royal Family are deposited.

At the Time of this Rebellion, it happened that one *Le Fort* a *French* Man, who had been Apprentice to a Merchant in *Amsterdam*, and was then a Captain in the *Russ* Army, was appointed one of the Officers

L   that

that commanded the Guards that were chosen to secure the *Czar's* Person in the said Monastery; and he being of an active and ingenious Temper, happened to be very much taken notice of by the *Czar*, who was then but 12 Years of Age, as has been mentioned; and he from that Time kept him always near his Person, and took a particular Affection to him, and was pleased with the Discourse that he often entertained him with; of the Countries he had been in, of the regular Discipline of the Armies, and of the Naval Powers; the Riches and Trade that was extended through *Europe*, by other Nations, over all the Parts of the World, by the means of Shipping. Whereupon the *Czar* at first ordered Ships to be built for his Pleasure, with Masts and Sails, and Guns, upon the *Perrislausky* Lake, not far from *Mosco*, where he often diverted himself with sailing upon the said Lake, and had several Sham-Fights perform'd, in which he acted and commanded as a Sea-Captain, from which Time he took that Title upon him.

And in the Year 1694, when the Emperor, the *Poles*, and the *Venetians* were jointly engaged in a War with the *Turks*, the *Czar* also declared War against them, and commanded several small Galleys and Vessels to be built and equipp'd on the River *Veronize*, which he employed in the taking of *Azoph*, together with some open Boats of the *Cossacks*, who inhabit 7 or
800

800 *Russ* Miles on the River *Don*, at the Mouth of which River *Azoph* is situated.

The first Summer, the *Czar* march'd against the Place with an Army of 80 or 90 thousand Men, (which was in the Year 1695) but the *Turks* got Succours into the Town by Water, made frequent Sallies, and held out a resolute Defence for above two Months. One *Jacob* a Foreigner, who served in the *Russ* Artillery, having been long held out of his Pay, and ill used by the *Boyar* whose Command he served under, nailed up the Canon upon the Batteries where he was entrusted, and in the Night deserted to the Enemy, informed them of the Treachery he had committed, and advised them thereupon immediately to make a vigorous Sally; which accordingly they put in Execution with such Success and Slaughter of the *Russes*, (who were brought into Confusion, when they found their Guns spiked up,) that they were obliged soon after to quit the Siege for that Year, and turn'd it into a Blockade.

But the second Year, the *Czar* having ordered a strong Recruit of his Army, and prepared a Fleet of small Vessels and Galleys, to prevent the Relief of the Town, when the *Turks* came with their Fleet, by way of the *Black Sea*, before the Bar, with a new Supply of Men, Provisions, and Money, and attempted with a great Number of half Galleys, Boats, and Vessels to have thrown fresh Succours into the Town, as they had done the Year before

L 2 fore:

fore: The *Czar* with his aforesaid Vessels and Boats, (on board of which he acted in Person) laid an Ambuscade behind a small Island, and after having first made Shew to retire before the Face of the Enemy, when they were got a little way within the River, he fell upon them, sunk and took several of their Vessels, with Soldiers, Provisions, and Money on board; and at another time, beat them back over the Bar, upon their making a second Attempt with their small Vessels and Boats, to which the *Czar*'s were at least equal in Force; besides a strong Battery that was placed upon the Island, where Canon would reach a-cross the Stream; at which Place the *Turks* were to pass, and there was not Water enough for bigger Ships or Vessels to attempt to come over the Bar. Soon after this Defeat, the Garrison finding themselves wholly disappointed of their Hopes of Relief, and the Siege having been vigorously carried on chiefly under the Conduct of General *Gordon*, a worthy and ingenious *North-Britain*, who on this Occasion to facilitate his Approaches, had kept rolling forwards a great Fence, or Bank of Earth, at several Places, of that Height, that the same looked into the Town over the Fortifications; so that no Man could stir in the Day-time, but they shot him down from behind the Top of these Banks; which they began first, and raised at some Distance from the Walls of the Town, out of the Reach of the Enemies Fire

Fire from their Small-Arms; and by great Numbers of Men, which the *Ruſſes* relieved every four Hours, and employed as thick as they could ſtand, without being in one another's way, they ſhovelled the Earth quite from the Bottom on the out-ſide, or off-ſide of the ſaid Fence, or Bank, and kept throwing it over at the Top, to that ſide next the Town, where it rolled and tumbled ſtill inwards; ſo that by this Method, in little more than a fortnight's Time, they advanced theſe Banks or Walls of Earth (which were much higher than the Enemies Baſtions) within half Musket-Shot of the Walls of the Town, until the Cannon from the ſeveral Batteries at other Places, had continued playing and made ſeveral Breaches in the Walls of the Town. The Enemy finding themſelves thus every way diſtreſs'd by the moſt ſurpriſing and vigorous Behaviour of the *Czar* and his Army, and no Proſpect of the Relief which they had expected by their Fleet, they were obliged to ſurrender themſelves, upon Conditions, that they ſhould have Liberty to march out of the Place without their Arms; and to deliver up the aforementioned *Jacob* (the Name he was known by) to be puniſhed according to the Extent of his Crime, and who was carried from thence to *Moſco* alive, where he was firſt three Times tortured upon the Pine, and then broke upon the Wheel, being told upon the Torture, that when he found himſelf aggrieved, as he complained, he ought to have had recourse to his Majesty for Justice, to whom he had always free Access, and not to have been guilty of so great a Treachery.

The *Czar* pleased with the Success of his new built Fleet, and the Reduction of so important a Place, which open'd a Way into the *Black Sea*; upon his returning to *Mosco* in Triumph, he was complemented upon this Victory by his *Boyars*, as being principally owing to his Fleet, and his Majesty's personal Vigour and Conduct on Board the same, by which he prevented the Relief of the Town. His Majesty on this Occasion finding the great Advantage of a Maritime Force, declared to his Lords that he was resolved to establish a Navy on that Side, that he might maintain this important Place, and be able to meet the *Turks* and oppose them in the *Black Sea*; and commanded them immediately to send for Builders and Artificers from *Holland* to build his Ships, and from *Italy* and *Venice* to build his Galleys; and resolved to have a Fleet of 40 Men of War, 10 Store Ships and Bomb Vessels, 20 large Galleys and Galleasses, and 30 Half Galleys and other Vessels to be built, and equipp'd with all things ready to put to Sea, within the time of three Years that was given for the doing it. A List accordingly was prepared and agreed on in Council, which the *Czar* called for this Purpose, by which several of the great Lords (who had great Estates, and a

great

great many Slaves at their Command, in which their Estates was accounted to consist) were obliged to build each of them a Man of War at their own Charge, and were at Liberty to call them after their own Names when built. The Monasteries also, and the Cities and Towns, the Merchants and the Gentlemen through all the Districts of his Dominions, were to pay their Proportion to the Charge of this new Undertaking, besides the ordinary Course of the Taxes for maintaining the Army, and carrying on the War that was then in hand. It was order'd, that if the respective Ships and Vessels were not ready within the time of three Years which was affix'd, then their Proportion was to be doubled. He permitted them on this Occasion to appoint Deputies to carry on the Work, and to hire and agree to have it done as they would. There were several *Dutchmen* and others who were accordingly forthwith employ'd as Agents in this Undertaking, and the same was perform'd with that Expedition as commanded. His Majesty declared also at the same time his Intentions to travel whilst this Fleet was preparing, and appointed several of the young Nobility and Gentry of his Countrey to go with him, to see and learn the Improvements of other Nations, commanding some of them to travel to one Place, and some to another, to make all the Observations were possible through all the Parts of *Europe*.

The building of these Ships, which had never been done in *Russia* before; and at the same time obliging the *Boyars* and Gentlemen of Estates to send their Sons abroad to travel, were both look'd upon as a great Grievance, the one being not only to entail a Charge upon them beyond the common Tax, but an Occasion of bringing in of Foreigners to build and sail their Ships; and the latter, the sending abroad their Children, was such an Innovation they could not well bear, for they feared, as was insinuated by the Priests, that it would be a means of corrupting them in the Principles of their Religion *, and which they held to be a Thing that was directly contrary to the Law of God, adhering to those Texts of Scrip-

---

* *Of the* Russ *Religion in general I must defer to speak till hereafter: I shall only here observe, that as it is the manner of all Men of all Religions in the World (or at least the Teachers of them) to reckon their own the only true Religion, and without scruple to condemn all the rest to Perdition (excepting the Charity of the* Church of England, *at least some Divines of it reckon, that an honest Man of any Religion may be saved) so the* Russes *are not behind hand with their Neighbours; they reckon every Man is directly in the way to Damnation that are not of their holy* Greek *Religion. And it has been therefore before this* Czar's *Time, accounted a great Merit among the great Lords and Men of Estates to gain over Proselytes to their Faith; and so irreconcileable are they towards all other Christians, that whenever any Man embraces the* Russ *Faith, he must be re-baptized, or he cannot be accepted or be accounted a Christian, but a Heathen: And in the Ceremony of being re-baptized, he must three times spit over his Left Shoulder, and repeat after the Priest these Words,* Cursed are my Parents that brought me up in the Religion that I have been taught, I spit upon them. *At the pronouncing of which Words, he must spit with his Mouth, and say,* I spit upon them,

Scripture, which forbid the Children of *Israel* to have any Communion with the Nations that were round about them, that they might not partake of their Idolatry; for which Reason, even Envoys that have been sent heretofore to Foreign Courts, have been denied to take their Sons with them, and upon Pain of Death it was forbid that any *Moscovite* should go out of the Countrey without especial Leave from the Patriarch. But they now murmur'd that the *Czar* wholly adher'd to Strangers, went himself daily to their Houses, and freely admitted them to his Conversation; which stir'd up the Discontents of the Party that were out of Favour at Court, and who had been made uneasy at their Disappointment since the last Rebellion, who were still in the Interest of the Princess *Sophia*, and wanted to be themselves at the Head of the Government; they therefore took this Opportunity in hopes to give a Turn to Affairs: And that they might effectually bring about their Purpose, a Conspiracy was held to set fire to some Houses that were near the *Czar*'s Residence, to murder him when he should be coming (as his usual way is) to quench it, to release the Princess *Sophia* out of Prison, to set the

---

them, and upon their Religion; *though all this want of Charity, and Things wherein they boast to be more religious than other Christians, proceeds merely from Superstition and Ceremony, the addressing to Saints, the keeping of Fasts, and the manner of holding their Fingers when they cross themselves, which is the height of what they dispute for, whilst they neglect the solid things of Christianity*

Crown

Crown upon her Head, to restore the ancient *Streletzes* to their Posts of the Guards, from whence they had been removed on account of their siding in the aforemention'd Rebellion at the *Czar*'s first coming to the Throne, and to have massacred all the *Czar*'s new Favourites and Foreigners that had ever been near him, and who were supposed by the *Russes* to have advised the *Czar* to those new Measures he intended.

In this Design, three great *Boyars*, one of the chief Colonels of the *Don Cossacks*, and four of the Captains of the *Streletzes* were engaged, and *February* 2, 1697. was set to have put this Tragedy in execution: But the very Day before the same was to be transacted, two of the said Captains being struck with Remorse of Conscience, went and threw themselves at the *Czar*'s Feet for Mercy, when he was at the House of his aforesaid Favourite *Le Fort*, confess'd their own Crimes, and discovered all the chief Persons concerned in the Conspiracy. Upon which the *Czar* rose from the Table without any great Surprize in his Countenance, and immediately went himself with only a few Persons with him, seized all the head Men who had associated together and plotted this Wickedness; amongst which, one of them was of his own Privy Council, who were all afterwards put to the Torture, and confess'd the whole Truth of their Design; and they were the Month following, being *March* 5, executed in the following

lowing manner, in the great Market-place before the Royal Castle. First, their Right Arms and Left Legs, and then their Left Arms and Right Legs were cut off, and afterwards their Heads sever'd from their Bodies, and fix'd upon Pinacles of Iron, on a tall Stone Column erected before the Castle for that purpose, with their Legs and Arms also hung round the same Statue or Column, and the Trunks of their Bodies were not suffered to be buried, but left expos'd in the Market-place to the view of all Spectators, till the Frost broke up, and the Scent became so nauseous to the Inhabitants, that they were order'd to be removed from thence, and cast into a Pit with common Rogues and Thieves. There were several others accused, but it not appearing that they had any Design against his Majesty's Life, they were pardon'd and acquitted.

His Majesty being thus happily deliver'd from this Conspiracy, he prepar'd in good earnest for his intended Journey. He resolved to travel *incognito*, that he might be freed from all Ceremony, and have a better Opportunity of making his Observations with Freedom. He took with him his aforementioned Favourite *Le Fort*, who was then made Lieutenant General of his Army, and Admiral of his Fleet; his present Favourite Prince *Menzicoff*, who had then no Character, together with Count *Gollovin*, the late Great Chancellor of *Russia*, and another great Lord;

which

which two last Persons, together with the above-mentioned *Le Fort*, were appointed to take upon them the Character of his Embassadors extraordinary, and acted as his publick Ministers in *Holland* and in *England*: There were with him also in his own Retinue several young Gentlemen and Favourites of lesser Note. He left the Administration of the Government in his Absence to three of his Lords, the first of which was his Mother's Brother, *Leof Corilich Nariskin*, (two of whose Sons were not long since in *England*;) the second, the aforemention'd Duke *Gollitzen*; and the third, the Lord *Peter Procorofsky*, to which three Lords he left the Care of his Son the present Prince of *Russia*, and the sole Management of all Affairs. He order'd the suspected *Streletzes*, many of whom had been found guilty and executed on account of the aforemention'd Rebellion, to be sent to the Frontiers against the *Turks*, with whom he left the War under the Command of *Generalissimo Allexfea Simmoniwitz Schein*, and appointed an Army of 12000 other Soldiers, of which most of the Officers were Foreigners, to be quarter'd in the Suburbs of *Mosco*, to keep the City in awe, commanded by General *Gordon*, who had enter'd in the *Russian* Service in the Time of his Father, and who, by his extraordinary Behaviour and Success, had acquired both the Love of the Army, and the Esteem of the whole Nation.

The

The *Czar* having thus dispos'd the Condition of Things in his Absence, in *May* 1697, he set forward upon his Journey. The first great City he came to was *Riga*, a very strong Place, regularly fortify'd after the Modern Way, then in the Hands of the *Swedes*. The *Czar* having not seen the like before, and his Curiosity leading him farther than the Town was willing to consent to, they either being cautious of their own Security, or fearing they should not be able to answer it to their King, they refused to give him the Liberty (in his Person) when he desired to view their Fortifications, &c. pretending that they did not know what he was, or whence he came. The *Czar* thereupon became disgusted and angry at the City, for their rough and uncourteous Behaviour to him; and upon his Return from his Travels back to *Mosco*, in the Articles which were drawn up, gave it for one of his Reasons why he declared War against the *Swedes*.

Whilst the *Czar* was upon his Way from this City, advice came to him by an Express, that the Elector of *Saxony* was chosen King of *Poland*; but that the Cardinal Primate had protested against the said Election in Favour of the Prince of *Conti*, who lay with a Squadron of *French* Men of War before *Dantzick*, and threaten'd the Town which refused to declare themselves as being a free People. Upon which the *Czar* dispatch'd Orders to his Embassador then residing at the Court of *Poland*,

to

to maintain the Right of the Election; to assure King *Augustus*, that he had 60000 Men in Readiness at his Service, in order to maintain his just Pretensions to the Crown; and that he had already sent Orders to his Troops about *Smolensky* and the *Ukrain*, to advance towards the Frontiers of *Lithuania* to retain that great Dutchy in his Interest: And 'twas believed, that the Regard which the *Poles* had to so near and powerful an Assistance, did not a little influence them on this Occasion: And from hence the *French* have never since had any Good-will towards the *Czar*.

The next Place of Consideration he came to was *Koningsberg*, in the Dominions of the King of *Prussia*, (then Duke of *Brandenburg*) which City was more regardful in complying with all his Curiosity and Desires. He had the King's (or Duke's) Yatchs order'd to attend him; and being the first Place where he had so agreeable an Opportunity, he staid some time and diverted himself there, and at the *Pillau*, and in sailing upon the *Haff*, which is a smooth Inland Water, that lies between *Dantzick* and *Koningsberg*, above 30 Leagues long, but not very broad. Here at *Dantzick*, and all the Maritime Places every where as he travelled, he had very handsome Presents brought to him, under the Name of being done to his Embassadors; who had the highest Marks of Honour shewn them, but his Majesty suffer'd no Ceremony at all to be paid

paid to himself. However, he was attended privately, without any Guards or Form, by the Governors, and great Men at every City: And the most ingenious Persons every where waited on him with such Curiosities in Art and Nature, as they believed might be acceptable to him, and oblige him.

His Humour did not lead him to the Courts of Princes to observe the Politeness of Government, or the Pleasures and Splendor there, but he employ'd his Time in conversing with common Artificers, that were Masters of such Arts as were wanting in his Countrey, (his People not being then Masters of the Grounds and Rules of any Art or Science whatsoever) but was most strictly curious in making his Inspections in the Improvements of Shipping and Trade, and the Arts and Discipline of War.

His Majesty travell'd sometimes in the same Cloaths with his own People, and sometimes in that of a Gentleman; but most commonly when he came to any Sea Port he went about in a *Dutch* Skipper's Habit, that he might go among the Shipping, and be the less taken Notice of. He did not stay long at any of the Sea Ports in the *Baltick*, nor many Days at *Hamburgh*, tho' that City is as beautiful and agreeable as most in *Europe*; and the Inhabitants having a very considerable Trade to *Archangel*, did their utmost to render every thing pleasing and acceptable to him. But the *Czar*

was

was defirous, above any other Place, to be at *Holland*.

For the *Dutch* Merchants in *Mofco* had, before his Majefty's Departure from thence, by means of his Majefty's prime Favourite *Le Fort*, who was bred at *Amfterdam*, (and now travell'd with him) recommended Men of their Countrey for the Building of his Ships as aforefaid, and had obtained a Commiffion from the *Czar* for fupplying fuch Neceffaries as were wanting to be fent for from Abroad for equipping his Navy.

And upon his Majefty's taking a Refolution to travel to fee the feveral Parts of *Europe*, the *Dutch* being jealous of the Impreffions that might be made on him by thofe who are their Rivals in the *Ruffia* Trade, ufed their utmoft Endeavours, by all poffible means, to engage him in the Efteem and Liking of their Countrey and People, and to perfuade him of their being Mafters of all the moft ufeful Arts and Sciences in the World. That their Shipping (wherein their Glory, Strength and Riches confifts, and which they knew the *Czar*'s principal Defign was to be inform'd of) was the moft numerous and powerful, built after the beft Manner, and the moft fit for Service of any in the World.

As his Majefty proceeded on his Journey towards the Frontiers of the *United Provinces*, there were Deputies appointed from the States-General to receive his Embaffy, (for under that Umbrage he travell'd *incognito*)

with

with very confiderable Prefents, with the highest Marks of Honour that they ever shew'd on such Occasions; and to declare, that their High Mightinesses had given Orders to defray the Charges of the Embassy whilst it was in their Dominions. The Magistrates made their Complements, the Soldiers were drawn out, and the Cannon were discharged from the Ramparts of all the great Towns through which they pass'd. And particularly at *Amsterdam*, all the young Men of the City mounted on Horseback with very splendid Equipages; and those of the first Rank and Quality went out Volunteers to meet this Embassy, that had the Fame of so great a Prince, to be cover'd in their Retinue. The Ladies, with whom the Windows and Balconies were crowded, made up part of the Shew of the Day: And the Night concluded with a very splendid Fire-work made upon the Water, before the House that was prepared for the Embassadors.

But the *Czar* himself, after he had travell'd some Leagues in the Territories of the *United Provinces*, left the Embassy, that he might with the more Speed reach the City of *Amsterdam*, and with freedom take his Observations of whatever he thought worth his Curiosity. He was met on the way by some considerable Merchants who had been in *Mosco*, who having private Notice of his coming, and being known to his Majesty, accompanied him in Disguise to the City, with only two or three Persons with him. The Magistrates, who also had Intimation of it, deputed some of their chiefest Members to wait upon him, with a Tender of all Things that were necessary and suitable for his high Character, and had prepared for him a very magnificent House for his Residence.

But the *Czar* having taken a particular Fancy and Resolution on his own part to learn the Art of Ship-building, that himself might be a Master therein: And for that End had, before he left *Mosco*, (amongst those Maritime Men whom he already had in his Countrey) learn'd to speak somewhat of the *Dutch* Language, with relation to the Terms in Shipping, he refused all Importunities made to him to accept of any Lodging in the City, and chose to take a small House on the *East-India* Wharf, (or Ship-Yard) just by the Water side, where there were strict Orders given, that neither any Mob from Abroad, nor the People in the Yard, should gaze and disturb him; a Thing he was the most averse to imaginable. Here he lived for some Months, with two or three of his Favourites, whom he took to be Partners with him in learning the Art of Ship-building. He wrought one part of the Day with the Carpenter's broad Ax among the *Dutchmen*; and for the better Disguise, wore the same sort of Habit which they did: And at other Times diverted himself with sailing, and rowing upon the Water.

He admitted nevertheless of the private Visits of some of the most considerable Men of the City, who brought to him all the Collections of Art and Nature that *Holland* could afford. He went often, during his Stay at *Amsterdam*, sometimes in one Habit, and sometimes in another, to Burgomaster *Whitson* *, and some others; to private Entertainments that were made for him; where he would be very free and merry with a few Persons, which to this Day is his way, and is most agreeable to him.

He had in this Time seen several of our *English* built Ships, and being pleased with the Proportion and Beauty of them, after he had been some Time at the *Hague*, (where his Embassadors made their publick Entry) and had had a private Interview with King *William*, he went to *England*, where a House was first provided for him in *York-Buildings* by the Water side. He spent some few Days in the City of *London*, and had several Interviews with the King, her Royal Highness the then Princess *Anne* of *Denmark*, and many of the *English* Nobility; but was more particularly, and above all, taken with the Conversation of the then Marquiss of *Carmarthen*, who complied with him in his Humour,

---

* *A Gentleman famed for his great Riches in Shipping, for his Love of all Arts, and his sending Men Abroad at his own Charge, to make Discoveries in all the Parts of the World; and he has been also at a great Charge in fixing large Telescopes for observing the Celestial Bodies.*

and assisted him in his Pursuit after the Knowledge of Shipping, and would row and sail with him upon the Water, which was his Delight; of which Obligations and Kindness of my Lord Marquiss to him, I have many times since heard him speak with great Affection; as indeed he often does of *England* in general, and what he observed here. And I have often heard him say, that he designs to take a Turn hither again when he has Peace settled in his own Countrey: And has often declared to his Lords, when he has been a little merry, that he thinks it a much happier Life to be an Admiral in *England*, than *Czar* in *Russia*.

A House in *London* not suiting his Humour and the Intentions of his Travels, some few Days after his Arrival, Mr. *Evelyn*'s House, an agreeable Seat at *Deptford*, was prepared for him, where there was a Back-Door open'd into the King's Yard, very convenient for his intended Business of conversing with our *English* Builders; who shew'd him their Draughts, and the Method of laying down by Proportion any Ship or Vessel, of what Body soever required, with the Rules for moulding and building a Ship, according as laid down in such Draught, which extremely took with and pleased his Majesty, and which he found every where practised, as well in the Merchants as the King's Yards. Which made him repent that he had spent so much time in *Holland*, where their Method is

much

much more unartificial and inferior to the *English* way of Building. And his Majesty, who is since become a great Master in Ship-building, and takes his chief Delight in it, often says, that if he had not come to *England* he had certainly been a Bungler as long as he had lived at that Art, which is now his Delight.

Upon his coming over to *England* he resolv'd to have none but *English* built Ships made in his Countrey, and was thereupon pleased to entertain several *English* Builders and Artificers for his Navy that he intended to establish. The chief of whom was Sir *Anthony Dean*'s Son, an ingenious Gentleman, whose Father Sir *Anthony* (being sent into *France* upon some Occasion by King *Charles* the Second) was said to have learn'd the *French* the Art of building Ships, for which he was several times mobb'd when he came back, and it had like to have cost him his Life.

The *Czar* was mightily pleas'd with our Armory in the *Tower*, and with our way of coining of Money, which is the most perfect in the World. He was about three Months in *England*, in which Time the King was pleased to send Admiral *Mitchel* down with him to *Portsmouth*, to put the Fleet that lay at *Spithead* to Sea, on purpose to shew him a sham Engagement; and which had before been shewn him in *Holland*, but not so satisfactory to him as that in *England*. He took also a Tour to *Oxford* to see the University.

versity. He was once to see the Archbishop of *Canterbury* at his Palace, and went often to our Churches and Cathedrals to see the Order of our establish'd Religion; and also had the Curiosity to see the Quakers and other Meeting-houses, in the Time of their Service.

He was likewise shewn both Houses of Parliament when they were Sitting, and was prevail'd upon to go once or twice to the Play, but that was what he did not like. He spent most of his Time in what related to War and Shipping, and upon the Water. He often took the Carpenters Tools in his Hands, and often work'd himself in *Deptford Yard*, as he had done before in *Holland*. He would sometimes be at the Smith's, and sometimes at the Gun-founder's, and there was scarce any Art or mechanick Trade whatsoever, from the Watch-maker to the Coffin-maker, but he more or less inspected it, and even caused a Model of an *English* Coffin to be sent into *Russia*, as he did also of many other things. Whilst he was in *England* he us'd to Dress himself after the *English* Fashion, sometimes as a Gentleman, and sometimes as a Seaman. He went Abroad with very little Attendance, as he did in *Holland*, that he might not be taken Notice of; and if at any time he was discover'd, and he found the Mob began to gather and gaze about him, he immediately, some Way or other, went off from the House or Place where he was. His Favourite, Prince *Menzi-*

Menzicoff, and one of his Embassadors, Count *Gollovin*, with several other Persons, were with him here in *England*; and his Majesty, whilst he was here, order'd his said Embassador to Contract with some Merchants for Exporting yearly into *Russia*, a considerable Quantity of Tobacco, upon Condition of being first licens'd by the Lord Marquess of *Carmarthen*; which he granted him, in return of the obliging Conversation he had receiv'd from him: The Benefit my Lord made of this Licence, was 5 s per Hogshead, Tobacco having before been prohibited in *Russia*, by order of the Patriach, as an unclean and irreligious Thing; and to this Day a Priest will not come into any Room where Tobacco is smoak'd.

The King's Cooks and Servants were appointed to attend him, and he and his Retinue were honourably entertain'd at the King's Charge, during the time he was in *England*, and in his Passage over from *Holland* and back again. Farther, the King gave him free Leave to take such of his Subjects into his Service as he should have Occasion for; and at his Departure made him a Present of the *Royal Transport*, which was much the finest and best Yatcht then in *England*, built Frigat fashion, carrying 24 Guns, and contriv'd by my Lord Marquess of *Carmarthen*, on purpose for the King's own Use, in crossing the Sea during the War.

When the *Czar* went out of *England*, King *William* gave him Leave to take two young Mathematicians out of *Christ-Church Hospital*; and he also took one *Fergharson*, a very ingenious Gentleman, Master of the Mathematicks, into his Service, who was bred at the University at *Aberdeen*, and was recommended to his Majesty to instruct and teach his Subjects in the Knowledge and Use of the Mathematicks.

The said Mathematicians, Ship-builders and Artificers, together with several other Officers, Bombardeers, and other Persons, who were entertain'd, were sent over in the *Royal Transport*, and by other Passages to *Archangel*; and within four Days after, an Agreement was made with me, his Majesty going over to *Holland*, as mention'd in the first Part of this Account. I was order'd to attend him in a Yatcht to *Helversluice*, and from thence to *Amsterdam*, where his Majesty procur'd an Order for me, and sent a Person with me to shew me all the Camels (which are flat Vessels made to be fix'd to the bottom of Ships, and to come up like a Chest on each side) with which the *Hollanders* are obliged to lift their Ships over the *Pampuss*, a large Flat that lies in the *Souda* Sea between the City of *Amsterdam* and the *Texel*. As also a Person was sent with me to shew me all the Engines and Instruments which the *Dutch* use in making their Sluices, several Artificers being already sent forward from thence into *Russia*, for

making

making the Sluices for the then intended Communication that I was to go upon between the River *Wolga* and the *Don*, upon the Defertion of *Breckel*, as has been before mentioned.

I had but seven or eight Days time given me in *Amsterdam*; and leaving the *Czar*, who design'd his Journey from thence to *Vienna* and other Parts, I was sent directly by the Way of *Narva* to *Mosco*, to survey the Work abovesaid, in Company with Sir *Anthony Dean*'s Son the *Czar*'s chief Builder, who died soon after in *Mosco*; upon which Mr. *Cozens*, whom I have formerly mention'd, was sent for over in his Place.

The first great Town I arriv'd at in *Russia*, was the City of *Novogorod*, situate at the Head of the River *Volcoff*, which falls out of the *Elmena* Lake into the *Lodiga Sea*. It is one of the most eminent and populous Cities in *Russia*. There was at that time a very considerable Trade carried on from thence to *Narva* and *New Shans*, on the River *Neva*, (where *Petersburgh* is now built,) but this City is since made a Rendezvouz of the Armies, and Stores and Magazines for carrying on the War on that Side, with Intention to make *Petersburgh* the Capital of the *Russian* Empire.

There are 72 Monasteries belonging to the District of the City of *Novogorod*, the Chief of which is dedicated to the famous St. *Anthony*, of whom the *Russes* relate this

Story;

Story; that he (being guided by the Vision of an Angel) came from the Mouth of the River *Tiber*, on the Coast of *Italy*, round thro' the great Ocean up the *Baltick*, and by Way of the *Lodiga Sea* and River *Volcoff*, to the said City of *Novogorod* in four Days, upon a Mill-stone; and by this Miracle occasion'd the thorough Conversion of the Country to the Christian Religion, which happen'd about 600 Years since. It was at the latter end of *June* when I came to this Place; at which time I happen'd to see the Effigies of the said Saint carried about the City in a very pompous annual Procession, in Commemoration of the Day of his Arrival.

The said Monastery is built on the side of the River *Volcoff*, a little way without the City, in the very Place where he landed; and the Mill-stone on which he Arriv'd, is still to be seen plac'd up upon one edge, in the Body of the Church belonging to the said Monastery. As also the Body of St. *Anthony* is laid in the same Church in a Stone Coffin, not far from the Mill-stone: And the *Russes* affirm as an undeniable Testimony of the Truth of this Miracle, that God has preserv'd his Body from being yet perish'd, and which they ordinarily expose to the view of such Persons who humbly come to pay their Devotions to his Tomb. It is not only at this Place, but at many others, that they pretend to the like Arguments and Demonstrations for the Confirmation of the Truth of their Religion; that many others of their

Saints

Saints though they have been buried many hundred Years, yet God doth not suffer their Bodies to decay, as particularly the Body of *Sergee*, lies without perishing in the Monastery of *Troitski*, 60 Miles from *Mosco*. And amongst others, the Place most fam'd for the miraculous Preservation of those Bodies of their Saints, is in a Monastery near *Kiow*, where there is a particular Register kept of the Merits of their Saints, and the Miracles of their Lives, which are preserv'd with great Care by their Priests, and which turns to a very good Account. For this Place being held in such great Veneration, there have been several Instances of Religious, and well-believing Persons that have Estates to answer it, who leave it in their Wills to have their Bodies carried from *Mosco* to *Kiow* to be buried there.

Dr. *Areskin*, a most ingenious Gentleman, who is chief Physician to the *Czar*, and a Member of the Royal Society in *England*, with whom the *Czar* usually informs himself in the Curiosities of Nature, being in the Year 1709, with his Majesty on that side the Countrey, he went on purpose by the *Czar*'s Order, to see the foresaid Saints that are laid in the Vault in a Monastery near *Kiow*; and in Discourse I have heard him say, that the *Russes* in their Pretences to these Miracles, sufficiently out-do whatsoever is pretended by all the Papists in *Europe*.

When I first went into the Countrey, I did not much mind the aforementioned Story of
St.

St. *Anthony*. But in the Year 1710, being sent upon a Survey upon that side of the Countrey, in order to make a Communication from the *Wolga* to *Petersburgh*, going down the River *Volcoff* into the *Lodiga Sea*, I sent a *Subdiack*, or Writer, that was appointed to go with me on that Service, to the foresaid Monastery near *Novogorod*, to desire leave that I, who was commissioned by the *Czar* on a particular Service relating to the making a Communication through that Part of the Countrey by Water, with an Order to all Governors, Deputy-Governors and Officers whatsoever, to be assisting to me, might have the Favour of coming and seeing the said Miracle of St. *Anthony* and the Millstone. I was accordingly admitted into the Monastery, and there was without any Difficulty shew'd me the Body of a Person which, as I remember, they told me had ordered the said Monastery to be built; and of another Saint, of whom they unveil'd to me the Face and Hands, which were something dry and wither'd, but look'd fresh. I saw also the Millstone which they shew'd me, and believe no Cork will swim like it. But whether the Monks which shew'd me thus far, thought my Faith not strong enough, or whether it was necessary that the Sight of the Body of St *Anthony* himself, should be regarded with a little more Ceremony, or be beheld with purer Eyes than mine, I cannot tell; for their

Monks

Monks or Priests, making me wait a longer Time than I thought was necessary, and the *Arkerea* (or Chief of their Order) being very tedious, without whom they told me they could not shew me St. *Anthony*, and it being then in the Morning, and he, it seem'd, not readily disposed to come out of his Lodgings; I thought I had seen enough already, and therefore with Decency took my leave till another Time, when he should be more at leisure.

I had at that Time one Captain *Alexander Gordon* along with me as an Assistant, who was of the *Romish* Faith, and who formerly had been appointed my Interpreter at *Camishinka*, at my first coming into the Countrey. I knew him to be a little superstitious and warm sometimes in his Temper about his Religion, and jesting a little freely with him upon this Occasion, he grew angry with the Priests and Monks, for turning us away without letting us see St. *Anthony*; and making some Excuse, he went back again into the Monastery, and when he returned to me, who was waiting for him at the Water side, and knew not where he was, he told me he had been and chid the Monks, as having been guilty of a great Sin in not shewing us the Body of St. *Anthony*; for that he told them, he had meditated on a short Prayer on purpose to have offered to him, but they had frustrated his Devotion.

About

About 100 *Russ* Miles from this Place, in the same District of *Novogorod*, by the River *Tiffin*, which falls likewise into the *Lodiga* Sea, and is one of those Rivers that were in my Orders to survey, there is a Monastery dedicated to the Blessed Virgin, whom they term the Mother of God Of which Monastery the *Russes* relate this farther Miracle; *viz.* That the Church which is now standing within the Walls of the said Monastery, was first built on the opposite side of the River; and that the Place where the Monastery now stands, was then a meer Swamp or Bog; but that the Mother of God came thro' the Air in 24 Hours from *Constantinople*, and in the Night removed the said Church over the River into the said Bog or Swamp, which thereupon became firm hard Land, such as it is at present. Whether it was swampy Ground before this Miracle I cannot swear; but I am sure when I was there, I observed the Banks of the said River to be firm, gravelly, hard Ground on both sides, both above it and below it to several Miles distance. They also affirm that the Virgin *Mary* her self appeared on this Occasion to an old Man who was praying in the Church; and declared that she removed the Church for this purpose, that the People from the Town might the easier come to offer up their Prayers to her there, and which she did in Testimony that she would not neglect to hear them whenever they had Occasion.

This

This Story of the Virgin *Mary*'s coming through the Air, from whence they call her the *Tiffinskee Bougharoditza*, (or *Tiffinskee* Mother of God,) the *Russes* advance as a Confirmation or Voucher to that of St. *Anthony*'s coming through the Water, and from thence they infer that both were equally possible with the omnipotent Power of God; and 'tis as much as a Man's Life is worth to dispute the Validity of these Things with them.

There is also another Part of *Russia* in the Kingdom of *Cazan*, of which the *Russes* relate a more trifling Miracle, *viz*. An Appearance of the Virgin *Mary* to a Painter who was drawing her Picture in the Kingdom of *Cazan*; which if you go about to doubt the Truth of, they presently account you an Atheist. The short of which Story is this. The Painter had been drawing the Virgin *Mary*'s Picture with our Saviour in her Arms, and had so disposed the Picture, as to make both her Hands appear. But the next time he came to finish the Picture in the Room where he had left it, he found three Hands regularly disposed about the Child; upon which, he believing that some other Person of the Trade had come and done this in the Night to put a Trick upon him, took his Pencil, and in a kind of Passion rubb'd out the third Hand, and when he had finish'd the Picture, which was drawn at large and fit for Sale, he lock'd the Door, and put the

key

Key in his Pocket, but coming the second Morning, he found a third Hand painted again as before, upon which he cross'd himself, and was greatly surprized. But after he had a little cool'd upon it, he still imagin'd that some Rogue or other had done it; he therefore rubb'd out again the Hand, and finish'd the Picture as before, and when he went out, took more exact Care to lock and seal his Doors, and secure his Windows. But coming the third Morning, to his still greater Surprize and Amazement, he found the third Hand painted a third time; and when he was *going again to put it out*, the Virgin *Mary* her self then appeared, and called to him to forbear, telling him 'twas her Will to have her Person so drawn, and which therefore the *Russes* to this Day follow, and paint her with three Hands, and when so done, they call her the *Cazansky Boagaroditza*, or *Cazansky* Mother of God. They cross themselves and fall down before this Picture, and knock their Heads to the Ground by way of Devotion to it; and in several Churches, as particularly at the *Jerusalem* Monastery, about 40 Miles from *Mosco*, there is in the Cathedral Church a large Description in writing of this Miracle placed by the side of her Picture, so drawn as she order'd; and in many other Places this Picture is set up. Pictures of their Saints are in every House, but no carved Images, the *Russ* Religion forbidding any but painted Saints, because of the Law of *Moses*, which

which has commanded not to bow down to or worship any graven Image: But this Miracle they maintain as one of the Proofs, that their worshipping of Pictures and sacred Things is approved of by God.

They also tell you that our Saviour himself whilst he was on Earth wrought this following Miracle, *viz.* That a Painter who had secretly fix'd himself several times to take our Saviour's Picture, was still disappointed in it, and found that the Likeness which he had taken at one time, did not at all agree with what he had taken at another, which caused great Surprize and Trouble to the Painter. At length our Saviour, who had Compassion on him, and who all the time knew what he was endeavouring to go about, call'd the Painter to him, and desiring him not to be uneasy at the Disappointment he had met with, ask'd him for his Handkerchief; which when the Painter had deliver'd him, he took and laid it upon his Face, and then gave it back immediately to the Painter, and told him there was his Picture, which was painted to the Life upon the said Handkerchief; from which Original, to this Day the *Russes* pretend that they copy our Saviour in the greatest Exactness. These Stories very much promote the Benefit of the Painter's Trade, the Truth of which is very dangerous to dispute.

I would give some farther Account of the Superstition of the *Russes* in Matters of Religion,

gion, and of the great Ignorance and Stupidity of their Priests, from whence proceeds the want of Honour and Honesty among them, and among the Laity, and of the Reformation which the *Czar* has endeavour'd in in order, to encourage Learning and better Education in his Country. But I shall first take notice, that whilst the *Czar* was making his Observations in foreign Parts of whatsoever he found worthy of Regard for the Purposes he design'd, there were repeated Advices came to *Mosco*, both from those who attended him in his Travels, and those who came thither from him, that his Majesty was extremely pleased and satisfied with what he observed in his Travels, and more particularly, that he had a Liking and Esteem of every thing in *England*, and that he was sending great Numbers of Officers and People from *England*, *Holland*, and other Parts, into his Service. Upon which Advices, the Malecontents and Adherents to the Princess *Sophia*, put the most evil Construction upon all his Majesty's Designs, and insinuated on these Occasions Jealousies in the Minds of the People which were fomented and spirited up by the Priests, that all his Majesty's Proceedings tended to the subverting of their holy Religion, by bringing in such a Number of Foreigners amongst them that would certainly be his Favourites and Counsellors; who would insult and domineer over the Natives at pleasure, extirpate the ancient Establishment

of

of the *Streletzes*, and change their beloved Customs and Manners, so as never to be recovered.

The Rumour of these Jealousies having pretty well taken place in the Minds of the People, a third Conspiracy was held, wherein many of the chief of the Clergy, as well as Nobility and great Men, who had been look'd upon to be in the *Czar*'s Interest, confederated together to cut the Throats of the Strangers, and all that stood in their way, to declare the Throne vacant by the Absence of the *Czar*, and to set up his Sister in his Room, who had been condemned to a Monastery on account of the first Rebellion that happen'd at the *Czar*'s coming to the Crown.

To effect this, the General and most of the Officers of a Party of about 10000 *Streletzes*, who were then in their Winter Quarters on the Borders of *Lithuania*, 500 Miles from *Mosco*; being made secure on their side, it was resolved, the better to palliate this Rebellion, that some Pretence should be made touching their Pay, upon which they should break up from their Quarters, and march directly to *Mosco*, where they were to be joined by other Malecontents, and to put their Design in execution.

The Regency to whom the Czar had left the supream Administration of the Government in his Absence, upon Advice of these Mutineers marching without Orders, and being apprehensive of their wicked Design, who had been twice concern'd in Rebellion not long before, to try to prevail with them by fair Means, deputed several Persons of Distinction to them to stop their March, with full Power and Money to pay them not only their Pretensions of Arrears, but every Man six Months Pay before-hand (which is sometimes the Custom of the Countrey,) and Courier after Courier was sent with Orders to persuade them to return and march (the Campaign then coming on) to join the other Forces that were to form the Army against the *Turks*. But they still persisted in their Resolution, that they would come to *Mosco* to visit their Friends, whom they had not seen in several Years, and to know whether the *Czar* was living or dead, or what was become of him.

Upon this Information, a general Consternation seized the People, and many of them left their Habitations and retired into the Countrey, dreading the Consequences of this March, the Revolt of others, and the Insolencies of these Mutineers, from whom they had seen a general Ravage and Desolation not many Years before. But to prevent such Insurrection if possible, and to stop the Mischief of their coming too near the City, the Army commanded by General *Gordon*, who had been many times in Action with him, and were for the most part old Soldiers, and Foreign Officers, were order'd to march and oppose these Mutineers.

They

They came up with the Rebels about 40 Miles from *Mosco*, near the *Jerusalem* Monastery, from whence the General first sent several Officers to them, with some considerable Lords that came out Volunteers with him, to persuade and assure them of honourable Satisfaction in whatever they desired, if they would return to their Duty; but they obstinately persisted in the Resolution that they would see *Mosco*, and know the Truth (as they pretended) whether the *Czar* was dead or living, and declared, that if their Brothers, meaning the Army that came out against them, did oppose them, they were resolved to resist, though the Army that was commanded by General *Gordon* was near double their Number.

Upon the return of this resolute Answer, General *Gordon* first fired some Cannon over their Heads, to awe and summon them to surrender; but they finding the Shot did not do Execution, the Priests immediately gave out that it was a Miracle, and that the Shot could not hurt them; upon which the Rebels gave a Shout, and run upon the General's Army, and thereupon began a very sharp Engagement, which lasted near two Hours. When the Rebels finding that the Battel was in earnest, and that they had between two and three thousand Men killed on the Spot, they surrendered themselves Prisoners, very few of them making their Escape.

General *Gordon*, according to the *Roman* way of Decimation, hang'd up every tenth Man after the Battel was over, and the rest he took Prisoners to *Mosco*, where several of the Ring leaders being examin'd upon the Pine (which is the being put to severe Torture, the Nature of which will be hereafter described) they confess'd their Crimes and the chief Persons concern'd with them; that their Design was to have released the Princess *Sophia* out of Prison, and to have put the Government into her Hands, to whom it of right belong'd in the *Czar*'s Absence, she having rul'd with general Satisfaction, when the Administration of Affairs was committed to her Hands, in the time of her Brother *Feodor*'s Minority.

The *Czar*, when the News of this Rebellion came to him, was at the Court of *Vienna*, where he was nobly entertain'd by the Emperor, with whom he was then in Alliance: and his Design was from thence to have taken a turn to *Venice*, whither he had prepar'd his Journey. But upon this News he alter'd his Resolution, and set out directly for *Mosco* by way of *Poland*, where he had a short Interview with King *Augustus*; and there being a Treaty of Peace on foot at that time with the *Turks*, by the Mediation of King *William*, which was then expected to be concluded, it was believed that a War was by these two Princes agreed on to be declared with *Sweden*, as it afterwards appeared

The

The *Czar* upon this News hasted forward to *Mosco*, and arrived with such Secrecy and Expedition, that there was no publick Notice of his coming, till he was arrived at *Mosco*, which gave great Joy and Pleasure to all his faithful Subjects and Friends, and added Terror and Confusion to such as wish'd ill to his Person and Government.

The first Day he arriv'd he immediately commanded a Reward to be given to those Soldiers who fought faithfully for him, and the next Day order'd that the principal Contrivers and Encouragers of the said Rebellion should be brought before him; and after he had himself re-examin'd them, they having before been condemn'd in a full Hearing before all the Lords, they were all sentenc'd to Death, among whom were Prince *Colorin*, General *Romanodoskowski*, with several Ladies of Quality, and Friars and Priests of the first Rank. Some of them were beheaded, some broke upon the Wheel, and others buried alive And the aforesaid *Streletzes* (or Soldiers) who had actually march'd and fought against the *Czar*'s Arms, and who had ever since the *Czar*'s first coming to the Crown, upon all Occasions, been in the Plots and Intrigues of the Princess *Sophia*, and the Party that adher'd to her, and had in several Instances shew'd their Will and Readiness to Revolt; upwards of 2000 of them were executed, some their Heads taken off in the publick Market-place, others hung up upon Gallowfes erected on purpose, at the Gates of all the three Walls round the City, with their Crimes writ upon the Gallows. This Execution being perform'd in the Depth of Winter, their Bodies were immediately frozen; those that were beheaded were order'd to lie in the same Posture as their Heads were cut off in Ranks upon the Ground, with their Heads lying by them; and those which were hang'd round the Walls of the City, were left hanging the whole Winter in the same Posture to the view of the People, till the warm Weather began to come on in the Spring, and then they were taken down and buried in a Pit together, to prevent the Infection of the Air.

There were likewise other Gallowses plac'd on all the publick Roads leading to *Mosco*, at about two Miles distance, where other Numbers of these Rebels were hang'd, and a large Monument of Stone erected upon the several Roads, with the Description of their Crimes deeply engraven, and order'd to be repair'd and kept up for ever; and the very Houses wherein they had liv'd, were order'd to be raz'd to the Ground, and the Name of *Streletzes* to be no more made use of in the Army of *Russia* for ever, but was chang'd, and from that time they were call'd *Soldatee* or Soldiers Such of the said *Streletzes* that were judg'd more innocent, or not so deeply involved in Guilt with the rest, having their Lives given them, were some sent to *Siberia*, others banish'd banish'd to *Astracan, Azoph*, and all the Outparts of the Kingdom, with their Wives and Families, and others of their near Relations to suffer with them, as is the Way of most of the Eastern Countries.

Thus his Majesty, upon his Return from his Travels, by the Example of so extensive a Punishment having suppress'd the Enemies to his Government, it was the more easie for him to go on with those things, which he had resolv'd upon for the reforming his Countrey. He began first and establish'd not only his Guards, which were those Regiments that were fix'd in the Place of the aforesaid *Streletzes*, but put his whole Army upon a new Foot, and a new Discipline, which he had collected from what he had observ'd abroad; and he order'd all his Army to be regularly cloath'd, with some Distinction in the Colour and Trimming of the Cloaths, like the Custom of other Nations of *Europe*, which had not till now been done, but every one wore his Cloaths according to his own Make and Fancy. He order'd also an Account to be brought to him of such Persons of the Nobility and Gentry of considerable Estates, who were not in any Service or Employment, out of which he chose and commanded a great Part to go and serve as Volunteers in the Army, and others he order'd to attend, and appointed them Duty in several Stations; some in the Equipping his Navy, and others he order'd to go and reside at the frontier Garrisons, that if they did no Good they might be out of the way of doing any Mischief.

When he had thus dispos'd things in *Mosco*, with relation to his Army, he went down himself to *Veronize* to view those Ships and Gallies that were built there by the *Dutch* in his Absence, and to hasten the Equipment of his Fleet that was preparing for the *Black Sea*. He made those *English* that he had brought over now his chief Master Builders, and he discharg'd all the *Dutch* Builders, except what were to finish the Ships which they had begun, and those who were left under the Command of the *English*; and that there should be none but *English* fashion Ships to be built for the future; one of which being a Ship of 50 Guns, his Majesty himself, immediately, as soon as he came there, set upon the Stocks, a Draught of which he had drawn with his own Hands, and so contriv'd her by an Invention of his own, that tho' the Keel should be knock'd off, the Ship should be tight (as he propos'd) which Ship when he had advanc'd a little way, he left to be carry'd on by two young *Ruß* Gentlemen that had been abroad, and in Company learn'd to build Ships along with his Majesty; only he left Orders for them to ask sometimes Advice of the *English* Builders when there was any Occasion for it. He left also Orders at *Veronize* with Vice-Admiral *Cruys*, and Rear-Admiral *Raes*, together with the Sea-Captains, Officers and Seamen that he had taken into his

Service

Service in *Holland*, before the time he came over to *England*, and who were now arriv'd in *Veronize*, to get those Ships and Gallies that were built to be rigg'd and ready fitted to carry down to *Azoph*, whither he intended to go with them in the Spring of the Year, together with his Favourite *Le Fort*, who tho' he knew nothing of the Sea, was declar'd Admiral.

When his Majesty had thus settled the Affairs of his Navy, as he had before done his Army, he return'd back again to *Mosco*; where, besides what he had done at his first coming over, he made a new Choice of Lords to be of his Council, and began to regulate Affairs in his Government, both in the Church, and in the State.

The Assessment of the Duties and Taxes to be laid upon the People, the collecting of the *Czar*'s Revenue, and the sole Decision of all Causes, (excepting those within the Ecclesiastical Jurisdiction) had formerly been wholly committed to such of the chief Lords who were Favourites, and commonly were of the greatest Families in *Russia*; who acted as sovereign Princes under the *Czar*, in the several Provinces into which the Empire was divided; who had the Liberty to make use of the *Czar*'s Name for their Authority in the issuing forth their Orders, and might be said to have the sole Power of Mens Lives and Fortunes in their Hands. And for the Examination of Causes, and for the Execution of their Orders, each

each of these Lords, or Princes, held apart an Office or Court of Justice in *Mosco*, where these great Lords usually resided, and to whom there was an Appeal from the District of all the lesser Towns and Cities in each respective Province. A Bench of *Diacks* (or Chancellors) sate as Judges in each of these principal Offices or Courts in *Mosco*, whose Business it was to hear and determine Matters; and to sign Orders, as well relating to the Treasury, and the Military, as to the Civil Matters; and to make Report from Time to Time of their Proceeding to their respective Lords, under whose Command they acted, and the said Lords seldom coming themselves in Person to hear any Causes, the *Diacks* represented Matters to them in such Forms and Colours, as they thought proper: And beyond which, in case of any Grievance, there was at that Time no higher Court of Appeal.

Each of these Lords had the sole Power also lodged in them, to appoint and send Governors to the several Towns and Cities, to which each Province was again subdivided into lesser Districts; and each of which Governors in their respective Stations had a *Diack*, or Petty-Chancellor, and an Office or Court of Justice erected under them in each City, called a *Precause*, (or Place for Command, as the Word signifies) where they sate both as Commissaries, to transact Business relating to the *Czar's* Revenue; and as Judges, with an absolute Power to determine all Causes, without

out any Jury affix'd, or Council to plead for unfortunate Men. Only in Cases of Life and Death they were obliged to make Representation by Letter to the Lord of the Province in *Mosco*, before any Man was executed; and which they never failed so to represent, as to make the Punishment fall as they would have it.

These Governors had their Commissions granted them, and usually held their Places at most but for three Years, if they did not practise such open Roguery and Oppression as to be turn'd out sooner. They never had any Salary appointed them; but on the contrary, it was the Custom to give the Lord of the Province where they were appointed, the Sum of 3 or 4000 Rubles upon their being advanced to their Governments, more or less, according to the Ability of the Place; besides what they privately gave in Presents to the *Diacks* or Chancellors belonging to the head Office, or *Precause*, in *Mosco*, from which they were sent; and yet these *Weywods*, or Governors, were commonly known to make themselves rich within the Term of three Years abovemention'd; by which (to say no more) it may easily be conjectured what Equity they practised towards the *Czar*, and towards the People committed to their Power. I shall not dwell upon many Particulars, but only observe to the Reader, that throughout all the Country of *Russia*, amongst the common People, in case of Injuries received, or Disputes

putes arising between Man and Man, the Bribery of the Judge is the first Step to go upon; Money is known to be taken on both Sides; and generally he who bids highest carries the Cause, whilst the Sufferer has no Remedy, but to be content. Which occasions a usual Saying among the People, when they complain of a Grievance done them, *That God is high, and the* Czar *is far off*.

But the Profits which these Governors usually received by Bribery, and which they are not yet deprived of, were not all the Advantages they made by their Commissions; there was another considerable Article which they found equally beneficial to them. These Governors, in their respective Districts throughout all the *Czar*'s Dominions, had the Power of the Assessment of the Taxes, and of appointing *Challavolnicks* (or Collectors) under them to receive the *Czar*'s Revenues, and to return such Sums as they collected (which they used to send under a Guard of Soldiers) into the grand *Precause*, or proper Office of each *Boyar*, residing in *Mosco*, where the Account of the Collections made in each Province was made out, (such as was thought fit) with the Account also of what was expended on the several pretended Occasions, for the Service of each respective Province; and the rest sent into the Office of the great Treasury in *Mosco*, as aforesaid.

Now the *Czar* believing that a more faithful Return might be made of his Revenue,
and

and to prevent the Oppression of these Governors in the unequal Assessment of the Taxes, his Majesty was pleased to call a grand Council of his Lords, and proposed to them, that there should be one general Office erected in *Mosco*, for the better Collection and Improvement of his Revenue; that the said Office should be called the Rate-House, (according to the *Dutch* Name and Model) and that a certain Number of reputable Men should be chosen out of the Merchants, who should be entitled *Burgomasters*, and that were to sit daily, five or more of them, to appoint Clerks and Officers in the first place to take an Account, and to collect the Revenue payable into their own Office, within the District of the City of *Mosco*; and from whence they were to impower and commission such other Persons as they should appoint, by the Name of *Burgomasters* also, in all the lesser Towns and Cities of his Majesty's Dominions, to collect and receive all Customs, with relation to publick Trade, as well as petty Toll, in the Market Places, and the Profit or Excise accruing to his Majesty from the Sale of Beer, Brandy and Mead, which in *Russia* is not permitted to be brewed or made, but by particular Licence, and to be sold for the immediate Profit of the *Czar*, at certain Rates that are set, at so much *per* Gallon, which is one of the principal Branches of the *Czar*'s Revenue.

The common People, or Peasants, were at that Time not permitted to brew any Beer, or to distil Brandy for their own Use, but only a certain Quantity, when they had Leave given them, against the Time of any great Holyday, (when the *Russes* are allowed by the Church to be merry) and were obliged to buy the rest that they had occasion for at the *Cobacks*, or publick Places of Sale. This was the State of this Branch of the *Czar*'s Revenue at that Time. But about 9 or 10 Years since a farther Restriction has been made, that no Person whatsoever, from the lowest to the highest Rank, shall be permitted at any time to brew any Beer for his own House and Family, without paying so much for a Licence to every Brewing; and that no Brandy at all shall be distilled in the Countrey, or Still bought or kept in the House of any Person, but who is commission'd to the distilling of Brandy for the Benefit of the *Czar*: And all the Stills in the Countrey (of which there were great Plenty in every Village) were ordered to be seized at the same Time when this last Order was made.

The Moneys, as abovesaid, to be collected through the several Districts of the *Czar*'s Dominions, his Majesty proposed to be return'd to the general Rate-House in *Mosco*, where the Accounts were to be adjusted, and from thence to be transmitted to the great Treasury, or otherwise, whither the *Czar*'s Orders, and the Emergencies of the State,
should

should require: And only the levying of the Land-Tax, (or Tax upon Houses) and Poll-Tax, to be levied by the Direction of the Governors, as before.

But this useful Proposition, when stated by the *Czar* to his Lords in a grand Council that was held for it, occasioned very great Strugglings amongst the Nobility, to have so considerable a Branch of their Power lopp'd off from them. They remonstrated to his Majesty, that this Honour and Trust of levying his Majesty's Revenue, had always been reposed in the Care of the Nobility, and that they hoped they had always discharged the same with Fidelity; and implored his Majesty's Favour and Justice, so as that his Majesty would not do them so much publick Dishonour and Affront, as to take away this Trust from them, and to lodge it in the Hands of Boors and Slaves that were not worthy to be named in Competition with them. But finding that these Pleadings did not prevail, they proposed several other Schemes and Methods to have given the *Czar* Satisfaction in this Point, or at least, that some of the Lords or Gentlemen of the first Families, might have the Honour to be commissioned in that general Office that was to be erected in *Mosco*; but finding all their Struggling to be in vain, and that the *Czar* at last began to grow so angry with them, that they feared some Heads would fly for their Shew of Disobedience, they were forced

ced to comply; and the same was accordingly put in Execution, and which continued for some Years with good Advantage to the *Czar*'s Revenue, till some wretched Politicians, who were the *Czar*'s Favourites, proposed other Methods to raise and force greater Sums into the *Czar*'s Treasury; whereby, though they succeeded two or three Years, they have at length so ruined Trade, and brought so general an Oppression upon the Subject thereby, that in several particular Articles, which by the good Management of the said Burgomasters, brought in before 100 or 200000 Rubles *per Annum*, brings in now not above half the Sum: But of this, more hereafter, when I come to speak of Trade.

The *Czar* also, soon after his Return from his Travels, gave Orders to the *Precause*, or Office belonging to the Monasteries, that for the Increase of his Revenue, to ease in some measure the trading Part of his People, a Tax should be levied upon the Monasteries through all *Russia*, they having a great Part of the best Lands and Villages belonging to them. As also soon after, his Majesty made an Order, that no Person but what exceeded the Age of 50, should be admitted into their Monasteries: For the *Czar* observed, that the shutting up of so many young People as they had in their Monasteries, made them useless, and prevented by so much the Increase of his People, which were wanting in his Wars. And besides this, the *Czar* had another political End in it, for he found that, by reducing their Numbers, he might take Part of their Revenue to himself, for a less Number of Villages would then serve to maintain them.

It had been the manner of the *Russes*, like the Patriarchs of old, to wear long Beards hanging down upon their Bosoms, which they comb'd out with Pride, and kept smooth and fine, without one Hair to be diminished; they wore even the Upper-Lip of that length, that if they drank at any time, their Beard dipp'd into the Cup, so that they were obliged to wipe it when they had done, altho' they wore the Hair of their Head cut short at the same time; it being the Custom only for the Popes or Priests, to wear the Hair of their Heads hanging down upon their Backs for Distinction sake. The *Czar* therefore to reform this foolish Custom, and to make them look like other *Europeans*, ordered a Tax to be laid, on all Gentlemen, Merchants, and others of his Subjects (excepting the Priests and common Peasants, or Slaves) that they should each of them pay 100 Rubles *per Annum*, for the wearing of their Beards, and that even the common People should pay a Copeck at the Entrance of the Gates of any of the Towns or Cities of *Russia*, where a Person should be deputed at the Gate to receive it as often as they had Occasion to pass. This was look'd upon to be little less than a Sin in the *Czar*, a Breach of their Religion, and held to be a great Grievance for some Time, as more particularly by being brought in by the Strangers. But the Women liking their Husbands and Sweet-hearts the better, they are now for the most part pretty well reconciled to this Practice.

It is most certain, that the *Russes* had a kind of religious Respect and Veneration for their Beards; and so much the more, because they differed herein from Strangers, which was back'd by the Humours of the Priests, alledging that the holy Men of old had worn their Beards acccording to the Model of the Picture of their Saints, and which nothing but the absolute Authority of the *Czar*, and the Terror of having them (in a merry Humour) pull'd out by the Roots, or sometimes taken so rough off, that some of the Skin went with them, could ever have prevailed with the *Russes* to have parted with their Beards. On this Occasion there were Letters drop'd about the Streets, sealed and directed to his *Czarish* Majesty, which charged him with Tyranny and Heathenism, for forcing them to part with their Beards.

About this Time the *Czar* came down to *Veronize*, where I was then on Service, and a great many of my Men that had worn their Beards all their Lives, were now obliged to part with them, amongst which, one of the first that I met with just coming from the Hands of the Barber, was an old *Russ* Carpenter

penter that had been with me at *Camishinka*, who was a very good Workman with his Hatchet, and whom I always had a Friendship for. I jested a little with him on this Occasion, telling him that he was become a young Man, and asked him what he had done with his Beard? Upon which he put his Hand in his Bosom and pull'd it out, and shew'd it to me; farther telling me, that when he came home, he would lay it up to have it put in his Coffin and buried along with him, that he might be able to give an Account of it to St. *Nicholas*, when he came to the other World; and that all his Brothers (meaning his Fellow-workmen who had been shaved that Day) had taken the same Care.

As to their Cloaths, the general Habit which the *Russes* used to wear, was a long Vestment hanging down to the middle of the Small of their Legs, and was gathered and laid in Pleats upon their Hips, little differing from the Habit of Womens Petticoats.

The *Czar* therefore resolving to have this Habit changed, first gave Orders, that all his *Boyars* and People whatsoever, that came near his Court, and that were in his Pay, should, upon Penalty of falling under his Displeasure, according to their several Abilities, equip themselves with handsome Cloaths made after the *English* Fashion, and to appear with Gold and Silver Trimming, those that could afford it. And next he commanded, that a Pattern of Cloaths of the *English* Fashion should
be

be hung up at all the Gates of the City of *Mosco*, and that Publication should be made, that all Persons (excepting the common Peasants who brought Goods and Provisions into the City) should make their Cloaths according to the said Patterns; and that whosoever should disobey the said Orders, and should be found passing any of the Gates of the City in their long Habits, should either pay 2 *Grevens* (which is 20 Pence) or be obliged to kneel down at the Gates of the City, and to have their Coats cut off just even with the Ground, so much as it was longer than to touch the Ground when they kneeled down, of which there were many hundreds of Coats that were cut accordingly; and being done with a good Humour, it occasioned Mirth among the People, and soon broke the Custom of their wearing long Coats, especially in Places near *Mosco*, and those other Towns wherever the *Czar* came.

The Women also, but more particularly the Ladies about Court, were ordered to reform the Fashion of their Cloaths too, according to the *English* Manner, and that which so much the more and sooner reconciled them to it, was this: It had been always the Custom of *Russia*, at all Entertainments, for the Women not to be admitted into the Sight or Conversation with Men; the very Houses of all Men of any Quality or Fashion, were built with an Entrance for the Women a-part, and they used to be kept up separate in an

Apartment

Apartment by themselves; only it was sometimes the Custom for the Master of the House, upon the Arrival of any Guest whom he had a Mind to Honour, to bring out his Wife the Back-way from her Apartment, attended with the Company of her Maids, to be saluted, and to present a Dram of Brandy round to the whole Company; which being done, they used to retire back to their own Apartment, and were to be seen no more. But the *Czar* being not only willing to introduce the *English* Habits, but to make them more particularly pleasing to the *Russ* Ladies, made an Order, that from thenceforward, at all Weddings, and at other publick Entertainments, the Women as well as the Men, should be invited, but in an *English* fashioned Dress; and that they should be entertained in the same Room with the Men, like as he had seen in foreign Countries; and that the Evenings should be concluded with Musick and Dancing, at which he himself often used to be present with most of the Noblility and Ladies about Court. And there was no Wedding of any Distinction, especially amongst the Foreigners, but the *Czar* had notice of it, and he himself would honour it with his Presence, and very often gave a Present to the Bride, suitable to the extraordinary Expence that such Entertainments cost them, especially when married to the Officers that were newly come into the Countrey. At these Entertainments, the *Russ* Ladies soon reconciled

reconciled themselves to the *English* Dress, which they found rendred them more agreeable.

There was another thing also which the Women very well liked in these Regulations of the *Czar*. It had been the Custom of *Russia*, in case of Marriages, that the Match used always to be made up between the Parents on each side, without any previous Meeting, Consent or Liking of one another, tho' they marry very young in that Countrey, sometimes when neither the Bride nor the Bridegroom are thirteen Years of Age, and therefore supposed not to be fit Judges for themselves. The Bridegroom on this Occasion was not to see nor to speak to the Bride but once before the Day that the Nuptials was to be performed; at which Meeting, the Friends on both sides were to come together at the Bride's Father's House, and then the Bride was to be brought out between her Maids into the Room where the Bridegroom was; and after a short Complement being made, she was to present the Bridegroom with a Dram of Brandy, or other Liquor, in Token of her Consent and Good liking of his Person. And afterwards all Care was to be taken that she was not to see the Bridegroom again until the Day of Marriage; and then she was to be carried with a Veil all over her Face, which was not to be uncover'd till she came into the Church. And thus this blind Bargain was made.

But

But the *Czar* taking into his Confideration this unacceptable way of joining young People together without their own Approbation, which might in a very great meafure be reckon'd to be the Occafion of that Difcord and little Love which is fhewn to one another afterwards, it being a thing common in *Ruffia* to beat their Wives in a moft barbarous manner, very often fo inhumanly that they die with the Blows; and yet they do not fuffer for the Murther, being a thing interpreted by the Law to be done by way of Correction, and therefore not culpable. The Wives on the other hand being thus many times made defperate, murther their Husbands in Revenge for the ill Ufage they receive; on which Occafion there is a Law made, that when they murther their Husbands, they are fet alive in the Ground, ftanding upright, with the Earth fill'd about them, and only their Heads left juft above the Earth, and a Watch fet over them, that they fhall not be relieved till they are ftarved to Death; which is a common Sight in that Countrey, and I have known them live fometimes feven or eight Days in this Pofture. Thefe fad Profpects made the *Czar* in much Pity to his People, take away the occafion of thefe Cruelties as much as poffible; and the forced Marriages being fuppofed to be one Caufe thereof, made an Order that no young Couple fhould be marry'd together, without their own free Liking and Confent; and that all

Per-

reconciled themselves to the *English* Dress, which they found rendred them more agreeable.

There was another thing also which the Women very well liked in these Regulations of the *Czar*. It had been the Custom of *Russia*, in case of Marriages, that the Match used always to be made up between the Parents on each side, without any previous Meeting, Consent or Liking of one another, tho' they marry very young in that Countrey, sometimes when neither the Bride nor the Bridegroom are thirteen Years of Age, and therefore supposed not to be fit Judges for themselves. The Bridegroom on this Occasion was not to see nor to speak to the Bride but once before the Day that the Nuptials was to be performed; at which Meeting, the Friends on both sides were to come together at the Bride's Father's House, and then the Bride was to be brought out between her Maids into the Room where the Bridegroom was; and after a short Complement being made, she was to present the Bridegroom with a Dram of Brandy, or other Liquor, in Token of her Consent and Good liking of his Person. And afterwards all Care was to be taken that she was not to see the Bridegroom again until the Day of Marriage; and then she was to be carried with a Veil all over her Face, which was not to be uncover'd till she came into the Church. And thus this blind Bargain was made.

But

But the *Czar* taking into his Confideration this unacceptable way of joining young People together without their own Approbation, which might in a very great meafure be reckon'd to be the Occafion of that Difcord and little Love which is fhewn to one another afterwards, it being a thing common in *Ruffia* to beat their Wives in a moft barbarous manner, very often fo inhumanly that they die with the Blows; and yet they do not fuffer for the Murther, being a thing interpreted by the Law to be done by way of Correction, and therefore not culpable. The Wives on the other hand being thus many times made defperate, murther their Husbands in Revenge for the ill Ufage they receive; on which Occafion there is a Law made, that when they murther their Husbands, they are fet alive in the Ground, ftanding upright, with the Earth fill'd about them, and only their Heads left juft above the Earth, and a Watch fet over them, that they fhall not be relieved till they are ftarved to Death; which is a common Sight in that Countrey, and I have known them live fometimes feven or eight Days in this Pofture. Thefe fad Profpects made the *Czar* in much Pity to his People, take away the occafion of thefe Cruelties as much as poffible; and the forced Marriages being fuppofed to be one Caufe thereof, made an Order that no young Couple fhould be marry'd together, without their own free Liking and Confent; and that all
Per-

Persons should be admitted to visit and see each other at least six Weeks before they were married together. This new Order is so well approved of, and so very pleasing to the young People, that they begin to think much better of Foreigners, and to have a better liking of such other new Customs as the *Czar* has introduced, than they ever did before, especially amongst the more knowing and better sort of People.

It had been a very pompous Custom among all the great *Boyars*, to retain in their Service, as a piece of State and Grandeur, a great Number of useless Servants or Attendants, which when they went any where abroad in the Streets of *Mosco*, some went before them bare-headed, and others follow'd after in a long Train, in all sorts of Dresses and Colours; and when the *Boyars* or Lords went either on Horseback, or in a Coach or Sled in *Mosco*, it was a piece of Grandeur to ride softly, though in the coldest Weather, that these People might keep Pace with them on Foot; and the great *Boyars* Ladies also used to have the like numerous Attendance.

But the *Czar*, who always rides swift, had set them another Pattern, for he went only with a few Servants on Horseback, cloath'd in a handsome uniform Livery; his Courtiers did the same; and commanded the Example to be follow'd among all the *Boyars* and Persons of Distinction; and that the same might be be the more effectual, the *Czar*, soon after he came from his Travels, order'd a List to be taken of all the loose Attendants that hung about these *Boyars* Houses, and order'd them to be sent into the Army. This went very much against the Grain, and great Interest and Intercession was made, and Sums of Money given for many of them to be excus'd, especially such of these Attendants as were really Gentlemen, and waited on these Lords only in expectation of Preferment; but however, the *Czar*'s Orders were to be obey'd, and there was a Draught made of several thousands of the unnecessary or supernumerary Attendants, and sent to serve in the Army.

Whilst the *Czar* was beginning these Regulations, within eight Months after his return Home from his Travels, a Truce by his Ministers at the Treaty of *Carlowitz* was separately concluded with the *Turks* for two Years, and it immediately follow'd that the *Poles*, the Emperor and the *Venetians* agreed on Preliminaries for Conditions of a perpetual Peace. Upon which the *Czar* found himself oblig'd to write to King *William*, who was accepted as Mediator at the said Treaty, to procure a farther Prolongation of the said Truce for his *Czarish* Majesty; accordingly the King of *England* was pleased to send Directions to my Lord *Pagett*, his then Embassador at the *Port*, to take the same Care of the *Czar* of *Muscovy*, as for the

the rest of the Princes of *Christendom*; and the *Czar*'s Truce was by the said Mediation prolong'd to the term of 25 Years, which was to the Satisfaction of his *Czarish* Majesty; and upon the Ratification whereof, in the Year 1700 a Peace was proclaim'd with the *Turks* upon one Day, and the very next Day after a War was declared by the *Czar* against the *Swedes*, and the strictest Orders were given to prosecute the same with all Expedition.

The *Czar* was at first very unfortunate in this new War, having the first Campaign at one Blow lost above half his Army, and his whole Artillery, in the memorable Battel of *Narva*. The various Transactions and Chances of the War, and the Successes which the *Czar* has since had, (which may in a great measure be ascribed to the rash Conduct of the young King of *Sweden*, and to his Contempt of the *Russ* Forces, whilst the *Czar* every Day gradually strengthned his Army, by retaining more Foreigners into his Service, and his own People growing every Day better Soldiers,) being a thing well enough known to all the World, I shall not go about to relate; only shall observe, that after the Loss of the said Battel, the *Czar* spent the greatest part of his Time in the effectually giving his Order for the raising of his Recruits, and in the placing his Officers, the seeing his Regiments exercised, and providing all things whatsoever that were necessary ry for his Army, the Care of which he would not trust to any of his Lords, but saw it all done himself, even to the minutest Particular.

As for his Artillery, for want of Metal, he order'd the Bells of several Churches to be pull'd down, and to be cast into Cannon, to supply the Place of those he lost, whereby he soon became able again to make a strong Head, and to act offensively against his Enemy. And though afterwards, during the course of the War, he spent most of his Time with his Army, yet all the while he neither neglected the Preparation of his Fleet at *Veronize* (whither during the first of the War he went every Winter) nor the carrying on his Resolution of reforming his People and Government.

I shall next speak of the Church or Religion of the *Russes*. It had been the Custom in the time of his Majesty's Predecessors, for the *Czars* of *Mosco* once every Year on *Palm Sunday*, to pass in solemn Procession through the Streets of *Mosco*, and to lead the Patriarch's Horse, the manner of which Procession was thus.

First there was a Horse covered with white Linen down to the Ground, his Ears being made long with the same Cloth, like to Asses Ears; upon this Horse the Patriarch sat on one side, like a Woman; in his Lap lay a fair Book with a golden Crucifix upon the Cover, which he held fast with his Left Hand, and in his Right Hand was a Cross of Gold, wherewith he bless'd the People as he rode through the Streets; a Nobleman (or *Boyar*) led the Horse by the Head for Security, and the *Czar* himself going on Foot, held the Horse by the Reins of the Bridle with one Hand, and carry'd a Branch of Palm-Tree in the other; then follow'd the Nobility and Gentry, with about 500 of the Priests in their respective Habits, and a great Crowd of many thousands of the common People. In this Order they went to Church (all the Bells in the Streets through which they pass'd clattering at the same time, not like our ringing) and from thence the *Czar* with some of his *Boyars*, and the Metropolitans and other Bishops used to go and dine at the Patriarch's House.

The *Russes* relate that their Patriarch deriv'd his Authority and Jurisdiction from the Patriarch of the *Greek* Church, who formerly resided at *Constantinople*, and afterwards at the Isle of *Scio*, to whom they had long paid their spiritual Subjection, and us'd to send Presents every Year; and being at length press'd and driven from thence by the *Turks*. *Hieronymo*, the *Greek* Patriarch, did in the Year 1588, being invited and encourag'd by the *Czar*, come to *Mosco*, and there resign his Patriarchal See to the Metropolitan of *Mosco*, as supreme Bishop and Pastor, or Head of the *Greek* Church However true this is I know not, but this may be said of the Patriarch

triarch of *Mosco*, that he was in very high Esteem with the People, and indeed might be said to bear a kind of Share in the Sovereignty of the Empire, having not only been supreme Judge of Ecclesiastical Causes, but had a Power also to reform whatever he thought prejudicial to good Manners, by his own Authority, and to pass Sentence on those he adjudg'd to Death, without acquainting the Court of it; and which had been the Orders of the former *Czars* of *Muscovy*, to be put in Execution without the least Contest or Hesitation.

But upon the Death of the late Patriarch, who was a very old Man, and who happen'd to dye soon after the *Czar* return'd from his Travels, the *Czar* refus'd to have any other Patriarch elected, and took upon himself to be the sole Head and Governor of his Church; only after the Death of the said Patriarch he appointed the present Metropolitan of *Razan*, whom he found to be the most learned and ablest among his Clergy, who was a *Pole* by Birth, and had his Education there, to take upon him the Administration of the Ecclesiastical Affairs, but so as that he should from time to time, in all Matters of Moment make a Representation of them to his *Czarish* Majesty, and receive his particular Directions and Orders therein.

This surprizing Turn in Ecclesiastical Affairs created a very great Uneasiness amongst the chief of the Clergy, and it coming

ming to his Majesty's Ear, that there was a Bishop that had talk'd a little too freely against this new Authority which the *Czar* had assum'd, his Majesty order'd him to be degraded; but none of the other Bishops readily complying to execute this Order of Degradation, but on the contrary representing to the *Czar*, that it was a thing never known that a Person of that high Dignity in the Church should be degraded: More especially they alledg'd, that they being all Bishops, and but of an equal Rank, it was not in their Power to do it, and therefore pray'd the *Czar* that he would be pleas'd to give them leave to proceed to the Election of a new Patriarch, and that then they would immediately go upon the Degradation of the Person accus'd: But the *Czar* resenting this their Evasion and Refusal, created a new Bishop on purpose, and order'd him to do it, and accordingly the Mitre was taken from him the by Hands of the said new Bishop, which as I remember was the present Metropolitan (or Archbishop) of *Razan*.

Upon this notable Resolution of the *Czar* very bold Writings were dropp'd in the City of *Mosco*, which is the way of *Russia* (for no Man ever dares to print or disperse any Libels there) whereupon there was a very large Reward publish'd to be given to any Person that should discover the Author, or any other Person concern'd therein, but no Discovery was ever made that I have heard of.

It

It was a very rare thing in *Russia* before this present *Czar*'s time to have found any Man, even among the highest and most learned of the Clergy, to have understood any Language but their own; and as they were themselves void of Learning, so they were wary and cautious to keep out all Means that might bring it in, lest their Ignorance should be discovered. To which End they insinuated to former Emperors, that the Introduction of foreign Languages might be a Means of introducing foreign Customs and Innovations, which might in time prove not only dangerous to the Church, but to the State too; for which Reason the learning of foreign Languages and Books were always formerly discourag'd; even as they are to this Day in the *Turkish* Empire, where neither Books of Learning nor Printing are suffer'd, or very little encourag'd.

There came once a Press and Letters out of *Poland* to *Mosco*, where a Printing-House was set up with the Approbation of one of the former *Czars*; but not long after the House was fir'd in the Night-time, and the Press and Letters were burnt, as was thought by the Procurement of the Priests; they looking upon all other Books, except the History of their own Countrey, and the Exploits and Victories of their *Czars*, and the Lives and Miracles of their Saints, to be as dangerous as Witchcraft. There is a Story affirm'd of an Envoy, that about 100 Years since was

P travelling

travelling from *Persia* through *Russia* in his Way to *Denmark*, and happening to be at *Mosco* at the time of an Eclipse of the Sun, and his Secretary, who was a Mathematician, having calculated how it would appear in that City, found it would be within a Digit or two of being total; and accordingly there was a Report spread through all the City, of the Day and Hour that it was to happen. Upon which at first it had no Credit, but occasion'd great Discourse how any Man could pretend to such Knowledge, or dare to prognosticate any such thing, which none but God could know. The Secretary observed, that after this Report had been spread, he had several times been gazed at by Crouds of People as he pass'd the Streets, which he took as a Mark of their Curiosity, that had no evil Meaning in it: But when the Day came, and the Sun happen'd to be fully as much darken'd as he had given out, the Mob the same Evening gather'd about the House, and demanded the Secretary that they might burn or tear him to pieces for a Sorcerer, because he had occasion'd the said Eclipse; but he was rescued by the Guards that Night, and the next Day privately convey'd out of the Countrey to save him from the Rage of the People, who, it is said, would undoubtedly have otherwise destroy'd him.

This Ignorance was not so much to be wonder'd at, when it is consider'd that they neither suffer'd their Sons to travel, nor was
there

there ever any University in the Countrey, or considerable School of any Learning, till this *Czar*'s Time.

I have already mention'd the ingenious Mr. *Fergharson*, and the other Persons whom the *Czar* entertain'd when he was in *England*, for teaching the Mathematicks in his Countrey. Soon after the *Czar* came over, he caused a large School to be erected for that Purpose, in which a great Number of Boys have been taught Arithmetick * at the *Czar*'s proper Charge, he allowing, besides their Free-schooling, Subsistence Money to such of them as will voluntarily come and learn. And out of them have been chose some of the most Ingenious to learn the Mathematicks; and near one hundred of these, who have been taught Navigation, have been sent abroad to *England*, to *Holland*, and to *Italy*, to qualify themselves to make Officers for the Service of his Majesty's Fleet. The *Czar* also employs the said *Fergharson* to teach Astronomy, and parti-

---

* *There never had been any School before to teach Arithmetick, nor did they know the Use of Figures, (I believe not 20 Men in the whole Countrey;) but they made use of a kind of Beads, an Invention of their own, which they set upon Wires in a Frame, like that which our Women in England use to set their Smoothing-Iron on, which they placed as Units, Tens, Hundreds, Thousands, and Tens of Thousands, by tossing of which Beads to and again, they could multiply and divide any Sum, after a very tedious way, and liable to gross Mistakes. Which Method they yet use in all the publick Offices of the Czar, excepting some very few Persons, who now reckon by Figures, and are remarkable amongst their Brethren for it as very ingenious Men.*

culaily

cularly has order'd him to calculate all the Eclipses how they will appear, that happen to be visible in his Countrey, which he has always done with very great Satisfaction to the *Czar*. His Majesty has order'd very good Telescopes to be brought into his Countrey, as well as all other useful Instruments and Books, for which the said *Fergharson* makes his Demand. His Majesty has always his Lords about him, and is himself very curious in observing the Eclipses that happen, and in describing and discoursing of the natural Cause of them to his Lords and People about him, and of the Motions of those other Heavenly Bodies within the System of the Sun, according as the great Sir *Isaac Newton* has indisputably demonstrated to the modern World. And wherever his Majesty is, or intends to be, whether in *Poland*, at *Petersburgh*, at *Veronize*, or at *Azoph*, he always appoints an Order to be writ to the said *Fergharson*, to send him a Draught and Account how the Eclipses, particularly those of the Sun, will happen in such Place where he is, or intends to be at the Time.

Since I am now speaking of the said *Fergharson*, I cannot forbear here to mention the hard Usage he, who is my Fellow-Sufferer, hath met with in the *Czar*'s Service, by his being long and unjustly kept out of his Pay, as we have often lamented our hard Fortunes together. The Case of the said *Fergharson*, in two Words, is this: There was an Agreement

ment made with him when he was entertain'd in *England*, that he should have his Charges defray'd to him to *Mosco*, and that he should have a handsome Allowance given him for his Subsistence when he came there, until he had learn'd the Language of the Countrey, for which he should have a *Latin* Interpreter appointed him, and until there was a fit School prepared: And that then, as often as ever he should teach and learn any Scholar, in particular the Art of Navigation, so as to be discharged from his School, and sent abroad beyond Sea further to learn the practical part of Navigation, the said *Fergharson* should have the Reward of a 100 Rubles in ready Money given to him for every such Scholar. But though he has, according to his said Contract, made perfect and discharged before I came out of the Countrey above 70 Scholars, yet he had not then, nor has not to this Day, (as I am told by the Persons who came latest from *Mosco*) received a Penny of the said Money for the Scholars he has taught and discharged from his School; but has been put off with fair Promises from Time to Time, notwithstanding all his Petitions and Solicitations, till the Death of Count *Gollovin*, (with whom his said Contract was verbally made;) and since his Death, upon renewing his Petition, he has been referr'd to my old Friend the present Admiral *Apraxin*, who pretends to know nothing of this Contract; but has lately, the same Year that I came out of the

P 3 Coun-

Countrey, given him some Addition to his Allowance of Subsistence Money. But yet this unfortunate but ingenious Gentleman lives in hopes, that though during the present War, whereby the Countrey is very much oppress'd, he cannot obtain his Money, yet that one time or other the *Czar*, in Justice to his Merit, may be prevailed upon to pay him the Money that is due to him, and to grant him Leave to return to his native Countrey.

As to the two Mathematicians which were taken from *Christ-Church* Hospital to assist Mr. *Fergharson*, one of them (about seven Years since) was attack'd by a Company of Rogues as he rode out from the School, and murder'd in the Streets about nine a Clock at Night; Mr. *Fergharson* himself also has since very narrowly escaped the same Fate: And Mr. *Guin*, the other Assistant that is left, who is a well-behaviour'd and ingenious Man, has only half the Allowance given him *per Annum*, that is allow'd to Mr. *Fergharson* for his bare Subsistence Money, though there is no question but he might have made much better Advantage of his Time, had he had the good Fortune to have continued in *England*. Begging Pardon for this Digression, I shall now speak again to the Religion and Principles of the *Russes*.

The Ministers of their Churches (which they call Popes and Proto-Popes, or Priests and Arch-Priests) never preach to the People, for that is a thing they have no Skill in;
only

only there are now some few of the chief Men, which sometimes preach before the *Czar*, and on great Holidays in Cathedral Churches; but the Height of the Learning which the common Clergy can be said to be Masters of, or indeed, that is required of them to be qualified with when they are admitted into Holy Orders by the Bishop, is this: That they can sing and read over distinctly the Service of the Church; that they stand in no evil Reputation with their Neighbours; have a good clear Voice, and can say over *Hospidi Pomilio*, (that is, *Lord have Mercy upon us*) as fast as ever they can utter it, 12 or 15 times in a Breath, which is their manner in their Churches, or elsewhere, when they are at Prayers. Nor do they much regard from whence they take their Priests; for I have known Men who have been bred to handicraft Trades, particularly a Smith in a Countrey Village, that has been admitted into the Priest's Office. There is no such thing as any College that ever I heard of, or School that was appointed for breeding up Men to be qualified for that holy Function in all the Countrey: Excepting at *Kiow*, 700 Miles from *Mosco*, which is in the *Cossacks* Countrey on the Borders of *Poland*, where the *Russes* seldom go for Learning. Nor are their Priests able to defend, or hold any tolerable Argument for, their Religion. And whenever you enter upon any Points of Divinity or Morality with them, the chief Things which they or the Laity reason for, is the addressing to Saints, the keeping of Fasts, that is, the abstaining from Flesh, which they must strictly do, at least half the Days in the Year: The doing some short Penance for Sins past, when enjoin'd; and the asking Forgiveness of the Priest, which when he has cross'd them and pronounc'd their Pardon, they go away as well satisfied as if they had never done any harm, though they have committed the most detestable Crimes in the World: Which as I have before observed occasions that Perfidiousness and Ungenerousness of Spirit, that the *Russes* are generally known to practise towards all that have to deal with them, in prevaricating and falsifying their Word; which occasions a Saying among the Foreigners in that Countrey, *That if you would know if a* Russ *be an honest Man, you must look if he has Hair grows on the Palm of his Hand; but if you find none there, don't expect it.* When they flatter and sooth, and profess with the highest Oaths and Asseverations, the Respect they have for you, which is their common way to lead you to a Dependence on them, (which too is their Practice with one another, as well as with Strangers) you must be sure to be upon your Guard, for then they have the greatest Intention to betray you. And so far are the Generality of the People from having any Sense of Shame for doing a base Thing, that to be a Sharper is a commendable Quality: And they say, *That such a Man understands*

the

the World, *and no doubt will thrive:* But of an honest Man they say, *Un Cloup nemeit shiet, he is a Blockhead, and does not know how to live.* And so little Regard have they for their Word, and so void of any Notion of Honour in the true and genuine Sense of it, that they have not so much as any Word in their Language that expresses it

Another Reason that may be alledg'd for the *Russes* having the want of the sense of Shame and Scandal for any the most wicked Thing, is, that after their being beat with the *Batoags* * or *Knout*, tho' done by the Hands of

---

* *The Punishment by way of* Batoags *is after this Manner, the Person to be punish'd is laid down flat on his Face with his Back all bare, and his Legs and Arms extended out, and two Persons are appointed to whip him on his Back with* Battocks, *which are Sticks or Rods at least the thickness of a Man's little Finger; one of them places himself at the Person's Head that is to be punish'd, to hold him down with his Head between his Knees, whilst the other kneels upon the Offender's Legs, and sometimes, if he struggles and does not take it patiently, two other Persons are appointed to his Hands to keep them down and extended, whilst the two plac'd at his Head and Feet continue striking his bare Back with their* Battocks, *keeping Time as the Smiths do at an Anvil, 'till their Rods are broken in pieces, and then they take fresh ones and keep striking on, although their Backs are all bruis'd and raw, until the Person who stands by and directs the Punishment says it is enough which is sometimes more and sometimes less severe. Both Lords and Peasants suffer this kind of Punishment, and sometimes it is done with that Severity that People dye of it; yet the Power of this sort of Punishment is lodg'd with all Persons that have the Superiority over others, as Lords, Gentlemen, Officers or Masters, who on any Displeasure or pretended Fault, without any Form of Tryal but Will, may exercise this piece of Cruelty. And there are two things always to be observ'd in this way of Punishment, the first is, that the Person so punish'd must cry out* Vinavat, *that*

of a common Hangman, there is no mark of Infamy set upon them for it; there is nothing more ordinary in *Russia* than to have them afterwards be again admitted into Places of Honour and Trust; and if they have but Money to bribe well for a new Place, they never blush for the Roguery they have committed, but when mention is made of what they

---

is, must own himself faulty, or he must be Battoag'd till he does. And the next is, that when his Punishment is over he must come and fall down on his Hands and his Knees, and knock his Forehead on the Ground, at the Feet of the Person who directs the Punishment, and thank him for the Favour that he has been beat no more; and 'tis very common to have Subdiack-flucks, *and Men in other like Posts often to receive this sort of Punishment with the* Botoags, *and yet to be continu'd in their Places, it being not the way of* Russia *to turn Men out for the lesser Crimes and knavish Tricks they are guilty of, but only to inflict corporal Punishment upon them, or to degrade them and put them in lower Places.*

The giving of the Knout *is of another Nature, and not to be put in Execution but by the Form of a Tryal before some Governor or Judge, or by the command of some great Man, and the Punishment is seldom executed but by the Hands of the common Hangman The* Knout *is a thick hard Thong of Leather of about three Foot and a half long, fasten'd to the end of a handsome Stick about two Foot and a half long, with a Ring or kind of Swivle like a Flail at the end of it, to which the Thong is fasten'd There are two ways of punishing with this Instrument, the first is for lesser Crimes, when the Man that has offended is hoisted up upon the Back of another with his Shirt stripped off, and the Hangman, or* Knoutavoit *Master, strikes him so many Strokes on the bare Back as are appointed by the Judge, first making a step back and giving a Spring forward at every Stroke, which is laid on with that force that the Blood flies at every Stroke, and Leaves a wheal behind as thick as a Mans Finger, and these Masters, as the* Russ *call them, are so exact at their own Work that they very rarely strike two Strokes in the same Place, but lay them on the whole breadth of a Man's Back, by the side of each other with great dexterity, from*

they have suffer'd, with a religious and demure Countenance they say, that it has been for their Sins, and that God and the *Czar* have been angry with them; although the *Czar* knows

---

the top of the Man's Shoulders down the Waste-band of his Breeches

The second and most severe way of giving the Knout (which is otherwise call'd the Pine) is when a Mans Hands are tied together behind his Body, and then drawn up by a Rope tied to his Hands, whilst at the same time a great Weight is fix'd to his Legs; and being thus hoisted up, his Shoulders turn out of Joint, and his Arms become right over his Head, which when done with the Weight still hanging to his Feet, the Executioner is order'd to lay on so many Strokes as are appointed by the Judge, in Manner as I have before describ'd This Punishment is commonly executed very leisurely, and between whiles a Subdiackshick (or Writer) examines the Sufferer how far he is guilty of the Crimes he stands accused of, or whether he has any Confederates, or is guilty of such other Crimes whereof he is then examin'd, such as treasonable Things, or Robbery and Murders that the Authors are not known This being done they are taken down, and their Arms put into joint again by the Hangman, and then perhaps dismiss'd or sent back to Prison. But if the Crime whereof any Person is accus'd be accounted Capital, and such as deserv'd Death, then there is a farther Punishment; there is a gentle Fire made just by the Gallows, and after the Offender (for it does not always prove that they are Criminal) is taken down from the Punishment, and denies the Fact or any part whereof he is accus'd, then his Hands and Feet are ty'd, and he is fix'd on a long Pole as upon a Spit, which being held at each end by two Men, the Person that stands charg'd with Guilt, has his raw Back roasted over the Fire, and is then examin'd and call'd upon by a Writer aforesaid to confess. The Writer takes down in writing all the Answers he makes, and if any Person charg'd with any capital Crime, in case when the Proof is not clear against him, cannot stand out this variety of Punishment three several times, which is order'd perhaps three or four Weeks one after the other, without confessing Guilt, or if his Answers that he has made in the time of his Punishment are not judg'd clear and satisfactory, he must after all this Torture suffer Death; but if he is so hardy as to stand it all out without owning himself or being otherwise proved guilty, he is acquitted.

knows nothing of their Roguery. Upon all Occasions, this is their common way of speaking, to join God and the *Czar* together; as, God and the *Czar* is strong, if God and the *Czar* permit; nay, even sometimes they attribute a kind of Divinity and Deference to the *Czar* as they do to God; as when they speak of things out of the reach of common Apprehension, and of what may come to pass, they say, God and the *Czar* knows.

The *Czar*, to instil Principles of Virtue into the Minds of his People, and to give them better Notions of Humanity and Conscience, has for 8 or 9 Years past imploy'd several Persons to translate out of foreign Languages, many excellent Books in Divinity and Morality, as well as relating to War and useful Arts and Sciences, and has set up Printing Houses, and caus'd them to be printed in *Mosco*, and dispers'd throughout his Dominions, maugre all the Opposition made thereto by the Clergy; and farther, has commanded several Schools of Learning to be set up, and made an Order, that whoever in his Countrey that is Master of an Estate to the Value of 500 Rubles *per Annum*, and doth not teach his Son to read and write, and learn *Latin*, or some other foreign Language, such Son shall not inherit his Father's Estate, but the same shall be forfeited to the next Heir of the same Family. As also his Majesty has commanded, that the Clergy of his Countrey for the future, shall be obliged to

learn

learn *Latin*, or not to officiate in the Priestly Office. Whereby it is to be hoped, that in time his People will be brought to a better Understanding in the Grounds of Religion and moral Virtues, as well as in the Art of War and Trade, and other useful Sciences.

His Majesty has not only done this, but takes Occasion in all his private Conversation to argue moderately with the chief Men of the Church, as well as his Nobility, desiring them to be very free in satisfying him in the Reasons they are able to produce for their Biggottry and Superstition, in adhering to their old Customs.

It was the manner of the *Russes* (especially those that were rich and could afford it) to have their Rooms, especially at the upper End and opposite to the Doors all hung, and as it were, cover'd with the Images or Pictures of their Saints; and it is still the Custom, that when any Person comes into a Room to pay a Visit or otherwise, the first thing they do as soon as they set their Feet within the Door, is to cross themselves, saying *Hospidi Pomilio*, that is, *Lord have Mercy upon me*; at the same time with great Reverence bowing to the Pictures, and then to turn and make their Complements to the Master of the House, and so round to the rest of the Company. But if it be in a poor Man's House, that has perhaps but one of these Images or Pictures, and it happens to be a little dark in the Room, and the

the Paint of the Picture perhaps half worn off, and become almost of the same Colour with the Wall, occasioned by the Smoak that is in the *Russes* Houses, and there be no Wax-Candle set up before the Picture (which is a thing done only on Holidays;) when I say it happens that a Man that is a Stranger comes into the Room, and does not at his first Entrance see the Picture or Image set up, he presently enquires *Ogdea Boag?* Where is God? Upon which some Body or other presently points at, and shews him the Picture that hangs on the Wall, and then they pay their Devotion as aforesaid, and sometimes as the Humour takes them, bow down to the very Ground, and knock their Heads on the Floor: This way of knocking their Heads on the Floor, is often done also to great Men. When you reason with them against this Idolatrous Way of bowing down to mere Pictures, they tell you, that it is absolutely necessary to have something to cross themselves to, and that it is a thing both very reasonable and decent, that you should first make your Complement to God, and then to the rest of the Company, at the Entrance into a Room or a House, for which they allege the Direction of their holy Saints, and the Customs of their Fathers: Not but that Men of tolerable Sense amongst them, will tell you, that at the same time they know that what they worship is a meer Picture, perhaps of St. *Nicholo* or some other Saint; yet that in doing

ing this Honour to them, you do it to God; and that as it is the moſt modeſt and ſucceſsful way to addreſs your ſelf to the Favourites of a Prince for what you deſire to obtain, ſo they make no queſtion, but that the Saints in Heaven do conſtantly make Repreſentation of their Prayers to the Almighty: And they hold, that as long as they make no graven Images of their Saints, the bowing down to the Pictures of them is not forbid. Some of the richer ſort of the *Ruſſes*, have the Picture of God Almighty himſelf in their Houſes, which is drawn in the Form of a very old Man with a great grey Beard; but when they draw the Virgin *Mary*, ſhe is painted young and beautiful, and in a better Dreſs, her Picture uſually being ſet off with Pearls and with Gold and Silver. Their manner is to exchange theſe Images in the Market-place for a Peice of Money; for to ſay that the Painter ſells them, or that they are bought with Money, is reckoned a Sin.

But the *Czar* who has a more rational Senſe of God and Religion, ſeeing the ſtupid Folly, as well as Bigottry of his Subjects in theſe Matters, and being willing to reform them from the Error of their Ways, has reduced the Number of his Saints in his own Houſes of Reſidence wherever he is, to the Croſs, or the Picture of our bleſſed Saviour only. And the Lords and other Perſons who are his Favourites, have been brought in a great Meaſure to follow his Example in it,

excepting

excepting some few of the old Lords, who notwithstanding they are his Favourites, will not be brought out of their old Way in this thing. His Majesty, the Summer after his Return from his Travels, going down himself with his Ships which were that Year carried from *Veronize* to *Azoph*, he appointed each Ship to be commanded by one of his own Lords, in conjunction with the foreign Officers which he brought over for that purpose; and when the *Czar* came on board to visit his Ships, he found that the said Lords had filled the Cabins of each Ship full of Pictures of their Saints, according to their usual Way in their Houses. Which when the *Czar* saw, he told them, that one of those Pictures or Images, was enough to cross themselves to, and therefore ordered that all the rest should be taken away, for he would have no more than one in each Ship; which has ever since been observed on board his Fleet at *Veronize* and at *Petersburgh*.

The *Russes* of all their Saints, hold St. *Nicholo* (or St. *Nicholas*) to be the greatest in Esteem, and often speak of him as they do of God: For instance, if you ask them as I have done going thwart the *Lodiga*, the *Onega*, and white Lakes, from the Mouth of one River to another, How far it is to such a Place? Or, How long they are usually with their Vessels upon the Voyage? They presently answer you, that if it pleases St. *Nicholo*,

or

or when *Nicholo* sends them a fair Wind, they then usually perform it in such a Time.

It is by reason of these foolish and abominable Superstitions, and the Illiterature of the Priests, and the general Perfidiousness of the People, as beforementioned, that not only the *Samoieds* and those *Tartars* that border on the *Czar*'s Dominions, of whom I have spoke in the foregoing Pages; but also the *Murdaw* and *Morsie*, and the *Cheremiss Tartars*, on this side the *Wolga*, who have been conquered above 140 Years since, who live in Villages intermix'd with the *Russians*, and are immediately under the Government of the *Czar* (for the most part within the Province of *Cazan*) absolutely refuse to embrace the Christian Religion in the Form which the *Russes* represent it to them, tho' they have been many times offered considerable Encouragement and Enlargement of their Privileges, in case they would be baptized into the *Russ* Faith; and though they daily suffer the Insults and Affronts of the *Russes*, so much the more for their Obstinacy in not doing of it.

When I was employed in making the Communication at *Camishinka*, above half of the Labourers that were sent to dig the Canal there, were of these *Tartars*, and most of the Horse that were sent to cover the Workmen, were composed of the Gentry, or better sort of the same People. I have often taken occasion to ask them about their Religion,

Q

ligion, and they say, that the *Russes* using of Images, is a Terror to them to think of embracing their Religion; for that there is but one God, and that he cannot be pictured or described by Men; they look up towards the Heavens, and say, that he resides there, and of whom they are afraid to do Evil; or to change their Religion for fear he will not afterwards bless them. Their Faith is something like the *Mahometan*; they explain their Notions very rationally, that God is the Eternal Maker of all Things, by whom they receive Life, and to whom they that live uprightly, return again after Death. And because of the Falsity of the *Russes* in the Practice of their Lives, they tell them to their Faces, (I mean the common People in their Discourse one with the other) that they will not believe there is any good in their Religion; and say to them, That if their Religion be right, why do they not do right? As to these *Tartars*, I must do them this Justice, that as often as I had occasion to trust, or make use of them, both I and all my Assistants have observed, that we have found them sincere and honest in their Lives, and ingenuous in their Conversation, above what we have in the *Russ* Nation; and I make not the least doubt, as I have often told these Men when I have discoursed with them, that were the Christian Religion laid down to them, in that Purity as it was delivered by our Saviour and his Apostles, and as it is

taught

taught by the Doctrine of the Church of *England*; and that were they intermixed in a Countrey where there was that Preaching, and where there is that Learning and Exemplariness of Life that is known among the Clergy, and that Honesty and Integrity towards each other, as may generally be said of the People of *England*, there is no doubt but the said *Tartars*, as well as the forementioned *Samoieds*, and other Borderers of *Russia*, would very readily and gladly, long e'er this, have embraced the Christian Religion

I shall conclude this Part of my Discourse, with this Observation of the *Russ* Way of Life; that notwithstanding their pretended Purity in keeping their Fasts, and abstaining from Flesh, there is nothing more common than to have both the People and the Priest too, go to Church on a Holiday in the Morning, and get drunk in the Afternoon long before Night; especially the greater the Holiday, the more it is excusable, and the Custom, to be drunk. It is very ordinary at such Times, if you ride through *Mosco* in the Evening on a great Holiday, to see the Priests, as well as other Men, lie drunk about the Streets, and if any one comes to speak to them and help them up when they are down, they say, *Wollatway Bachca Prosnick ya Pean*, What you will, Father, it is Holiday, and I am drunk; it being the common way of *Russia* to accost any Man with the Appellation of Father that does one a Kindness And so

Q 2 far

far it is from being accounted any Scandal to be drunk, that the very Women, not only the meaner fort, but even Women of Diſtinction and Faſhion, will make no Scruple to own, that they have been very drunk; and in publick Company will thank them for the Civility and Kindneſs, as they call it, of making them drunk, when they have been entertained at any Place, the next time they meet them. And indeed, when I firſt went into the Countrey, and for ſome Years after, it was the common Way, not only at all great Entertainments where the Court was invited and preſent, but even among private Friends, to make their Viſitants drunk before they parted, or it was not accounted that they had been made welcome; and it was the way to preſs and force them to it, even to that Degree that it was uſual to lock up the Gates and Doors, and to ſet a Guard that no Man ſhould go away before he had his Load, or it was otherwiſe thought niggardly, and that their Friends had not been heartily entertain'd, and which Cuſtom extended even amongſt the Foreigners as well as the *Ruſſes*. But in the Year 1705, upon the coming of the Honourable Mr. *Whitworth*, her late Majeſty's Envoy Extraordinary into the Countrey, he made ſuch effectual Repreſentations againſt his own not having his Liberty at his firſt Audience with the prime Miniſter, and gave himſelf ſuch an Example at all the noble and agreeable Entertainments which he frequently made,

made, that it thereupon gave Occasion of breaking the Neck of this most destructive Custom, and for some Years past there has been no force us'd at any publick Entertainments any more, but every Man has Freedom to drink what is agreeable to his own Inclinations; and the like Liberty is now generally become the Fashion in all private Conversation amongst the best sort of Gentlemen who have regard to their own Health, and to Reason. But it is still the prevailing Custom among the generality of the common People, who hold as it were Religious, and that they shew a Respect for the Saints to be drunk upon their Holy-days, of which they have a great many in the Year. What Obscenities, Murthers and Wickedness attend this Custom for want of being better taught by the Priests, who even join with them in the Example, for I am sure I have a thousand times seen them so drunk that they could not stand, I will leave the Reader to judge; even the horrible Sin of Sodomy being scarce look'd on as a Crime in this Countrey, which they are very much addicted to in their Drink; and there is nothing more common in the time of the *Russ* Carnavals, and the next Morning after great Holy-days, than to hear of Murders that have been committed, and to see People lie stript and dead in the Streets of *Mosco*, it being very rare but that the *Russes* kill those whom they rob, barbarously saying that the Dead tell no Tales.

There is no great difference between the *Russ* Religion and that of the Papists, with respect to their holding their Adoration of Saints, and keeping of Holy-days; in their Belief that it is in the Power of the Priest to forgive Sins, and in the Point of their damning and inveighing against all People of any other Religion but their own: And herein the *Russes* are pretty even with the Papists, for they hold that the Pope of *Rome* is an Usurper, and Blasphemer of God, in taking upon him the Style of the Head of the Church, which they say only belongs to Christ himself. They condemn the Papists for not marrying, when St. *Paul*, in his Epistle to *Timothy*, has positively determin'd, that a Priest shall be the Husband of one Wife; and according to which Text of Scripture a *Russ* Priest is oblig'd to marry one Wife, and no more, and if she dies he must not any longer than one Year officiate in the Priest's Office, nor is then any longer called Pope, but *Ruspopa*, or *quondam* Priest, and then usually goes into a Monastery for his Bread; for which Reason it is remarkable that the Priests use their Wives better than any Men in the Countrey. They differ with the Papists in the Administration of the holy Sacrament, which the *Russes* administer to the Laity in both Kinds. They hold also two other Sacraments, *viz.* Baptism and extream Unction. They have not the same Opinion of Purgatory with the Papists, tho' they pray for the Dead;

they

they believe if a Man has receiv'd the Blessing of the Priest before his Departure from this World, and has a small Billet or Certificate for St. *Nicholas*, written by the Priest that he dy'd in the true Christian Faith, and put between his Fingers when he is laid in his Grave, he shall be admitted into Heaven: They hold with the Papists, that the Traditions of the Church are at least of equal Authority with the Scriptures, and as the Papists so they believe it no Sin to break Faith with Hereticks and Heathens. Concerning the holy Trinity they differ both from the Papists and the Reform'd Churches, believing that the Holy Ghost proceeds from the Father only, and not from the Father and the Son; and so much they reverence the Holy Ghost descending in the Form of a Dove, that there are very few of them that eat a Pidgeon. They above all believe that the Purity of their Religion consists chiefly in strictly keeping their Fasts, of which they have four great Fasts or Lents in the Year, besides two Days in every Week, which they punctually keep in abstaining from Flesh, or any thing that comes from it, as even Eggs or Milk which they will not touch; and if they are sick they will rather die than take any sort of Physick, unless they first ask and are assur'd that it is not *Scorumno*, that is, not polluted with any thing that proceeds from Flesh; and they account all others, both Papists and Protestants Hereticks, and say of them, that they are Heathens and eat Flesh like Dogs, who do not keep their Fasts. One of the strongest and hottest Disputes they have among them about any difference in their Religion, is in the Manner of holding their Fingers when they Cross themselves; the Patriarch having not long since establish'd a Law, that the Lay-men should only Cross themselves with two Fingers; but notwithstanding this Order there is an obstinate Sect among them who will do it with three Fingers, of which one *Jacob Nurſoff*, who rais'd the late Rebellion at *Aſtracan*, was a great Stickler, and who led a considerable Party after him, but came to Destruction.

No Man who would not embrace the *Ruſs* Faith, was formerly permitted to come into their Churches, or but very rarely, and if they did it was look'd upon as a great Favour, and the Church was afterwards to be purify'd with holy Water, and burning of Incense; nor would they formerly permit any Foreigner to be bury'd in their Church-yards, but the present *Czar* as he now goes often himself to the foreign Churches, which are in the Suburbs of *Moſco*, with several of his Lords, especially when there is any Burial of a Stranger for whom he had an Esteem, so it is now become a thing freely permitted for Strangers to go into the Churches of the *Ruſſes*; and I have known Foreigners bury'd in the Church-yards of the *Ruſſes*, by an Order of the *Czar*, in particular a young Gentleman who was his Favourite, who was kill'd by Accident at *Veronize*,

ronize, over whose Grave there is a Monument erected.

There is a known Story of a Monkey belonging to an *English* Embassador that was sent to one of the former *Czars*, which is this: The Monkey one Day getting loose, got into a Church that was near where the Embassador lived, and threw down some of the Pictures which were placed on a Shelf in the Church, it being the *Russ* way not to hang up the Pictures of Saints, for they reckon that not honourable, but to place them on a Shelf. There was a Complaint made to the Embassador on occasion of this Accident, as if the Monkey had been let loose by design to put this Affront upon the Church, and led by the Devil to defile their Saints. The Church was purified with the extraordinary Ceremony of sprinkling of Holy Water, and Prayers on this Occasion were made to the Saints, and the Devil was conjured to go out of the Church. For which the Monkey was condemn'd; and by peculiar Order from the Patriarch carried in publick View as a Criminal through the Streets, and afterwards put to Death.

There is also another Story to which I will here give a place, that is positively related of a *German* Surgeon who was formerly in the *Czar*'s Service, who had a Skeleton hanging up in his Room near his Window, and which as the Wind moved always gave it Motion. And one Evening as this Surgeon was sitting and

and playing on his Lute, the Agreeableness of the Musick drew some of the *Streletzes*, or Guards of the *Czar*, who were passing by to come and listen to it; and at the same time peeping in at a Crevis of the Door they saw the Skeleton have a Motion, which so affrighted them, that they ran immediately to Court, and told some of the Favourites of the *Czar*, that they had seen the dead Bones dance to the Musick of the Surgeon; and which being also confirm'd by others, who were thereupon sent to observe the Truth, the Surgeon was adjudg'd and condemn'd to Death as a Sorcerer; and had certainly suffer'd, had not the *Boyar*, who was his Patron, and a Favourite of the *Czar*'s, interceded for his Life, and by remonstrating to his Majesty, that the Surgeons only made use of and kept these Skeletons in their Houses, that they might know and be the better Masters in their Business, by seeing the Composure and Joints of a Man's Body before them: But notwithstanding which, the Surgeon was however obliged thereupon to leave the Countrey, and the Skeleton was dragg'd about the Streets and burnt.

When I first went into the Countrey the *Russes* dated their Year from the Creation of the World, which they reckon'd 7206; but from whence, or what Assurance they had for their Account, beside the Tradition of their Fathers, I could never understand from them. They also reckon'd the first Day of their Year on the first of *September*, which they kept with very great Solemnity. The Reason which they give for this Beginning of their Year on the first of *September*, and which their Disputants thought to be a most convincing Reason, and prided themselves in being Masters of their Argument, was this; That God, who was all-wise and good, created the World in the Autumn, when the Corn was in its full Ear, and the Fruits of the Earth were ripe, and fit to take and eat; and not as other *Europeans* reckon'd, in the very Depth of Winter, when the Earth was all frozen and cover'd with Snow. But the *Czar* (sensible of their mistaken Notion) desired his Lords to view the Map of the Globe, and in a pleasant Temper gave them to understand, that *Russia* was not all the World; that what was Winter with them, was at the same time always Summer in all those Places beyond the Equator. Besides that, according to the common Way of computing the Termination of the Year, the Seasons are considerably alter'd since the Creation of the World, through those odd Minutes that happen in every Year over and above 365 Days and six Hours: And therefore the *Czar*, to conform his Countrey to the rest of *Europe*, so far as in reckoning the first Day of the Year on the first of *January*, and in dating the Year with other Christians from the Incarnation of our Saviour, he took the following Method.

The

The first of *January* 1700, Old Stile, he proclaimed a Jubilee, and commanded the same to be solemnized a whole Week together, with the firing of Guns, and ringing of Bells; and the Streets to be adorn'd with Colours flying in the Day, and Illuminations at Night, which all Houses of any Distinction were to observe; and made an Order, that from that time forward, in all Laws and Writings whatsoever, no Person, under a Penalty, should date the Year any longer according to the old way which the *Russes* had used. This he did, notwithstanding it was look'd upon by the Malecontents as another considerable Innovation, and striking at the Ground of their Religion They comply with this Order out of mere Fear; but there are still some of the old *Russes* who will get together on the first Day of *September*, and with warm Zeal still solemnize that as the first Day of the new Year, and privately will assert, that the World is just as old as they reckon it, which according to their Account is now 7223 Years.

It had been the Custom in the Time of the *Czar*'s Predecessors, for all the Subjects of *Russia*, as well the highest Lords as the meanest Peasants in all Petitions and Business of Law, or otherwise to write themselves *Golups*, or Slaves to the *Czar*, and in all Petitions and other Matters, tho' never so trifling, both in the beginning and the Prayer of the Petition to write the *Czar*'s Dignities and Titles at
large

large, which were long and tedious; and if any Man fail'd in naming his Titles right, he was to be punish'd. But the *Czar*, the better to reconcile his People to this Alteration that he had made of the new Year, order'd that from the Date aforesaid none of his People throughout his Dominions should any more write themselves his Slaves, but Subjects; and that the word *Raab*, which signifies Subject, should be used in the place of *Golup*, or Slave; which although there is no real Advantage to them in it, (for they are but Slaves still) yet the very Sound or Change of the Word has pleased them. And his Majesty also ordered, that in all Causes, both Military and Civil, and in all Cases of Law whatsoever, where they were obliged to exhibit Petitions as to his *Czarish* Majesty, (and which is in the nature of an Action or Writ enter'd or taken out in *England*) his Titles at large should not any more be set forth in full length as usual, but be directed only in these Words, *Voffsea Millistea Vishia Sudaria*; that is in *English*, *To his most highly gracious Majesty*.

There are a great many other Things which his Majesty has done to reform and convince his People of the Folly of being bigotted to their old Ways and Customs, and that there was no real Evil in changing them for new, that are either more reasonable, or more becoming and decent. The Account of which would be too tedious to the Reader, as well as my self, to relate. I shall therefore only mention one thing more which the *Czar* did to shew his People that the Customs of *Russia* had been chang'd, and Improvements really made for the better in the Course of Time, and that there was no more Ill in the doing of it at once, than in the Course of 500 Years, of which he made them this following Representation.

In the Year 1701, one of his Jesters being to be married to a very pretty Woman, he ordered all his Lords and Gentlemen that were in his Favour, with several Foreigners, to be invited to the Wedding; and gave his Commands that every Person who was invited (whose Names of both Sexes were set down in writing) should provide themselves with the same Habit that was worn in *Russia* in the Days of their Fathers about 200 Years before; and that the whole Ceremony should be perform'd after the same manner as it was at that time; of which I shall only give this short Account. The *Boyars*, who wore long Caps upon their Heads at least a Foot higher than was then the Fashion, had on a gawdy aukward Dress that I cannot here easily describe, and rode on Horseback. The Furniture of their Horses was fix'd after a very unusual manner, some of the *Boyars* who were of the first Rank, had for the Reins of their Bridle a silver Chain, the Jinks of which were about an Inch and a half or two Inches broad, made of thin Silver beat out flat, and

the

the Breast-plate and Crupper were drest with little square Pieces of the same thin Silver, which with the Motion of the Horse struck against each other, and made a kind of jingling like Bells as they rode; amongst which Rank was his Majesty in the same Habit with his Lords, there being another Person who was one of the old *Boyars* appointed for representing the *Czar* for that Day in a mock Dress. Persons of meaner Rank, who could not have their Horses Furniture fix'd with Silver, had it with Tin lacquer'd over.

The Women who were invited to this Wedding, were order'd to be dress'd after the old *Russ* Manner, their Smock sleeves were at least 12 Yards long, contracted into a Ruff, as much as would lie between their Shoulders and their Wrists, with their upper Vestment only covering their Bodies, and the Heels of their Shoes or Slippers near 5 Inches high; they rode in Machines or Waggons set only upon Axletrees and Wheels, without any Leathers or Swing to make 'em easy, and there were short Ladders ty'd on the side of each Waggon (like the present way of the *Tartars*) to get up, which Waggons were hoop'd over at one end, where the Women sat cover'd with red Cloth. In this Order I saw them march to the House of the deceas'd General *Le Fort*, which was a House built at the *Czar*'s Charge.

There were several Tables spread in a very large Hall, according to the Degrees and
Ranks

Ranks of the Guests, and at the upper end there was one Table placed upon a Throne, about 3 Foot higher than the rest, at which sat the Mock *Czar* with a Mock Patriarch, to whom the Company advanced by gradual Steps, and bowed their Heads to the Ground at several proper Distances as they advanced; being call'd by Name, to kiss, first the Mock *Czar*, and then the Patriarch's Hands, upon which a Dram of Brandy was presented to every Man, both from the *Czar* and the Patriarch, and then they went backwards from the Throne to about 20 Foot distance, and all the way made their Bows as they went back. A splendid Entertainment was prepared for the Company; but the Victuals, and way of serving it to the Table, was, on purpose for Mirth made irregular and disagreeable, and their Furniture poor and mean, their Liquor also was as unacceptable, the best of which (as in the Days of old) was made of Brandy and Honey, and yet they were obliged to drink it, for though there was a grievous begging and complaint made in jest and in earnest, yet there was not one Glass of good Beer, nor one drop of any Wine to be had that Day, for they were told, that their Fathers had not drank any, neither must they; the Dancing and Musick in the Evening was after the *Russ* Fashion. And lastly, though it was in the depth of Winter, and the Frost was very severe, there was a Bed provided for the married Pair in the Summer-house in the Garden, where there was neither Fire nor Stove to keep the Room warm, according as it had been a superstitious Custom in that Countrey. For by reason the *Russ* Houses are built without any Chimney or Fire-place in any of their Rooms, but have Stoves built in them to keep them warm in the Winter, and a considerable quantity of Earth laid always above the Cielings on the top of the Room to keep in the Heat (as has been before observed in another Discourse) the *Russes* therefore look'd upon it as ominous, and a thing that favour'd too much of Death and the Grave, for a young Couple to lie the first Night with Earth over their Heads, for which reason it had been their Manner, though they happen'd to be married in the depth of Winter, to lie, as the *Czar* now order'd his Jester, and as some of the *Russ* still superstitiously follow, always the first Night with the Bride in a cold Room.

The next thing I shall speak of is the Trade of *Russia*, and the several Discouragements and Hindrances to Industry which the *Czar*'s Subjects labour under, through the arbitrary Constitution and ill Administration of the Government, which hath been, and is still like to be injurious to his Countrey; and shall also name a few Particulars, which have been directly contrary to the *Czar*'s immediate Interest.

Russia, to speak of it in general, is a very level and fertile Country, abounding with whatsoever is necessary for human Life; and as there are no burning hollow Mountains, and being far from those deep Places of the Sea where there is no Depth to be found till you come near the Shore, so there is never any undermining or falling in of the Land from the Surface, nor any Earthquakes ever felt in this Countrey. The Air is serene and good, with not the 20th part of the Fogs, and I believe at least one fifth part less Rain than we have in *England* or *Ireland*. The Countrey is intermix'd with Pasture and Arable Land, with Woods, Lakes and Rivers, and every where through all the Parts that I have travell'd (which has been almost on all the Sides of the *Czar*'s Dominions,) there are to be seen many pleasant and delightful Situations. The *Russes* have a Saying, that they are very rich in Fish and in Bread; and I may add that they have good store of Horses and of Cattle; and of wild Game, they have of all sorts the greatest plenty in the World, and particularly what is very surprizing and wonderful in its Nature, is this, that one sort of the Hares, of which they have the greatest Plenty in *Russia*, every Winter turn Milk white as soon as the Snow lies on the Ground, and again change their Colour in the Spring of the Year, and are then like our Hares. There are two sorts of Hares in *Russia*, that sort which turn white in the Win-

Winter, the *Russes* call *Zaits*; and the other sort, which are found mostly in the Southern Parts, they call *Rossac*. It is remarkable that the Bears which are in the extreme Northern Parts of the *Czar*'s Dominions, are most of them white, as are most of the Weasels, the Skin of which is call'd the Ermine, of which sort I have seen in the Winter, but never any of them in the Summer.

By reason of the Severity of Cold in this Countrey, not only the Water-Fowl, Cranes, Swans, Ducks, Geese, Snipes, with other great variety of Water-Fowl, of which no Countrey produces more, but almost all sorts of Land Birds fly to the Southward in the Winter in infinite Numbers, and back again in the Spring when the Snow melts from off the Ground, and the bare Places of the Earth begin to appear: Which in the Latitude of *Mosco* is usually not till about the middle or towards the latter end of *April*, when the Days are long, and the Sun has taken a considerable Power, before the Snow which has lain a very great thickness on the Ground can be melted through; then in ten Days or a Fortnight's time at most, the Fields are all perfectly green, the Weather at once becomes sensibly warm, the Trees bud, the Grass springs, the Flowers immediately begin to appear, and the Nightingales and other Birds which then come on from the Southward, every where chirp and sing.

There are two remarkable Times of the Year when the *Russes* express their Joy upon the Alteration of the Seasons; the one is when the Snow first falls on the Ground, and the Winter is so strongly set in, that the Rivers are so frozen up, that they can pass with their Horses and Sleds upon the Ice; which Change, when the Wind shifts about and blows from the Northward, happens so suddenly, that sometimes within 24 Hours there is no Ice to be seen, and the next Day a Horse and Sled may drive over the Rivers; and when the Winter is thus strongly fix'd, they have on all sides across the Land, the Lakes, and the Rivers, wherever the nearest Way lies, an Opportunity of Land-Carriage by Sleds, which is certainly the most commodious and swiftest travelling in the World either for Passengers or for Goods; the Sleds being light and conveniently made, and with little Labour to the Horses, slide smooth and easy over the Snow and the Ice; and the Snow by often passing of the Sleds upon it wherever there is a Way made, becomes smooth and hard like Ice. Against which Season of the Year, great quantities of Goods are laid up in most Places of *Russia*, for the Easiness and Cheapness of Carriage in the Winter, excepting where there is Opportunity of Water Carriage by their Floats, their Boats and their Vessels. The whole Winter through when once the Sled way is fix'd, there come several thousand Sleds every Day laden into *Mosco*,

drawn

drawn usually but with one Horse; and it is remarkable that in *Russia* the price of Land-carriage in the Winter upon Sleds, is not above the fourth or fifth part so much as it is in the Summer upon Wheels. The *Russes* also usually use but one Horse for their common Carriage by Waggons in the Summer, their Waggons being made light and the Roads thereby preserv'd smooth, and are not cut deep

The other time of their Rejoycing is in the Spring of the Year, after the Ice has been some Days rotten and dangerous and then breaks away, the Rivers become open and free for their Boats and Vessels to pass On these two Occasions the *Russes* hold a kind of Festival, and are merry with their Neighbours.

The Product or Manufactures of *Russia* with which Commerce is principally maintain'd with foreign Parts, is Pot-ash, Weed-ash, *Russia* Leather, Furs, Linen, Flax, Hemp, Seal-skins, Train-oyl, Rosin, Pitch, Tar, Caviar, Tallow, Honey, Wax, Isinglass of both sorts (the one of which is us'd in Windows for Ships, &c. and the other for making of Glue;) as also Masts, Timber, Plank, Oak and Firr; and if the *Czar* does ever live to perform the Communication which is his Intention to make for free Water-carriage between the *Wolga* and *Petersburgh*, he will then be able to bring Oak and Timber with plenty of Corn to that Place at very easie Rates, that the same may both pay a considerable Duty to the *Czar*, and turn very much to the Advantage of his Countrey, by the being exported from thence to other Parts of *Europe*; for Corn may then be loaded much cheaper there than can be deliver'd, either at the Ports of *Riga*, *Dantzick*, or *Konigsberg*, from whence and other Places in the *Baltick*, the *Hollanders* alone load every Year eight hundred or a thousand sail of Ships with Corn

The *Russes* make the most part of their Bread with Rye, which they reckon to be the most strengthning for Men, and in many Places on the *Wolga*, between the Mouth of the *Shacksna* and *Cazan*, Rye is usually sold for the Value of an *English* 6 d. or 7 d. per Bushel, according to *English* Measure, Wheat at about 9 d. per Bushel, and all other Grain is there in Price proportionable.

There is also Brimstone and Salt Petre made in the *Czar*'s Dominions, and there are Powder Mills built on several small Rivers near *Mosco*, where a sufficient Quantity of Powder is by Foreigners made, not only to supply the *Czar*'s Occasions, but may be spar'd to other Nations: As also some Copper Mines are found in the Province of *Cazan*, and there are a great many Iron Mines and Works in the *Czar*'s Countrey, particularly near *Venize*, and near *Mosco*, and on the Side of the *Onega* Lake; at each of which very great Quantities of Iron-work are made for all manner of Occasions in *Russia*, with all sorts of
Arms

Arms for supplying the *Czar*'s Army, the making of which is now brought to pretty good Perfection; and it is even pretended, that by reason of the Price of Provision being less, and Labour cheaper than in other Parts, they will supply other Nations with Arms and other Iron Manufacture, of which some Patterns have been sent Abroad, before I came from *Russia*.

These are the Produce of the *Czar*'s Countrey for War and for Trade; and if the Advantage of the Situation be consider'd by Means of those grand Rivers which every where spread their Branches, flowing thro' the Heart of *Russia*, and fall into four several Seas, as I have already mention'd in another Place, was but Industry cultivated and incouraged as it is in *England* and other free Countreys, the Product of it might, it is certain, be much farther improv'd, Trade be extended, the People made happy, and the *Czars* of *Muscovy*, as the Extent of their Countrey is very great, might in a short time become equal in Power and Strength to any Monarch on Earth; more particularly by reason of the great Cheapness and Plenty of Timber and Naval Stores for equipping out a Fleet, and by reason of its being easie to maintain an Army on the Side of *Azoph*, they would undoubtedly be more able to shake the Empire of the *Turks* than any of those Princes of *Europe* who usually have War with them.

But I must here observe two or three Instances of the Disadvantages to the *Czar*'s Revenue, thro' the vitiated Temper and injudicious Administration of his *Boyars*, and of the general Oppression which his People (notwithstanding all the Reformations which the *Czar* has endeavour'd) do and are like still to groan under, and from whence it will always appear, that wherever Trade is oppress'd the People must be poor, and by consequence the Prince must be so too.

The first Instance I shall name which has in my time prov'd very detrimental to the *Czar*'s Revenue, and injurious to his People, is this; When I first went into the Countrey the biggest piece of Silver of the Coin of *Russia* was only *Copeeks* or Pence; and the least was some Half-pence and Farthings of the same Metal; and this Coin was of very good Silver, and of full Weight in Proportion to the best Money of other Countreys, so that in return of some little Mony that I had occasion to send to *England*, the Exchange was then at two or three *per Cent* advance. But after the Misfortune which the *Czar* sustain'd of losing almost all his Army, with his whole Artillery and Baggage before *Narva*, which was the Winter *Anno* 1700, being afterwards somewhat straightned to raise new Forces to carry on the War; and a Resolution being taken to have still a greater Number of Foreigners brought into the *Czar*'s Service; it was propos'd by one of his favourite *Boyars*, and seconded

conded by the rest, that all the *Czar*'s old Money should be call'd in and melted down, and that new Copeeks and half Copeeks should be coin'd in the place of the old, not three fifths of the Weight, and yet to pass for the same Value as before; and which is still worse, an Allay has been since order'd to be mix'd with the Copeeks.

After this recoining of the Money had gone on for about a Year's Time, and finding that the People hoarded up their old Money, and did not care to part with it, and bring it into the Mint, a farther Order was made, whereby 10*l per Cent.* was given in new Money to every one that should bring in the Old, and larger Pieces of Money were ordered to be coined, such as Rubles, half Rubles, quarter of Rubles, 10 and 5 and 3 Copeek Pieces; and on this Occasion a Rix Dollar (in which Money the foreign Merchants are obliged to pay all the *Czar*'s Customs for Goods imported) and which in the Time of old Money being current, was but at the Value of about 55 Copeeks, was now recoined, and with some Allay, made a Ruble, which is 100 Copeeks.

By this recoining of the *Russ* Money, not only my self, (which was one great Occasion of the Dispute that first arose about the Payment of my Arrears) but a great Number of other Foreigners suffered in the Payment of their Wages: But since that time, Men have been more cautious who have entred into the

Czar's

Czar's Service, particularly those who have since made their Contract in *England*, have had Merchants engaged for the Payment of their Money, according to Sterling Value.

The Exchange on which Trade more particularly depends, after this, soon fell to between 30 and 40 *per Cent* and the Price of every thing, more especially what there was occasion for from foreign Parts, was soon advanced in proportion to the Exchange; and a great deal of ill Money, mix'd with an Allay, has since that time been believed to have been coined by other Hands, and crowded upon the Government, whereby the Exchange still suffers, and will inevitably become worse and worse till remedied. Nor has it in any respect proved any other than false Policy, at the Foot of the Account; for whatsoever the *Czar*'s own immediate Affairs require from abroad, whether for the cloathing of his Army, or for all other foreign Commodities which there is a Demand for, and are sent to *Russia*, the Price has been since raised according to the Course of the Exchange: But in a more particular manner this Evil hath been felt in the late maintaining of the *Czar*'s Army in *Pomerania*, when 40 and 45 *per Cent.* was given for the Return of Money thither; as also has been experienced in the Purchase of those Ships which the *Czar* has had occasion to buy in *England* and in *Holland*; so that the *Czar*'s own immediate Affairs have suffered their full Share in this piece of ill Conduct

Conduct, as well as Foreigners who have been wrong'd in their Pay, and Merchants and Trade in general been injured thereby.

But this is not the only Misfortune which the Countrey Labours under thro' the *Czar's* Want of honest and able Ministers to advise and assist him in Things relating to Trade, and the Management of his Revenue; which for the most part he leaves to his Lords, who make such Representations from time to time to him, as they think fit; whilst his Majesty busies himself principally in the Disposition of Affairs relating to his Army, and in his Naval Preparations, in drawing the Draughts, which he does often with his own Hands, and in building and ordering the Proportion of the Masts, the Sails, and the Rigging of his Ships of War, Yatchts, Brigantines, Gallies, half-Gallies, and several other sorts of Vessels of which his Fleets are composed, in which he chiefly takes his Delight; and his *Boyars*, who are content to have him diverted this way, in the mean time take care to keep to themselves the modelling of Things more immediately belonging to Trade, and the Taxes laid upon the People.

I have before mentioned a new Office that was created by the *Czar*, at his first coming from his Travels; in which Office he impowered some of the principal Merchants to make the Assessments and Collection of Duties, which related to Trade But not long after this, it was in a great measure laid by, and

and there were other Projects set on foot; several new Officers were created, called *Prebulshicks* (or Advancers of Profit to be brought into the *Czar*'s Treasure) and these Persons had a full Power given them, in several Schemes which were laid down (according to the old ways of *Russia*) to manage some one Branch, and some another Branch of the Duties and Customs to be paid to the *Czar*; whereby they proposed to bring more speedy and greater Sums into the Treasury: And the things wherein the Trade has been directly injur'd and obstructed have been as follow.

First, By forestalling and monopolizing many of the principal Commodities, the Growth of the *Czar*'s Countrey. such as Pot-ash, Tar, &c by buying up large Quantities of Goods, and then setting an extraordinary Value upon them, and forbidding any *Russ* Merchant to sell the same sort of Goods, until all Goods thus bought for the *Czar* (as they call it) are first sold at the Rate that is set upon them. Besides this monopolizing and raising the Price of Goods whereby Trade is immediately deaden'd and oppress'd: It is also practised in *Russia* to lay on new Duties on several Species of Goods, without giving timely Notice of it; and often done after the Factors in *Mosco* have written to their Principals abroad, and the Ships with their Orders have been on their Voyage too, and at other Times even after they have been arrived at *Archangel*: In which Cases the foreign Merchants have

have been put under the greatest Difficulties; for they have been obliged either to comply and take the Goods at the Price that has been advanced upon them by the new Duties imposed, or the Ships must go home again without Freight, and their Correspondents be disappointed of the Goods that they have expected, and been perhaps under an Engagement to deliver.

Secondly, When the *Czar*'s Occasions have been declared to require it, and Goods from foreign Markets have arrived at *Archangel*, it has been often order'd that no *Russ* Merchant, or other Person whatsoever, should dare buy any such Goods as are come into Port, until what the *Czar* has occasion for is first bought; whereby foreign Merchants have often been constrained to deliver their Goods at such Prices as have been offer'd them by the Persons who are commission'd to buy them for the *Czar*. So that in the first of these Instances, the Native, who is a Merchant, does not know how to encourage Goods to be prepared, nor what Price he shall shall give for them at any time, lest he should be afterwards restrained from selling them to his own Advantage. And secondly, foreign Merchants have often, by these Monopolizings, and by Imposition of new Duties, without timely Notice given, been considerably injured and disappointed, which I will leave to the Merchants themselves to relate; and how very scandalously, by cavilling

Pre-

Pretences, they have been often dealt with, even in Instances where the most firm Contract and Agreement has been made with them in the Name and publick Offices of the *Czar*. For obtaining Right in which several Cases, publick Complaints and Remonstrances have been strongly made, before they have in any Measure been relieved, and often never redress'd. For which Reasons, and to prevent these Evils for the future, pressing Instances have been made for a Treaty of Commerce to be settled, at least that tho' the *Czar* might from time to time appoint such Duties on Goods either imported, or exported, as should be thought fit, yet that 10 or 12 Months Notice should be given of it, that Merchants might regulate their Affairs accordingly: But the Lords and Favourites of the *Czar* have oppos'd it; for they would thereby lose the Opportunity which they now have of being sought to and enriching themselves by constant Presents and Bribes.

Thirdly, The aforesaid *Prebulshicks* have been farther empower'd to go into all Houses to search after Goods, to assess and levy severe Duties in all Inland Markets and Trade, and to trouble and vex the People to the last degree through all the *Czar*'s Dominions, beside the general Tax which every House and Family is obliged to pay: So that through these things, the arbitrary Practices, together with the Oppression of the Governors, of the *Diacks*, and petty Officers subordinate

to

to them, the common People have but very little Heart or Desire to any Industry, farther than Necessity drives them. For if at any time by their Ingenuity and Endeavours they do get Money, it cannot rightly be said they can call it their own; but with Submission they say, *All that they have belongs to God and the* Czar: Nor do they dare to appear as if they had any Riches, in their Apparel, or in their Houses, it being counted the best way to seem poor, lest there should be any Notice taken of them that they have Money; and they are troubled and harrass'd till they must part with it, and always be making Bribes and Presents to be at rest; of which there are ten thousand Instances. So that every where as you travel through the Villages in *Russia*, for this reason you will see the general part of the common People idle in the Streets, and in the Houses, especially in the Winter; the chiefest Things which they take Care for, being in the Affairs of their Husbandry, to sow and to reap in their Seasons, and to make a coarse sort of Cloaths to defend themselves from the Cold. What Money the common People get, it is their way often to hide it under the Earth, so that 'tis certain great Sums are thereby wholly lost when Men come to dye.

There are very many sinister Ways which the Governors and Men in Power take to oppress the People; among which the general and common Way is to contrive some pretended

tended Fault to be charged upon a Man, and to send for and examine him, with Threats of the *Knout* or *Battocks*; or otherwise to encourage some Petition or Information against him; in which Case, let Justice be as it will, every Man according to his Substance must either suffer Stripes, or buy off his Punishment with Money.

The common Boors or Peasants, who have been sent upon the Works under my Command, have complained to me with Tears of Wrongs and Injuries that have been done them by the Governors of Towns, and the Officers in the Districts who have been under the Governors, particularly when I was at *Veronize:* And when I have offer'd to represent the Injustice done them to the present Admiral *Apraxin,* (who had then the Command of that Province) and have promised them that I would do my utmost, and engage to obtain Right for them, they have thereupon earnestly begg'd of me by no means to mention the Things which they have complained of; alledging this for their Reason, That even tho' they should obtain Right at that Time, yet that they were sure afterwards to suffer, and to be ruin'd for their complaining of those in Power over them, who would mark them out as Informers.

There is this Instance more that I cannot but mention, touching the Misery of these People; namely, that if any poor Man be naturally ingenious, or a better Workman than
his

his Neighbours in a Countrey Town or Place, or be sent upon any of the *Czar*'s Works, he usually endeavours to conceal it, and pretends to be ignorant, for these two following Reasons.

First, If it be known in a Countrey Town or Place where a Man lives that he is ingenious, he gets no rest, but is constantly sent for and employ'd, either by the Governor or petty Officers under him, or by the Gentlemen of the Countrey, whose Slaves they are, without being able to call their Time their own, or having any suitable Encouragement to themselves; but in the place thereof, if they do not please, or murmur, and are not content, they often get Stripes for their Labour.

Secondly, In case of any Number of Men being sent from the Places where they live to go upon any of the *Czar*'s Works, if any Artificers are more ingenious than their Fellow-Workmen, unless it be where the *Czar* himself is present, and takes Cognizance of it, they have oftentimes more Labour and Care of Work committed to their Charge, but have no Encouragement given them for their Ingenuity more than another Man. When I was at *Veronize*, I order'd a *Dutch* Master Carpenter who was under my Command, upon Occasion of an Engine that was to be made, to chuse out two or three of the most ingenious Persons that he could find among the *Russ* Carpenters to be employ'd in it; upon which, among others, he named one to me, who

who, he told me, he believed was the best Workman of them all: But I happening to differ with him in Opinion, because he had never discover'd himself, he answer'd me, That he was assured the Person whom he had named to me was a Workman, by what he had observ'd of him in the handling of his Tools, but that the Man was in the right of it not to discover himself, for the Reason abovemention'd; and when it came to be try'd, it proved to be as the *Dutchman* had represented it to me.

And notwithstanding all that I could do by the Representations I have made on the Works that I have been employ'd on, to have some small Encouragement to be given to such as I found deserving out of the *Czar*'s Treasure, yet I could never obtain so much as one single Copeek a Day Encouragement for any one Person; it being not the Manner of *Russia*, on any such Works as I was employ'd on, to pay any Money or Wages at all to common Artificers and Labourers out of the *Czar*'s Treasure.

But that the Reader may the better understand how such Men, who are employ'd and sent on publick Works are paid, it will be necessary to give the following Account:

All the common People, or Peasants of *Russia*, (who dress and till the Land, &c.) are Slaves, either directly to the *Czar* himself, to the *Boyars*, to the Monasteries, or to the Gentlemen of the Countrey; and when the *Czar* either gives any Person a Village, (which is often forfeited, and taken from one Man and given to another,) or when any Village or Estate is bought and sold in *Russia*, the Way of reckoning the Value of the same, is not according to the Extent of Land that belongs to the same, but according to the Number of Inhabitants or Slaves there are upon it; each House or Family have their Portion of Land alotted to them, and are obliged to pay to their proper Landlord such a Proportion of Money, of Corn, and all manner of Provision in Specie. Besides the common Taxes that are laid on them by the *Czar*'s particular Orders for carrying on his Wars; it is the manner of *Russia*, upon Occasion of all Works and Business belonging to the *Czar*, where any Number of common Labourers, Carpenters, Masons, or Smiths, are required, to send an Order into such Provinces and Districts for the respective Governors of the Towns, as is thought fit, to levy them from among such of the Peasants or Slaves, according as the Order directs; which sometimes falls out, that every third, fifth, or tenth House, shall find a Man, whether Carpenter, Smith, or Labourer, sometimes with a Horse, and sometimes without, for so many Months or so much Time as such Order appoints, to be paid at the proper Expence and Charge of the Towns and Villages from whence they are appointed to be levied, till they are order'd to be relieved, and other Numbers of fresh Men, either from the same or some other Districts are sent in their Places. And I have known it sometimes, that even one half of the Men belonging to all the Villages in some particular Districts, have been sent alternately to relieve one another, without having any Wages allowed them. And therefore this being the Custom of *Russia*, when I have made my utmost Application for the Encouragement of some few Persons who have been really ingenious, that they might have but a Copeek a Day Reward allow'd them to animate the rest, I have received for Answer, particularly by my Lord *Apraxin*, when I was employ'd at *Veronize*, that there was no such Precedent for the giving of Money out of the *Czar*'s Treasure for Men to do their Duty for which they were sent; but in the place of it they had *Batoags* that grew in *Russia*, and if they did not do their Work when required, they must be beaten to it.

Upon these Considerations, it is no great wonder that the *Russes* are the most dull and heavy People to attain to any Art or Science of any Nation in the World, and upon every Opportunity are the most apt to rebel, and to engage in any the most barbarous Cruelties, in hopes of being reliev'd from that Slavery that is hereditary to them.

The *Czar*, where he is present, does indeed give Encouragement to some of those common Atificers and Workmen, who have the Happiness to be under his Eye, and whom he finds deserving, as particularly in the building and equipping of his Ships, where he is daily among the Artificers, and will often take the Tools in hand, and work himself along with them. But his *Boyars* are quite of another Temper, and in all other Places and Occasions, through all the Parts of the *Czar's* Dominions, the generality of his Subjects remain still under the same Check and Discouragement to Ingenuity: And this is certain, that if the present *Czar* should happen to die, without the greatest part of his present old *Boyars* go off before him, the generality of Things wherein he has taken so much Pains to reform his Country, will for the most part revolve into their old Form. For it is believed that his Son, the present Prince of *Russia*, who is of a Temper very much differing from his Father's, and adheres to Bigottry and Superstition, will easily be prevailed on to come into the old Methods of *Russia*, and quit and lay aside many of those laudable Things that have been begun by the present *Czar*.

Which leads me here to mention, that among some other Causes, one of the chief which makes the generality of the Nobility at present uneasy, is, that the *Czar* obliges them against their Will, to come and live at *Petersburgh*, with their Wives and their Families, where they are obliged to build new Houses for themselves, and where all manner of Provisions are usually three or four times as dear, and Forage for their Horses, &c. at least six or eight times as dear as it is at *Mosco*; which happens from the great Expence of it at *Petersburgh*, and the small quantity which the Countrey thereabouts produces, being more than two thirds Woods and Bogs; and not only the Nobility, but Merchants and Tradesmen of all sorts, are obliged to go and live there, and to trade with such things as they are order'd, which Crowd of People enhances the Price of Provisions, and makes a Scarcity for those Men who are absolutely necessary to live there, on account of the Land and Sea Service, and in carrying on those Buildings and Works which the *Czar* has already, and farther designs to make there. Whereas in *Mosco*, all the Lords and Men of distinction, have not only very large Buildings within the City, but also their Countrey Seats and Villages, where they have their Fishponds, their Gardens, with plenty of several sorts of Fruit and Places of Pleasure; but *Petersburgh*, which lies in the Latitude of 60 Degrees and 15 Minutes North, is too cold to produce these Things. Besides, *Mosco* is the Native Place which the *Russes* are fond of, and where they have their Friends and Acquaintance about them; their Villages are near, and their Provision comes easy and cheap to them, which is brought by their Slaves.

As for the *Czar*, he is a great Lover of the Water, and entirely delights in Ships and Boats, and in sailing, even to that degree,
that

that in the Winter, when both the River *Neva*, and the Head of the East Sea is frozen over, that he can no more go upon the Water, then he has his Boats made on purpose, and ingeniously fix'd for sailing upon the Ice; and every Day when there is a Gale of Wind, unless some very extraordinary thing happen to prevent him, he sails and plies to Windward upon the Ice with his said Boats, with Jack-Ensign and Pennant flying in the same manner as upon the Water. But his Lords have no Relish nor Pleasure in those Things, and though they seemingly compliment the *Czar* whenever he talks to them of the Beauties and Delights of *Petersburgh*; yet when they get together by themselves, they complain and say that there are Tears and Water enough at *Petersburgh*, but they pray God to send them to live again at *Mosco*.

Mosco is situated near the Centre of *Russia*, on a River of that Name that falls into the *Acca*, and stands upon a large piece of Ground, where every Man of distinction hath (though in the midst of the City) both a Garden and an outward Court belonging to his House. Whenever any Traveller comes within a fair view of the City, the numerous Churches, the Monasteries, and Noblemen and Gentlemens Houses, the Steeples, Cupolos and Crosses at the tops of the Churches, which are gilded and painted over, makes the City look to be one of the most rich and
beau-

beautiful in the World, as indeed it appeared to me at first sight coming from the *Novogorod* Road, which is the best view of it; but upon a nearer view, you find your self deceived and disappointed in your Expectation. When you come into the Streets, the Houses, excepting those of the *Boyars*, and some few rich Men, are every where built of Wood, particularly those that front the Streets, after a very mean Fashion: The Walls or Fences between the Streets and the Houses are made of Wood, and the very Streets, instead of being pav'd with Stone, are lin'd or laid with Wood, being done with Fir Baulks of about 15 or 16 Foot long, laid one by the side of another across the Street, upon other Baulks that lie underneath them lengthways in the Street, and lie generally above the Dirt which is on each side, so that the Wet presently runs off from them, and they generally lie dry; which gives me an Occasion to speak of the frequent and destructive Fires in this Countrey, not only in *Mosco*, but generally all the Buildings in every Town and City of *Russia*, being made after the same manner, occasions those often and dreadful Fires, that the like is not to be found in any other Countrey in the World.

Particularly in *Mosco*, it is common when a Fire begins, especially in the Summer Season, when every thing is dry and ready to kindle, to have a Fire spread on all sides, and burn on so furious, that there is no standing before

before it; and in this Extremity, it is the way of the *Ruſſes*, in hopes to put a ſtop to the Fire, to pull down the Houſes and Fences that are made of Wood, tho' they often have not time to carry it off, but as it lies upon the Ground together with the Wood with which the Streets are lined, gives a Train to the Fire; ſo that I have known it in leſs than half a Days time, when there has been a Gale of Wind, burn above a *Ruſs* Mile in length, and deſtroy many thouſand Houſes before it has been quench'd, and often without giving the Inhabitants opportunity to carry off the tenth part of their Goods. This has often brought many People to the laſt degree of Poverty, when all that they have had has been burnt; and it is one great Cauſe that the Houſes appear ſo poor in *Moſco*, when they cannot raiſe Money to build them better, and by reaſon of their being very often, as ſoon as they are built up, burnt down again to the Ground.

The *Czar*, as well as his Subjects, ſuffers extremely by thoſe general Conflagrations; particularly once I remember when I was in *Moſco*, there was in one Ware-houſe near the *Moſco* River above 100000 Rubles worth of Tobacco which belong'd to the *Czar* burnt; beſides, his Subjects are often rendred by thoſe Fires unable to pay the Duties and Taxes. It is certain, that during the time that I was in *Ruſſia* the City of *Moſco* in particular has ſuffer'd five times more by the Accidents
of

of Fire, than by all the Taxes and Charges of the War. And this brings me again to my Observations of the Stupidity and Injudiciousness of the *Russ* Lords and Counsellors, and their Creatures, call'd *Prebulshicks*; for notwithstanding these repeated Losses and Destructions by Fire are so great that I believe in twenty Years time, they are more than would have Rebuilt the City of *Mosco* with Stone or Brick; (which one would think should long since have put either them or their Fathers (whom they so much revere) upon such a Calculation, and by it upon thinking of Methods to prevent so great an Evil, by a general Tax and common Consent, to have rais'd a Fund to have made the Price of Bricks easie, and to have allow'd them to those who had the Misfortune to have their Houses burnt down, at less than the prime Cost, whereby to have encourag'd the rebuilding at least the capital City of *Russia* with Bricks; where not only the Houses but great Quanties of Corn and Provision, and rich Goods and Merchandize, are continually burnt, and the *Czar*'s Revenue and the whole Kingdom in some measure suffering Ruin thereby:) Yet so far have the *Czar*'s present Counsellors been from considering of any Means to remedy this great Evil, that they have practis'd the very reverse of it, and about eight Years since have laid such a Tax upon Bricks, and set *Prebulshicks* to levy the same, that Bricks are now very near double what they were before thro' all the *Czar*'s Dominions, whereby by many Men who would otherwise willingly build their Houses with Brick to preserve themselves from Ruin by Fire, are become unable to do it.

The *Russes*, to secure their Houses, which they make with Brick from Fire, build the Walls very thick, arch them over at the top, and bind the sides together with Bars of Iron, and likewise have Iron Doors and Shutters made to all their Windows; so that in the time of general Fires the top of the House only is burnt off, which is usually cover'd with Fir Boards, excepting some few Houses in *Mosco*, which are lately cover'd with Pantiles, and others of the great *Boyars* with Sheets of Iron.

I might by many other Instances shew, that the Methods that have been put in practice by these *Prebulshicks* have really very much lessen'd the *Czar's* Revenue, deaden'd the Trade, and ruin'd the People, but I believe I have said enough to let the Reader see the Happiness of living in a free Countrey.

Another thing which I shall here take notice of, and which has been very injudiciously put in practice, upon a Scheme that was laid down to be of considerable Advantage to the *Czar's* Countrey, but has come very short of the Benefits that were proposed by it, is this; About 12 or 14 Years since, an Estimate was deliver'd in at the Council Table, of the great Quantities of Cloth that there was a Demand for and brought into the Countrey every

Year

Year from *England* and *Holland*, and that it would be of great Advantage to *Russia* to have Cloth made in *Mosco*, to save this Charge, particularly for cloathing the *Czar*'s Army. Upon which, though they were told by Foreign Merchants, that their Wooll was abundantly too coarse, and not possible to answer the making of Cloth with it: Yet a Resolution was taken to try the Experiment, and Orders were forthwith given to send for Spinners, Weavers, Sheerers, Dyers, &c. to come over from *Holland*, with all manner of Instruments compleat for setting up a Woollen Manufactury in *Russia*. A large Square for this Purpose was projected and built with Brick, on the side of the *Mosco* River, with Workhouses for employing several hundred Persons, who were to be directed by Master Artificers, who accordingly came over from *Holland*, to teach the *Czar*'s People to make, dress, and dy Cloth; the Charge of doing which, amounted to several hundred thousand Rubles, before the Experiment of making one Yard of Cloth was produced; and when it came to be fully try'd, it was found that the *Russ* Wooll, which is very short, and as coarse almost as Dog's Hair, would not make any Thread for Cloth; so that afterward they were obliged to send to *Holland* for Wooll to mix with it; and at the foot of the whole Account, it is found that even such coarse Cloath, as has been made only fit for Soldiers, can be deliver'd ver'd much easier to the *Czar*, than to have it made in *Russia*.

This is a thing that they would have forced against Nature and against Reason, when they have no Wool for it; whereas on the other hand Flax is the growth of *Russia*, wherewith other Nations are supply'd from thence; and there is no doubt, had the *Czar* been but at the 40th part of the Charge to have brought in a few Foreigners to have instructed his People in the making and improving the Linen Manufacture, but with a very little teaching, and the use of the proper Instruments to spin and to weave Linen Cloth, which hitherto they have not had, nor do not know the use of, his own Subjects might long e'er this (with Encouragement and Protection) have brought it to tolerable Perfection, and have been a Means to have vended much greater Quantities abroad into Foreign Countries, and at easier Rates than from any other Nation whatsoever. The want of which improving of the *Russ* Linen, and making of it of a proper breadth, like what is done in other Countries; the Linen which they make for ordinary shirting, being not made above twenty Inches broad, so that four Breadths must be used for that purpose, is what is generally complain'd of by all those who purchase *Russ* Linen, or know any thing of that Trade. And yet this thing still remains unattempted: And notwithstanding all the Persuasions of foreign Merchants, the *Russes* still obstinately

obstinately persist in their own Way, and will make their Cloth to narrow for any Use.

There are many other like Instances of their Errors and Obstinacy that I could name, which are contrary to the Advantage and Interest of *Russia*: But I fear I have been already too tedious, and therefore shall only now give a very short Account of the Regulations made in the *Czar*'s Army, which by his own Care and good Management has been brought to much better Perfection than ever was before done, or attempted by any of his Predecessors.

I have already mention'd how the *Russ* Army was cloath'd in their long Habits, and when this *Czar* return'd from his Travels, how he then cloath'd the several Regiments in regular Liveries, like the Forces of other Princes of *Europe*; as also observ'd his establishing a new Discipline in their Exercise, which he had taken from other Nations, and his receiving foreign Officers into his Service; I think it may not be unacceptable to the Reader, to shew what Temper and Method he took to make his own People Soldiers, Seamen, &c.

In doing of which, that he might have Men fit to serve him in his Army, Navy, and in all manner of Business, he order'd a List to be taken of all the Lords and Gentlemen of his Countrey, how many Sons they had, and what their Estates were. Some he sent to travel, others he appointed to his Army and Navy,

Navy, there to serve at their own Charge, until they had fitly qualified and signalized themselves by their Behaviour, so as to be recommended as deserving of some Post, and to be enter'd into his Majesty's Pay; and that the greatest Lord's Son, after some time serving Volunteer, should only first be made an Ensign, and so to rise gradually, acording to his Behaviour; and not to be taken Notice of, or have any Respect paid him, (at publick Entertainments, or the like) but according to the Post that they were in, and had merited in his Service.

And that this Order might the better take effect, and that all Persons, whether those he sent into his Army or Navy, might be the better contented with it, he set an Example, by taking upon himself both a Post in his Navy, and in his Army, wherein he acted and took the gradual Steps of Preferment, like another Man. Of which it will be necessary to be a little more particular.

The first Title he took upon him was that of a Sea Captain, at the Time when he first built Ships upon the *Pereslavski* Lake; and afterwards, when he went against *Azoph* in the Year 1695, he enter'd himself an Ensign before his Travels into *Europe*. Upon his Return, when he changed the Establishment and Name of the *Streletzes* to that of Soldiers, he took upon himself the Command of a Company in the first Regiment of his Guards. And I have seen him march as a private Captain

tain at the Head of his Company through the City of *Mosco*, on occasion of going to bless the Waters of that River, which is constantly done with a great Procession of the Clergy twice every Year; as likewise is done every where else in *Russia*.

Upon his Majesty's Return from his Travels, he drew a Draught with his own Hands, and set up a Man of War of fifty Guns upon the Stocks at *Veronize*, and caused himself to be declared Master Builder, (by his Mock *Czar* beforemention'd) in Presence of all his Lords. His Jester harangu'd him on this Occasion for his Ingenuity, and the several Degrees of Knowledge that he had attain'd to in his Travels, and the Mock *Czar* assured him of his Favour, and that he might expect farther Preferment according to his Merit.

These three Titles he took upon him when I first came into the Countrey; and no Man was to accost him in any publick Company, as at Entertainments, or the like, but by the Name of Captain. He continued above eight Years before he attained to the Degree of Colonel, which was upon his having some signal Success in an Action against the *Swedes* in *Poland*; and after he obtain'd the great Victory at *Poltava*, and came to *Mosco* in Triumph, he was made Lieutenant-General; and, as I remember about two Years before that, was made Rear-Admiral of his Fleet, and hoisted his Flag accordingly: And this Summer I
hear

hear he is made Vice-Admiral, with the ufual Ceremony.

In all thefe feveral Stations, as he was from time to time gradually preferr'd, he conftantly received his Pay, and gave a Receipt for his Money, which was always brought and deliver'd to him at fome great Entertainment, when all his Lords were prefent; upon which the Mock *Czar* ufually complemented him as deferving well of the Publick for his good Service; and his Health was thereupon drank as Captain, or Ship-builder, or Colonel, or General, according as he took his Money that Day. More particularly at any time when he launches a Ship that is of his own Building, or that he takes the Name of doing it upon him, and has been carry'd on by his *Rufs* Affiftants; then his Mock *Czar* and his Lords always make him Prefents of Plate, and of Money, and of Cloth, to make him new Cloaths, which by his own Acting and Labour among the Carpenters, is commonly made pretty dirty on that Day, and is ufually done after the Ship is launch'd, when they are feafting and merry.

His Jefter on thefe Occafions is always very bufy, fometimes praifing him, and at other times telling him that he is ufed too well, and preferred too foon; and reckoning up many other Services that ought to be done, before he is juftly entitled to fo much Encouragement, and always makes oblique Strokes at the fame time on the Ways of the former *Czars*, the

T ill

ill Management and bad Conduct of their Armies, and the Bigottry of the old *Boyars*.

These are the Methods which the *Czar* has taken, with Mirth and Good-humour, to make his Lords see that he expects they shall not think themselves nor their Sons too good to serve their Countrey, and take their Steps gradually to Preferment: And he has not only done this, but taken indefatigable Pains to examine into the Merit and Behaviour of all who serve in his Army, and to reward and punish those who deserve it, of which there are several remarkable Instances. Whereby he has now very well furnish'd his Army with good Officers of his own Nation, who are Gentlemen of the first Rank, and ought to be Men of Spirit and Bravery.

Next as to his Troops and common Soldiers, of whom his Regiments are composed: Those who serve as Horse are a great part of them Gentlemens Sons of the lower Rank, who have but small Estates, with several Sons of the Clergy: For the *Czar* observing that his Countrey was over-stock'd with Priests of but very little Learning, and that they usually bred up their Sons in the same Ignorance to the same Office, order'd a Draught of them to be made, and sent into his Army; and has also several times sent considerable Numbers of the *Subdiackshicks*, which were supernumerary, about the *Precauses*, and from others taken among petty trading People: So that there are but very few of the common Peasants or Slaves

found

found among the *Czar*'s Troops, who are Light Horse and Dragoons.

As to the common Foot Soldiers, there are some very remarkable Things which render them as fit for Service as any in the World.

First, It is the Manner of all *Russia*, for the common People, (Men and Women) to go at least once, if not twice a Week, into their Bagnio's or Sweating Houses; and it is their Manner, even in the Depth of Winter, to come naked out of their Bagnio's, and either to jump into the River, or if there be no River open, to pour two or three Pails full of cold Water directly upon their Heads: And by their being thus used from their Infancy to these Extremes of Heat and Cold, it is common for them when they travel in the open *Step* where there are no Houses, to make a Fire in the Night, and to lie round it and sleep in the time of the severest Frosts, and not to catch cold, or known to be troubled with Coughs in that Countrey; and their being thus enured to Hardships, is one thing that renders them fit to be Soldiers. Another is, that a *Russ*, if you give him but *Sucarie*, (which is Rye-Bread first baked and minced in small square Bits, and then dry'd again in the Oven) if they have but Water to drink with it, they will march fourteen Days together, and be very content: But if they get now and then a Dram of Brandy, they think they fare well.

Secondly, The *Russes* do not seem to value or be discouraged at Death; as commonly is observed of them when they go to be executed, they do it with the least Concern in the World. I have seen several of them go together with the Chains on their Legs, and Wax Candles burning in their Hands: And as they pass by the Crowds of People they bow to them, and say, *Proftee Brats*, that is, *Adieu Brothers*; and the People make the like Reply to them, bidding them adieu: And so they lay down their Heads on the Blocks, and with a steady Countenance resign their Lives.

On these Accounts it is that the *Russes* are esteem'd by those who are better Judges than I, that if their Officers are good, they will not fail to make good Soldiers: And it has in many Actions been lately proved, that those that have been well led on, and used to Action, will stand as firm, and fight as well, as any other Nation.

The *Czar*'s Army, besides his own People, is composed of several Regiments of *Cossacks*, commanded by their own Officers. They are all Light Horse, and have been very useful in the *Russ* Wars against the *Turks* and *Tartars*, and in the present War against the *Swedes*, have been usually sent out with Parties of *Russ* Horse upon any Expedition, to raise Contributions, and to burn or plunder the Countrey. The *Czar* has always a Party of *Cullmicks* who are obliged to attend his Army, according to a Treaty of Alliance made with them. They are a robust, War-like People, who only want Discipline to make them
Soldiers.

Soldiers. They once occasion'd a considerable Victory, which the *Czar* obtained over a Party of *Swedes* near *Plesco*, soon after the Loss of the Battel of *Narva*.

The Dromedary, which I have before spoken of, which the *Cullmicks* use to draw and carry their Baggage on the East side of the River *Wolga*, is a Creature, that a Horse that has not seen them before, is extremely frighten'd at, and will startle and run from with very great Precipitation; and upon the *Russes* coming up with a Party of *Swedes*, which they march'd to attack, the *Cullmicks*, with several of these Dromedaries in the Front, were order'd in the Attack, who, when they came near, so affrighted the *Swedish* Horse, that they gave way and broke their Ranks, and the *Russes* fell in upon them and routed them. The *Cossacks* were usually reckon'd about 10000 Men, and the *Cullmicks* about 6000, and the *Czar*'s Army which he has in Pay at all Places, and on all Occasions, is in the whole about a hundred and twenty or thirty thousand Men.

There is one thing more wherein the present *Czar* has very much improved his Army. Before his time, the *Russes* had no regular Artillery, nor were ever known to form a Siege with any Effect, against any Place of Importance, nor had they any proper Officers peculiar to the Artillery; but the present *Czar*, about two Years after his Return from his Travels, establish'd a regular Artillery,

and

and made it Regimental, like those of other Nations, and has now several of his own Subjects, who are Captains and Officers in his Artillery, and have learnt the Art of Gunnery, and are good Bombardeers, and many others are daily sent from his Mathematical School in *Mosco* to serve in his Artillery, as well as in his Navy, besides those who have been, and are still sent abroad to learn Mechanick Arts and Sciences, who have been only learnt Arithmetick and Geometry, of whom particularly there are about a Month since come over to *England* twenty Persons, who are order'd to be put Apprentices to several mechanick Trades, as Shipwrights, Block-makers, Rope-makers, Sail-makers, Smiths, &c. relating to Shipping and to Gunnery.

As the *Czar* has taken particular Regard to have his own Subjects qualify'd to serve him on all these Occasions, and has spared no Pains for it, but continually busies himself amongst these Men, in ordering and giving his Directions in every thing that relates to his Army and his Navy, and delights in it, so that it may be said of him, that he is from the Drummer to the General, a compleat Soldier; besides his being Engineer, Cannoneer, Fire-worker, Ship-builder, Turner, Boatswain, Gun-founder, Blacksmith, &c. All which he frequently works at with his own Hands, and will himself see that every thing be carried on and perform'd to his own Mind, as well in

these

these minutest things, as in the greater Disposition of Affairs.

One thing more I will mention, the Places where his Naval Preparations are made, and where his Armies are disposed, being very far distant sometimes one from another, which requires him very often to undertake long and tedious Journeys from Place to Place. He has, I believe (for the Proportion of Time that I was in the Countrey) travell'd twenty times more than ever any Prince in the World did before him, and which in no Countrey, but by Sled Way, could be perform'd; his usual Method of travelling in the Winter, being after the rate of more than a hundred *English* Miles a Day, which he does by fresh Sets of Horses. But though this travelling by Sleds in the Winter be thus commodious in *Russia*, yet there are no Inns or Places of any tolerable Entertainment by the way, excepting in great Towns, which are generally 100 Miles distant one from the other.

Therefore the *Czar* to make his Journeys the more agreeable to him, and his Officers and Lords who travel, has upon the Road to *Veronize*, *Kiow*, *Smolensky* and *Petersburgh*, order'd convenient Houses of Entertainment to be built at every 20 or 30 Miles distant upon all the said Roads, and has likewise caused handsome Posts to be set up at every Mile, with the distance from Place to Place legibly written, both in *English* Figures and *Russ* Characters, that Travellers as they are upon
the

the Road may easily know how far they have to go: And particularly, to the End that *Petersburgh* may be render'd more agreeable, about seven Years since he order'd Mr. *Fergharson* and Mr. *Gwin* to take an exact Survey of the Road between *Petersburgh* and *Mosco*, to find the Bearing of one Place from another, in order to make a Road the whole Way, by a streight Line through all the Woods, and over all the Lakes, Morasses and Rivers, by which it will happen about one fifth part nearer than it now is; and a Tract has since been mark'd out through the Woods for making the Way on a direct Line, which was finish'd in the Year 1710. And the *Czar* does design to have a Road accordingly made, when he has Peace, and can better spare Men and Money for it.

FINIS.